# Frommer's®

# Spanish Phrasebook & Culture Guide

## Mexican / Latin American Edition

### 1st Edition

**WILEY**

Wiley Publishing, Inc.

Published by:

## Wiley Publishing, Inc.

111 River St.
Hoboken, NJ 07030-5774

ISBN-13: 978-0-471-79298-7
ISBN-10: 0-471-79298-5

Series Editor: Maureen Clarke
Travel Tips and Culture Guide: Haas Mroue
Travel Content Editor: Michael Spring
Editorial Assistant: Melinda Quintero
Photo Editor: Richard H. Fox
Cover design by Fritz Metsch

With special thanks to Charlie O'Malley.

Interior Design, Content Development, Translation, Copyediting, Proofreading,
Production, and Layout by:
Publication Services, Inc., 1802 South Duncan Road, Champaign, IL 61822
Linguists: Nanette Monet & Justin Serrano

For information on our other products and services or to obtain technical support,
please contact our Customer Care Department within the U.S. at 800/762-2974, outside the U.S. at 317/572-3993 or fax 317/572-4002.
Wiley also publishes its books in a variety of electronic formats. Some content that
appears in print may not be available in electronic formats.

Manufactured in the United States of America

5  4  3

# Contents

## An Invitation to the Reader

In researching this book, we discovered many wonderful sayings and terms useful to travelers in Latin America. We're sure you'll find others. Please tell us about them, so we can share the information with your fellow travelers in upcoming editions. If you were disappointed with an aspect of this book, we'd like to know that, too. Please write to:

*Frommer's Spanish Phrasebook & Culture Guide*,
Mexican / Latin American Edition, 1st Edition
Wiley Publishing, Inc.
111 River St. • Hoboken, NJ 07030-5774

## An Additional Note

## Frommers.com

Now that you have the language for a great trip, visit our website at **www.frommers.com** for travel information on more than 3,000 destinations. With features updated regularly, we give you instant access to the most current trip-planning information available. At Frommers.com, you'll also find the best prices on airfares, accommodations, and car rentals—and you can even book travel online through our travel booking partners. At Frommers.com, you'll also find:

- Online updates to our most popular guidebooks
- Vacation sweepstakes and contest giveaways
- Newsletter highlighting the hottest travel trends
- Online travel message boards with featured travel discussions

# INTRODUCTION: HOW TO USE THIS BOOK

As a Romance language, Spanish is closely related to Latin, French, Italian, Portuguese, and Romanian. But not one of these European tongues is used with half the frequency of Spanish—with more than 332 million speakers, including more than 23 million in the United States. Variations spoken by Mexicans, Spaniards, Ecuadorians, Puerto Ricans, and other Latino ethnic groups are considerable. For simplicity's sake, we have used a universal form of Latin American Spanish throughout this book. But a native Spaniard has reviewed our translations, noting where they're radically different from what is spoken in Spain.

Our intention is not to teach you Spanish; we figure you'll find an audio program for that. Our aim is to provide a portable travel tool that's easy to use. With most phrasebooks, you practically have to memorize the contents before you know where to look for a term on the spot. This phrasebook is designed for fingertip referencing, to help you find the language you need fast.

Part of this book organizes terms by chapters, as in a Frommer's guide—getting a room, getting a good meal, etc. Within those sections, we tried to organize phrases according to how frequently readers are likely to use them. But let's say you're in a cab and received the wrong change, and don't know where to look in the money chapter. With Frommer's PhraseFinder, you can quickly look up "change" in the dictionary, and learn how to say "Sorry, but this isn't the right change." Then you can follow the cross reference for numbers, and specify how much you're missing.

What will make this book most practical? What will make it easiest to use? These are the questions we asked ourselves as we assembled these travel terms.

Our immediate goal was to create a phrasebook as indispensable as your passport. Our far-ranging goal, of course, is to enrich your experience of travel. And with that we offer the following wish: *¡Que tenga un buen viaje!*

# CHAPTER ONE

## SURVIVAL SPANISH

If you tire of toting around this phrasebook, tear out this chapter. You should be able to navigate your destination with only the terms found in the next 35 pages.

### BASIC GREETINGS

*For a full list of greetings, see p127.*

| | |
|---|---|
| Hello. | **Hola.**<br>*OH-lah* |
| How are you? | **¿Cómo está?**<br>*KOH-moh ehs-TAH* |
| I'm fine, thanks. | **Estoy bien, gracias.**<br>*ehs-TOY BYEHN, GRAH-syahs* |
| And you? | **¿Y usted?**<br>*ee oos-TEHD* |
| My name is ____. | **Me llamo ____.**<br>*meh YAH-mo* |
| And yours? | **¿Y usted?**<br>*ee oos-TEHD* |
| It's a pleasure to meet you. | **Es un placer conocerle.**<br>*EHS oon plah-SEHR koh-noh-SEHR-leh* |
| Please. | **Por favor.**<br>*pohr fah-VOHR* |
| Thank you. | **Gracias.**<br>*GRAH-syahs* |
| Yes. | **Sí.**<br>*see* |
| No. | **No.**<br>*noh* |

| | |
|---|---|
| Okay. | **OK.**<br>*OH-keh*<br>**De acuerdo.**<br>*deh ah-KWEHR-doh*<br>**Okay.**<br>*OH-keh* |
| No problem. | **No hay problema.**<br>*noh aye proh-BLEH-mah* |
| I'm sorry, I don't understand. | **Lo siento, no entiendo.**<br>*loh SYEHN-toh no ehn-TYEHN-doh* |
| Would you speak slower, please? | **¿Puede hablar un poco más lento?**<br>*PWEH-deh ah-BLAHR oon POH-koh mahs LEHN-to* |
| Would you speak louder, please? | **¿Puede hablar un poco más alto?**<br>*PWEH-deh ah-BLAHR oon POH-koh mahs AHL-toh* |
| Do you speak English? | **¿Usted habla inglés?**<br>*oos-TEHD AH-blah eeng-GLEHS* |
| Do you speak any other languages? | **¿Usted habla otro idioma?**<br>*oos-TEHD AH-blah OH-troh ee-DYOH-ma* |
| I speak ____ better than Spanish. | **Yo hablo ____ mejor que español.**<br>*yoh AH-bloh ____ meh-HOHR keh ehs-pah-NYOL* |

*For languages, see English-Spanish Dictionary.*

| | |
|---|---|
| Would you spell that? | **¿Puede deletrear eso?**<br>*PWEH-de deh-leh-treh-AHR EH-so* |
| Would you please repeat that? | **¿Puede repetir, por favor?**<br>*PWEH-deh rreh-peh-TEER pohr fah-VOHR* |
| Would you point that out in this dictionary? | **¿Puede señalarlo en este diccionario?**<br>*PWEH-deh seh-nyah-LAHR-loh ehn EHS-deh deek-syoh-NAHR-yoh* |

SURVIVAL SPANISH

## THE KEY QUESTIONS

With the right hand gestures, you can get a lot of mileage from the following list of single-word questions and answers.

| | |
|---|---|
| Who? | **¿Quién? ¿Quiénes?** |
| | *KYEHN? KYEH-nehs?* |
| What? | **¿Qué?** |
| | *keh* |
| When? | **¿Cuándo?** |
| | *KWAHN-doh* |
| Where? | **¿Dónde?** |
| | *DOHN-deh* |
| To where? | **¿Adónde?** |
| | *ah-DOHN-deh* |
| Why? | **¿Por qué?** |
| | *pohr-KEH* |
| How? | **¿Cómo?** |
| | *KOH-moh* |
| Which? | **¿Cuál?** |
| | *KWAHL* |
| How many? / How much? | **¿Cuánto? ¿Cuántos?** |
| | *KWAHN-toh, KWAHN-tohs* |

## THE ANSWERS: WHO

*For full coverage of pronouns, see p21.*

| | |
|---|---|
| I | **yo** |
| | *yoh* |
| you | **usted / tú** |
| | *oos-TEHD, too* |
| him | **él** |
| | *ehl* |
| her | **ella** |
| | *EH-yah* |
| us | **nosotros** |
| | *noh-SOH-trohs* |
| them | **ellos / ellas** |
| | *EH-yohs, EH-yahs* |

## THE ANSWERS: WHEN

*For full coverage of time, see p12.*

| | |
|---|---|
| now | **ahora** |
| | *ah-OH-rah* |
| later | **después** |
| | *dehs-PWEHS* |
| in a minute | **en un minuto** |
| | *ehn oon mee-NOO-toh* |
| today | **hoy** |
| | *oy* |
| tomorrow | **mañana** |
| | *mah-NYAH-nah* |
| yesterday | **ayer** |
| | *ah-YEHR* |
| in a week | **en una semana** |
| | *ehn OO-nah seh-MAH-nah* |
| next week | **la próxima semana** |
| | *lah PROHK-see-mah seh-MAH-nah* |
| last week | **la semana pasada** |
| | *lah seh-MAH-nah pah-SAH-dah* |
| next month | **el próximo mes** |
| | *ehl PROHK-see-moh MEHS* |
| At _____ | **A las _____** |
| | *ah lahs* |
| ten o'clock this morning. | **diez en punto esta mañana.** |
| | *DYEHS ehn POON-toh EHS-tah mah-NYAH-nah* |
| two o'clock this afternoon. | **dos en punto esta tarde.** |
| | *dohs ehn POON-toh EHS-tah TAHR-deh* |
| seven o'clock this evening. | **siete en punto esta noche.** |
| | *SYEH-teh ehn POON-toh EHS-ahOH-cheh* |

*For full coverage of numbers, see p7.*

## THE ANSWERS: WHERE

| here | aquí / acá |
| | *ah-KEE, ah-KAH* |
| there | allá / allí |
| | *ah-YAH, ah-EE* |
| near | cerca |
| | *SEHR-kah* |
| closer | más cerca |
| | *mahs SEHR-kah* |
| closest | lo más cerca |
| | *loh MAHS SEHR-kah* |
| far | lejos |
| | *LEH-hohs* |
| farther | más lejos |
| | *mahs LEH-hohs* |
| farthest | lo más lejos |
| | *loh MAHS LEH-hohs* |
| across from | atrás de |
| | *ah-TRAHS deh* |
| next to | al lado de |
| | *ahl LAH-doh deh* |
| behind | detrás de |
| | *deh-TRAHS deh* |
| straight ahead | adelante / siguiente |
| | *ah-deh-LAHN-teh, see-GYEHN-teh* |
| left | la izquierda |
| | *lah ees-KYEHR-dah* |
| right | la derecha |
| | *lah deh-REH-chah* |
| up | arriba |
| | *ah-RREE-bah* |
| down | abajo |
| | *ah-BAH-hoh* |
| lower | más abajo |
| | *mahs ah-BAH-hoh* |

| higher | **más arriba** |
| | *mahs ah-RREE-bah* |
| forward | **hacia delante** |
| | *AH-syah deh-LAHN-teh* |
| back | **hacia atrás** |
| | *AH-syah ah-TRAHS* |
| around | **alrededor** |
| | *ahl-reh-deh-DOHR* |
| across the street | **al cruzar la calle** |
| | *ahl kroo-SAHR lah KAH-yeh* |
| down the street | **calle abajo** |
| | *KAH-yeh ah-BAH-hoh* |
| on the corner | **en la esquina** |
| | *ehn lah ehs-KEE-nah* |
| kitty-corner | **la esquina diagonal** |
| | *lah ehs-KEE-nah dee-ah-* |
| | *goh-NAHL* |
| _____ blocks from here | **a _____ cuadras de aquí** |
| | *ah _____ KWAH-drahs deh ah-KEE* |

*For a full list of numbers, see the next page*

## THE ANSWERS: WHICH

| this one | **éste / ésta** |
| | *EH-steh, EH-stah* |
| that (that one, close by) | **ese / esa** |
| | *EH-seh, EH-sah* |
| (that one, in the distance) | **aquel / aquella** |
| | *ah-KEHL / ah-KEH-yah* |
| these | **éstos / éstas** |
| | *EHS-tohs, EHS-tahs* |
| those (those there, close by) | **ésos / ésas** |
| | *EH-sohs, EH-sahs* |
| | *ehl heh-REHN-teh* |

# NUMBERS & COUNTING

| | | | |
|---|---|---|---|
| one | **uno** <br> *OO-noh* | seventeen | **diecisiete** <br> *dyeh-see-SYEH-teh* |
| two | **dos** <br> *dohs* | eighteen | **dieciocho** <br> *dyeh-SYOH-choh* |
| three | **tres** <br> *trehs* | nineteen | **diecinueve** <br> *dyeh-see-NWEH-veh* |
| four | **cuatro** <br> *KWAH-troh* | twenty | **veinte** <br> *VEH-een-teh* |
| five | **cinco** <br> *SEENG-koh* | twenty-one | **veintiuno** <br> *veh-een-TYOO-noh* |
| six | **seis** <br> *SEH-ees* | thirty | **treinta** <br> *TREH-een-tah* |
| seven | **siete** <br> *SYEH-teh* | forty | **cuarenta** <br> *kwah-REN-teh* |
| eight | **ocho** <br> *OH-cho* | fifty | **cincuenta** <br> *seen-KWEHN-tah* |
| nine | **nueve** <br> *NWEH-veh* | sixty | **sesenta** <br> *seh-SEHN-tah* |
| ten | **diez** <br> *dyehs* | seventy | **setenta** <br> *seh-TEHN-tah* |
| eleven | **once** <br> *OHN-seh* | eighty | **ochenta** <br> *o-CHEHN-tah* |
| twelve | **doce** <br> *DOH-seh* | ninety | **noventa** <br> *noh-VEHN-tah* |
| thirteen | **trece** <br> *TREH-seh* | one hundred | **cien** <br> *syehn* |
| fourteen | **catorce** <br> *kah-TOHR-seh* | two hundred | **doscientos** <br> *doh-SYEHN-tohs* |
| fifteen | **quince** <br> *KEEN-seh* | one thousand | **mil** <br> *meel* |
| sixteen | **dieciséis** <br> *dyeh-see-SEH-ees* | | |

## FRACTIONS & DECIMALS

| | |
|---|---|
| one eighth | **un octavo** |
| | *oon ohk-TAH-voh* |
| one quarter | **un cuarto** |
| | *oon KWAHR-toh* |
| one third | **un tercio** |
| | *oon TEHR-syoh* |
| one half | **medio** |
| | *MEH-dyoh* |
| two thirds | **dos tercios** |
| | *dohs TEHR-syohs* |
| three quarters | **tres cuartos** |
| | *trehs KWAHR-tohs* |
| double | **doble** |
| | *DOH-bleh* |
| triple | **triple** |
| | *TREE-pleh* |
| one tenth | **un décimo** |
| | *oon DEH-see-moh* |
| one hundredth | **un centésimo** |
| | *oon sehn-TEH-see-moh* |
| one thousandth | **un milésimo** |
| | *oon mee-LEH-see-moh* |

## MATH

| | |
|---|---|
| addition | **la suma** |
| | *SOO-mah* |
| 2 +1 | **dos más uno** |
| | *dohs mahs OO-noh* |
| subtraction | **la resta** |
| | *RREHS-tah* |
| 2 - 1 | **dos menos uno** |
| | *dohs MEH-nohs OO-noh* |

| | |
|---|---|
| multiplication | **la multiplicación** |
| | *mool-tee-plee-kah-SYOHN* |
| 2 × 3 | **dos por tres** |
| | *dohs pohr trehs* |
| division | **la división** |
| | *dee-vee-SYOHN* |
| 6 ÷ 3 | **Seis dividido entre tres** |
| | *SEH-ees dee-vee-DEE-doh EHN-treh TREHS* |

## ORDINAL NUMBERS

| | |
|---|---|
| first | **primero -a** |
| | *pree-MEH-roh / pree-MEH-rah* |
| second | **segundo -a** |
| | *seh-GOON-doh / seh-GOON-dah* |
| third | **tercero -a** |
| | *tehr-SEH-roh / tehr-SEH-rah* |
| fourth | **cuarto -a** |
| | *KWAHR-toh / KWAHR-tah* |
| fifth | **quinto -a** |
| | *KEEN-toh / KEEN-tah* |
| sixth | **sexto -a** |
| | *SEHK-sto / SEHK-stah* |
| seventh | **séptimo -a** |
| | *SEHP-tee-moh / SEHP-tee-mah* |
| eighth | **octavo -a** |
| | *ohk-TAH-voh / ohk-TAH-vah* |
| ninth | **noveno -a** |
| | *noh-VEH-noh / noh-VEH-nah* |
| tenth | **décimo -a** |
| | *DEH-see-moh / DEH-see-mah* |
| last | **último -a** |
| | *OOL-tee-mo / OOL-tee-mah* |

## MEASUREMENTS

Measurements will usually be metric, though you may need a few American measurement terms.

| inch | **la pulgada**<br>*pool-GAH-dah* |
| foot | **el pie**<br>*PYEH* |
| mile | **la milla**<br>*MEE-yah* |
| millimeter | **el milímetro**<br>*mee-lee-MEH-troh* |
| centimeter | **el centimetro**<br>*sehn-tee-MEH-troh* |
| meter | **el metro**<br>*MEH-troh* |
| kilometer | **el kilómetro**<br>*kee-LOH-meh-troh* |
| hectare | **la hectárea**<br>*hehk-TAH-reh-ahs* |
| squared | **cuadrado -a**<br>*kwah-DRAH-doh / kwah-DRAH-dah* |
| short | **corto -a**<br>*KOHR-toh / KOHR-tah* |
| long | **largo -a**<br>*LAHR-goh / LAHR-gah* |

### VOLUME

| milliliters | **mililitros**<br>*mee-lee-LEE-trohs* |
| liter | **litro**<br>*LEE-troh* |
| kilo | **kilo**<br>*Kee-loh* |
| ounce | **onza**<br>*OHN-sah* |

| | |
|---|---|
| cup | **taza** |
| | *TAH-sah* |
| pint | **pinta** |
| | *PEEN-tah* |
| quart | **cuarto (de galón)** |
| | *KWAHR-toh deh gah-LOHN* |
| gallon | **galón** |
| | *gah-LOHN* |

## QUANTITY

| | |
|---|---|
| some | **algún -a / algunos -as** |
| | *ahl-GOON / ahl-GOO-nah /* |
| | *ahl-GOO-nohs / ahl-GOO-nahs* |
| none | **nada / ninguno -a / ningunos -as** |
| | *NAH-dah / neeng-GOO-noh /* |
| | *neeng-GOO-nah / neeng-* |
| | *GOO-nohs / neeng-GOO-nahs* |
| all | **todo -a / todos -as** |
| | *TOH-doh / TOH-dah / TOH-dohs /* |
| | *TOH-dahs* |
| many / much | **mucho -a / muchos -as** |
| | *MOO-cho / MOO-cha /* |
| | *MOO-chohs / MOO-chas* |
| a little bit (can be used | **un poco / una poca** |
| for quantity or for time) | *oon POH-koh / oo-nah POH-kah* |
| dozen | **docena** |
| | *doh-SEH-na* |

## SIZE

| | |
|---|---|
| small | **pequeño -a** |
| | *peh-KEH-nyoh / peh-KEH-nyah* |
| the smallest (literally | **el / la / lo más pequeño -a** |
| "the most small") | *ehl / lah / loh mahs peh-KEH-* |
| | *nyoh / peh-KEH-nyah* |

| medium | **mediano -a** |
| | *meh-DYAH-no / meh-DYAH-na* |
| big | **grande** |
| | *GRAHN-deh* |
| fat | **gordo -a** |
| | *GOHR-doh / GOHR-dah* |
| wide | **ancho -a** |
| | *AHN-cho / AHN-cha* |
| narrow | **angosto -a** |
| | *ahng-GOH-stoh / ahng-GOH-stah* |

## TIME

Time in Spanish is referred to, literally, by the hour. What time is it? translates literally as "What hour is it? / What hours are they?"

*For full coverage of number terms, see p7.*

### HOURS OF THE DAY

| What time is it? | **¿Qué hora es?** |
| | *keh OH-ra ehs* |
| At what time? | **¿A qué hora?** |
| | *ah KEH OH-rah* |
| For how long? | **¿Por cuánto tiempo?** |
| | *pohr KWAHN-toh TYEHM-poh* |
| It's one o'clock. | **Es la una en punto.** |
| | *ehs lah OO-nah ehn POON-toh* |

### A little tip

By adding a diminutive suffix -ito / -ita, -ico / -ica, or a combination of the two, you can make anything smaller or shorter. These endings replace the original -o and -a.

| advice, tip | **consejo** (*kohn-SEH-hoh*) |
| a little tip | **consejito** (*kohn-seh-HEE-toh*) |

| It's two o'clock. | **Son las dos en punto.** |
| | *sohn lahs DOHS ehn POON-toh* |
| It's two thirty. | **Son las dos y media.** |
| | *sohn lahs DOHS ee MEH-dyah* |
| It's two fifteen. | **Son las dos y cuarto.** |
| | *sohn lahs DOHS ee KWAHR-toh* |
| It's a quarter to three. | **Son las tres menos cuarto** |
| | *sohn las TREHS MEH-nohs* |
| | *KWAHR-toh* |
| | **Falta un cuarto para las tres.** |
| | *FAHL-tah oon KWAHR-toh pah-* |
| | *rah lahs trehs* |
| It's noon. | **Es mediodía.** |
| | *ehs MEH-dyoh DEE-ah* |
| It's midnight. | **Es medianoche.** |
| | *ehs meh-dyah-NOH-cheh* |
| It's early. | **Es temprano.** |
| | *ehs tehm-PRAH-noh* |
| It's late. | **Es tarde.** |
| | *ehs TAHR-deh* |
| in the morning | **de la mañana** |
| | *deh lah mah-NYAH-nah* |
| in the afternoon | **de la tarde** |
| | *deh lah TAHR-deh* |
| at night | **de la noche** |
| | *deh lah NOH-cheh* |
| dawn | **la madrugada** |
| | *lah mah-droo-GAH-dah* |

## DAYS OF THE WEEK

| | |
|---|---|
| Sunday | **el domingo** |
| | *ehl doh-MEENG-go* |
| Monday | **el lunes** |
| | *ehl LOO-nehs* |
| Tuesday | **el martes** |
| | *ehl MAHR-tehs* |
| Wednesday | **el miércoles** |
| | *ehl MYEHR-koh-lehs* |
| Thursday | **el jueves** |
| | *ehl HWEH-vehs* |
| Friday | **el viernes** |
| | *ehl VYEHR-nehs* |
| Saturday | **el sábado** |
| | *ehl SAH-bah-doh* |
| today | **hoy** |
| | *oy* |
| tomorrow | **mañana** |
| | *mah-NYAH-nah* |
| yesterday | **ayer** |
| | *ah-YEHR* |
| the day before yesterday | **anteayer** |
| | *ahn-teh-ah-YEHR* |
| one week | **una semana** |
| | *OO-nah seh-MAH-nah* |
| next week | **la próxima semana** |
| | *lah PROHK-see-mah seh-MAH-nah* |
| last week | **la semana pasada** |
| | *lah seh-MAH-nah pah-SAH-dah* |

## MONTHS OF THE YEAR

| | |
|---|---|
| January | **enero** |
| | *eh-NEH-roh* |
| February | **febrero** |
| | *feh-BREH-roh* |

| March | **marzo** |
| | *MAHR-soh* |
| April | **abril** |
| | *ah-BREEL* |
| May | **mayo** |
| | *MAH-yoh* |
| June | **junio** |
| | *HOO-nee-oh* |
| July | **julio** |
| | *HOO-lee-oh* |
| August | **agosto** |
| | *ah-GOHS-toh* |
| September | **septiembre** |
| | *sehp-TYEHM-breh* |
| October | **octubre** |
| | *ohk-TOO-breh* |
| November | **noviembre** |
| | *noh-VYEHM-breh* |
| December | **diciembre** |
| | *dee-SYEHM-breh* |
| next month | **el mes entrante** |
| | *ehl MEHS ehn-TRAHN-teh* |
| | **el próximo mes** |
| | *ehl PROHK-see-moh MEHS* |
| last month | **el mes pasado** |
| | *ehl MEHS pah-SAH-doh* |

## SEASONS OF THE YEAR

| spring | **la primavera** |
| | *lah pree-mah-VEH-rah* |
| summer | **el verano** |
| | *ehl veh-RAH-noh* |
| autumn | **el otoño** |
| | *ehl oh-TOH-nyoh* |
| winter | **el invierno** |
| | *ehl een-VYEHR-noh* |

## Falsos Amigos

If you try winging it with Spanglish, beware of false cognates, known as falsos amigos, "false friends"—Spanish words that sound like English ones, but with different meanings. Here are some of the most commonly confused terms.

| | |
|---|---|
| **suburbio** | slum |
| **barrio** | suburb |
| **bomba** | pump / tank / bomb |
| **explosivo** | bomb |
| **arma** | weapon |
| **brazo** | arm |
| **constipado -a** | congested |
| **estreñido -a** | constipated |
| **embarazada** | pregnant |
| **avergonzado -a** | embarrassed |
| **injuria** | insult |
| **herida** | injury |
| **parientes** | relatives |
| **padres** | parents |
| **largo** | long |
| **grande** | large |
| **actual** | now, current |
| **verdadero -a** | actual |
| **asistir** | to attend |
| **ayudar** | to assist |
| **sopa** | soup |
| **jabón** | soap |
| **ropa** | clothing |
| **ropa vieja** (lit. old clothes) | delicious Cuban dish of stewed, shredded beef |
| **cuerda** | rope |

## SPANISH GRAMMAR BASICS

Classified as a Romance language, descended from the Latin spoken when Spain was part of the Roman Empire, Spanish is a linguistic amalgamation closely related to Latin, French, Italian, Portuguese, and Romanian. Spanish was strongly affected by the Arabic of Spain's Moorish conquerors, who occupied the country from A.D. 711 to 1492. When Spain conquered what is today Latin America, it imposed its language on millions of Native Americans, from the Caribbean to Tierra del Fuego. But the indigenous languages they spoke, in turn, affected the local spoken Spanish, accounting for some of the rich diversity of the language.

## THE ALPHABET

Spanish is a straightforward language with a simple alphabet. If foreign letters (k and w) are counted, the alphabet has 27 letters (ñ, in addition to the English alphabet).

Spanish also has two double letters: ll (elle), pronounced like y in English "yes," and rr (erre), pronounced like an English r trilled by vibrating the end of the tongue against the hard palate, just above the upper teeth. There is also ch, as in chipmunk.

| Letter | Name | Pronunciation of Letter Name |
|--------|------|------------------------------|
| a | a | *ah* |
| b | be | *beh* |
| c | ce | *seh* |
| d | de | *deh* |
| e | e | *eh* |
| f | efe | *EH-feh* |
| g | ge | *heh* |
| h | hache | *AH-cheh* |
| i | i | *ee* |
| j | jota | *HOH-tah* |
| k | ka | *kah* |
| l | ele | *EH-leh* |
| m | eme | *EH-meh* |
| n | ene | *EH-neh* |

| Letter | Name | Pronunciation of Letter Name |
|--------|------|------------------------------|
| ñ | eñe | *EH-nyeh* |
| o | o | *oh* |
| p | pe | *peh* |
| q | cu | *koo* |
| r | ere | *EH-reh* |
| s | ese | *EH-seh* |
| t | te | *teh* |
| u | u | *oo* |
| v | ve, uve | *veh* |
| w | doble u, ve doble | *DOH-bleh oo, veh DOH-bleh* |
| x | equis | *EH-kees* |
| y | i griega | *ee GRYEH-gah* |
| z | seta | *SEH-tah* |

## PRONUNCIATION GUIDE

### Vowels

| | |
|---|---|
| a | ah as the a in father: abajo *(ah BAH hoh)* |
| au | ow as in cow: automático *(ow-to-MAH-tee-koh)* |
| ay | aye as in "All in favor, say aye": hay *(aye)* |
| e | eh to rhyme with the e in nestle: espera *(ehs PEH rah)* |
| i | ee as in feed: pasillo *(pah SEE yoh)* |
| o | oh as in boat: modismo *(moh DEES moh)* |
| oy | oy as in boy: hoy *(oy)* |
| u | oo as in the word coo: buscar *(boos KAHR)* |

### Consonants

| | |
|---|---|
| b | as in bean, but softer with less explosion than in English: buscar *(boos-KAHR)* |
| c | before e and i as English initial s; ce is pronounced as seh: necesito *(neh seh SEE toh)*; ci is pronounced as see: cinco *(SEENG-koh)*; before a, o, u as English k, but softer with less explosion: caballero *(kah bah YEH roh)*; consejo *(kohn SEH hoh)*; Cuba *(KOO bah)* |

| | |
|---|---|
| cu | in combination with a, e, i, o pronounced like the qu in quick: cuándo *(KWAHN doh)*; cuestión *(kwehs TYOHN)* |
| d | as the d in day, but softer with less explosion than in English. Some final ds can be pronounced as the th in the: usted *(oo STEHTH)*. If you pronounce Spanish d like the English d, you will be understood: ciudad *(see-oo-DAHD)*; de *(deh)* |
| f | as in fox: favor *(fah-VOHR)* |
| g | before e and i as English h; ge is pronounced like he in hen: emergencia *(eh-mehr-HEHN-syah)*; gi is pronounced like English he: puerta giratoria *(PWEHR-tah hee-rah-TOHR-yah)* |
| | before a, o, u as initial hard g in English as in gate: llegar *(yeh GAHR)*; tengo *(TEHN-goh)*; seguridad *(seh-goo-ree-DAHD)* |
| h | silent; hizo *(EE-soh)*, hasta *(AHS-tah)*; hi before a vowel is pronounced like English y: hielo *(YEH-loh)* |
| j | as English h in hot: equipaje *(eh-kee-PAH-heh)* |
| k | as in English: kilómetro *(kee-LOH-meh-troh)* |
| l | as in English: ala *(AH-lah)* |
| ll | as the initial y in yeah: llegada *(yeh-GAH-dah)* |
| m | as in English: aeromozo *(eh-roh-MOH-soh)* |
| n | as in English: negocios *(neh-GOH-syohs)* |
| ñ | as ny in canyon: cañón *(kahn-YOHN)* |
| p | as in English but softer: pasaporte *(pah-sah-POHR-teh)* |
| q | qu is pronounced as k: máquina *(MAH-kee-nah)* |
| r | as in English but more clipped: puerta *(PWEHR-tah)* |
| rr | as a trilled r sound, vibrating the end of the tongue against the area just above the top teeth: perro *(PEH-rroh)*. A single r that starts a word is pronounced like the double r: rayos X *(RRAH-yohs EH-kees)* |
| s | as in English: salida *(sah-LEE-dah)* |

| t | as in English but softer: tranvía *(trahn-VEE-ah)* |
|---|---|
| v | as in English: vuelo *(VWEH-loh)* |
| w | as in English: waflera *(wah-FLEH-rah)* |
| x | like English x: próximo *(PROHK-see-moh)*; in some old names and some names of Native American origin, like h: Don Quixote *(dohn kee HOH teh)*, México *(MEH-hee-koh)* spelled with j in Spain; before a consonant, like s: Taxco *(TAHS-koh)* |
| y | as in English: yo *(yoh)*; by itself, as the ee sound in bead: y *(ee)* |
| z | like English s: aterrizaje *(ah-teh-rree-SAH-heh)* |

## WORD PRONUNCIATION

Syllables in words are also accented in a standard pattern. Generally, the last syllable is stressed except when a word ends in a vowel, n, or s; then the stress falls on the second to last syllable. If a word varies from this pattern, an accent mark is shown. Examples:

**Ending in r**
comer                    *koh-MEHR*

**Ending in a**
comida                   *koh-MEE-dah*

**Ending in s**
comemos                 *koh-MEH-mohs*

**Ending in n but with an accent mark**
comilón                  *koh-mee-LOHN*

## GENDER, ADJECTIVES, MODIFIERS

Each noun takes a masculine or feminine gender, most often accompanied by a masculine or feminine definite article (el or la). Definite articles ("the"), indefinite articles ("a," "an"), and related adjectives must also be masculine or feminine, singular or plural, depending on the noun they're modifying.

## The Definite Article ("The")

|  | Masculine | Feminine |
|---|---|---|
| Singular | *el* perro (the dog) | *la* mesa (the table) |
| Plural | *los* perros (the dogs) | *las* mesas (the tables) |

## The Indefinite Article ("A" or "An")

|  | Masculine | Feminine |
|---|---|---|
| Singular | *un* perro (a dog) | *una* mesa (a table) |
| Plural | *unos* perros (some dogs) | *unas* mesas (some tables) |

## PERSONAL PRONOUNS

| | AMAR: "To Love" | |
|---|---|---|
| **I love.** | *Yo amo.* | AH-moh |
| **You** (singular familiar) **love.** | *Tú amas.* | AH-mahs |
| **He / She loves. You** (singular, formal) **love.** | *Él / Ella / Ud. ama.* | AH-mah |
| **We love.** | *Nosotros -as amamos.* | ah-MAH-mohs |
| **You** (plural, familiar) **love.** | *Vosotros -as amáis.* | ah-MAH-ees |
| **They / You** (plural, formal) **love.** | *Ellos / Ellas / Uds. aman.* | AH-mahn |

### Hey, You!

Spanish has two words for "you"—tú, spoken among friends and familiars, and Usted (abbreviated Ud. or Vd.), used among strangers or as a sign of respect toward elders and authority figures. When speaking with a stranger, expect to use Usted, unless you are invited to do otherwise. The second-person familiar plural form (vosotros) is rarely used, and then only in Spain, Argentina, and Chile. Ustedes (abbreviated Uds. or Vds.) is used instead, even among friends, especially in Latin America.

## REGULAR VERB CONJUGATIONS

Spanish verb infinitives end in AR (hablar, to speak), ER (comer, to eat), or IR (asistir, to attend). Most verbs (known as "regular verbs") are conjugated according to those endings. To conjugate the present tense of regular verbs, simply drop the AR, ER, or IR and add the following endings:

**Present Tense**

| AR Verbs | HABLAR "To Speak" | |
|---|---|---|
| I speak. | Yo hablo. | AH-bloh |
| You (singular familiar) speak. | Tú hablas. | AH-blahs |
| He / She speaks. You (singular formal) speak. | Él / Ella / Ud. habla. | AH-blah |
| We speak. | Nosotros -as hablamos. | ah-BLAH-mohs |
| You (plural familiar) speak. | Vosotros -as habláis. | ah-BLAH-ees |
| They / You (plural formal) speak. | Ellos / Ellas / Uds. hablan. | AH-blahn |

**ER Verbs** · COMER "To Eat"

| I eat. | Yo como. | KOH-moh |
|---|---|---|
| You (singular familiar) eat. | Tú comes. | KOH-mehs |
| He / She eats. You (singular formal) eat. | Él / Ella / Ud. come. | KOH-meh |
| We eat. | Nosotros -as comemos. | koh-MEH-mohs |
| You (plural familiar) eat. | Vosotros -as coméis. | koh-MEH-ees |
| They / You (plural formal) eat. | Ellos / Ellas / Uds. comen. | KOH-mehn |

**IR Verbs** · ASISTIR "To Attend"

| I attend. | Yo asisto. | ah-SEES-toh |
|---|---|---|
| You (singular familiar) attend. | Tú asistes. | ah-SEES-tehs |
| He / She attends. You (singular formal) attend. | Él / Ella / Ud. asiste. | ah-SEES-teh |
| We attend. | Nosotros -as asistimos. | ah-sees-TEE-mohs |
| You (plural familiar) attend. | Vosotros -as asistís. | ah-sees-TEES |
| They / You (plural formal) attend. | Ellos / Ellas / Uds. asisten. | ah-SEES-tehn |

## Simple Past Tense

These are the simple past tense conjugations for regular verbs.

| AR Verbs | HABLAR "To Speak" | |
|---|---|---|
| I spoke. | Yo hablé. | ah-BLEH |
| You (singular familiar) spoke. | Tú hablaste. | ah-BLAHS-teh |
| He / She/ You (singular formal) spoke. | Él / Ella / Ud. habló. | ah-BLOH |
| We spoke. | Nosotros -as hablamos. | ah-BLAH-mohs |
| You (plural familiar) spoke. | Vosotros -as hablasteis. | ah-BLAHS-teh-ees |
| They / You (plural formal) spoke. | Ellos / Ellas / Uds. hablaron. | ah-BLAH-rohn |

| ER Verbs | COMER "To Eat" | |
|---|---|---|
| I ate. | Yo comí. | koh-MEE |
| You (singular familiar) ate. | Tú comiste. | koh-MEES-teh |
| He / She / You singular formal) ate. | Él / Ella / Ud. comió. | koh-mee-OH |
| We ate. | Nosotros -as comimos. | koh-MEE-mohs |
| You (plural familiar) ate. | Vosotros -as comisteis. | koh-MEES-teh-ees |
| They / You (plural formal) ate. | Ellos / Ellas / Uds. comieron. | koh-MYEH-rohn |

| IR Verbs | ASISTIR "To Attend" | |
|---|---|---|
| I attended. | Yo asist*í*. | ah-sees-TEE |
| You (singular familiar) attended. | Tú asist*iste*. | ah-sees-TEES-teh |
| He / She / You (singular formal) attended. | Él / Ella / Ud. asist*ió*. | ah-sees-TYOH |
| We attended. | Nosotros -as asist*imos*. | ah-sees-TEE-mohs |
| You plural familiar) attended. | Vosotros -as asist*isteis*. | ah-sees-TEES-teh-ees |
| They / You (plural formal) attended. | Ellos / Ellas / Uds. asist*ieron*. | ah-sees-TYEH-rohn |

## The Future

For novice Spanish speakers, the easiest way to express the future is to conjugate the irregular verb IR (to go) + a + any infinitive ("I am going to speak," "you are going to speak," etc.).

| I am going to speak. | Yo *voy a* hablar. | voy ah ah-BLAHR |
|---|---|---|
| You (singular familiar) are going to speak. | Tú *vas a* hablar. | vahs ah ah-BLAHR |
| He / She is going to speak. You (singular formal) are going to speak. | Él / Ella / Ud. *va a* hablar. | vah ah ah-BLAHR |
| We are going to speak. | Nosotros -as *vamos a* hablar. | VAH-mohs ah ah-BLAHR |

| You (plural familiar) are going to speak. | Vosotros -as *vais a* hablar. | VAH-ees ah ah-BLAHR |
| They / You (plural formal) are going to speak. | Ellos / Ellas / Uds. *van a* hablar. | vahn ah ah-BLAHR |

## TO BE OR NOT TO BE (ESTAR & SER)

There are two forms of "being" in Spanish. One is for physical location or temporary conditions (estar), and the other is for fixed qualities or conditions (ser).

| | |
|---|---|
| **I am here.**<br>(temporary, estar) | Yo estoy aquí. |
| **I am from the United States.**<br>(fixed, ser) | Yo soy de los Estados Unidos. |
| **Norman is bored.**<br>(temporary, estar) | Norman está aburrido. |
| **Norman is boring.**<br>(quality, ser) | Norman es aburrido. |
| **The TV is old.**<br>(quality, ser) | La televisión es vieja. |
| **The TV is broken.**<br>(condition, estar) | La televisión está rota. |

## Present Tense

| Estar "To Be" (conditional) | | |
|---|---|---|
| I am. | Yo esto*y*. | ehs-TOY |
| You (singular, familiar) are. | Tú est*ás*. | ehs-TAHS |
| He / She is. You (singular formal) are. | Él / Ella / Ud. est*á*. | ehs-TAH |
| We are. | Nosotros -as est*amos*. | ehs-TAH-mohs |
| You (plural familiar) are. | Vosotros -as est*áis*. | ehs-TAH-ees |
| They / You (plural formal) are. | Ellos / Ellas / Uds. est*án*. | ehs-TAHN |

## Simple Past Tense

| Estar "To Be" (conditional) | | |
|---|---|---|
| I was. | Yo est*uve*. | ehs-TOO-veh |
| You were. | Tú est*uviste*. | ehs-too-VEES-teh |
| He / She was. You (formal) were. | Él / Ella / Ud. est*uvo*. | ehs-TOO-voh |
| We were. | Nosotros -as est*uvimos*. | ehs-too-VEE-mohs |
| You were. | Vosotros -as est*uvisteis*. | ehs-too-VEES-teh-ees |
| They / You (plural formal) were. | Ellos / Ellas / Uds. est*uvieron*. | ehs-too-VYEH-rohn |

## Present Tense

|  | Ser "To be" (permanent) |  |
|---|---|---|
| I am. | Yo *soy*. | soy |
| You (singular familiar) **are**. | Tú *eres*. | EH-rehs |
| He/ She is. You (singular formal) **are**. | Él / Ella / Ud. *es*. | ehs |
| We are. | Nosotros -as *somos*. | SOH-mohs |
| You (plural familiar) **are**. | Vosotros -as *sois*. | SOH-ees |
| They / You (plural formal) **are**. | Ellos / Ellas / Uds. *son*. | sohn |

## Simple Past Tense

|  | Ser "To be" (permanent) |  |
|---|---|---|
| I was. | Yo *fui*. | FOO-ee |
| You (singular familiar) **were**. | Tú *fuiste*. | foo-EES-teh |
| He/ She was. You (singular formal) **were**. | Él / Ella / Ud. *fue*. | FOO-eh |
| We were. | Nosotros -as *fuimos*. | foo-EE-mohs |
| You (plural familiar) **were**. | Vosotros -as *fuisteis*. | foo-EES-teh-ees |
| They / You (plural formal) **were**. | Ellos / Ellas / Uds. *fueron* | foo-EH-rohn |

# IRREGULAR VERBS

Spanish has numerous irregular verbs that stray from the standard AR, ER, and IR conjugations. Rather than bog you down with too much grammar, we're providing the present tense conjugations for the most commonly used irregular verbs.

**TENER "To Have" (possess)**

| I have. | Yo *tengo*. | TEHNG-goh |
|---|---|---|
| **You** (singular familiar) **have.** | Tú *tienes*. | TYEH-nehs |
| He / She has. **You** (singular formal) **have.** | Él / Ella / Ud. *tiene*. | TYEH-neh |
| We have. | Nosotros -as *tenemos*. | TYEH-neh |
| **You** (plural familiar) **have.** | Vosotros -as *tenéis*. | teh-NEH-mohs |
| They / **You** (plural formal) **have.** | Ellos / Ellas / Uds. *tienen*. | TYEH-nehn |

---

### Tener

*Tener* means "to have," but it's also used to describe conditions such as hunger, body pain, and age. For example:
**Tengo hambre.** I'm hungry.
(Literally: I have hunger.)
**Tengo dolor de cabeza.** I have a headache.
**Tengo diez años.** I am ten years old.
(Literally: I have ten years.)

## HACER "To Do, To Make"

| I make. | Yo ha*go*. | AH-goh |
|---|---|---|
| **You** (singular familiar) **make.** | Tú ha*ces*. | AH-sehs |
| **He / She makes. You** (singular formal) **make.** | Él / Ella / Ud. ha*ce*. | AH-seh |
| **We make.** | Nosotros -as ha*cemos*. | ah-SEH-mohs |
| **You** (plural familiar) **make.** | Vosotros -as ha*céis*. | ah-SEH-ees |
| **They / You** (plural formal) **make.** | Ellos / Ellas / Uds. ha*cen*. | AH-sehn |

## COMENZAR "To Begin"

| I begin. | Yo com*ienzo*. | koh-MYEHN-soh |
|---|---|---|
| **You** (singular familiar) **begin.** | Tú com*ienzas*. | koh-MYEHN-sahs |
| **He / She begins. You** (singular formal) **begin.** | Él / Ella / Ud. com*ienza*. | koh-MYEHN-sah |
| **We begin.** | Nosotros -as comenz*amos* | koh-mehn-SAH-mos |
| **You** (plural familiar) **begin.** | Vosotros -as comenz*ais*. | koh-MEHN-says |
| **They / You** plural formal) **being.** | Ellos / Ellas / Uds. com*ienzen*. | koh-MYEHN-sahn |

## QUERER "To Want"

| I want. | Yo qu*ie*ro. | KYEH-roh |
|---|---|---|
| You (singular familiar) **want.** | Tú qu*ie*res. | KYEH-rehs |
| He / She wants. You (singular formal) **want.** | Él / Ella / Ud. qu*ie*re. | KYEH-reh |
| We want. | Nosotros -as quer*e*mos | keh-REH-mohs |
| You (plural familiar) **want.** | Vosotros -as quer*é*is. | keh-REH-ees |
| They / You plural formal) **want.** | Ellos / Ellas / Uds. qu*ie*ren. | KYEH-rehn |

## PODER "To Be Able"

| I can. (I) | Yo p*ue*do. | PWEH-doh |
|---|---|---|
| You (singular familiar) **can.** | Tú p*ue*des. | PWEH-dehs |
| He / She can. You singular formal) **can.** | Él / Ella / Ud. p*ue*de. | PWEH-deh |
| We can. | Nosotros -as pod*e*mos. | poh-DEH-mohs |
| You (plural familiar) **can.** | Vosotros -as pod*é*is. | poh-DEH-ees |
| They / You (plural formal) **can.** | Ellos / Ellas / Uds. p*ue*den. | PWEH-dehn |

| | HABER "To Have" (with past participle) | |
|---|---|---|
| I have. | Yo he. | eh |
| You (singular familiar) have. | Tú has. | ahs |
| He / She has. You (singular formal) have. | Él / Ella / Ud. ha. | ah |
| We have. | Nosotros -as hemos. | EH-mohs |
| You (plural familiar) have. | Vosotros -as habéis. | ah-BEH-ees |
| They / You plural formal) have. | Ellos / Ellas / Uds. han. | ahn |

| | PEDIR "To Ask" | |
|---|---|---|
| I ask. | Yo pido. | PEE-doh |
| You (singular familiar) ask. | Tú pides. | PEE-dehs |
| He / She asks. You (singular formal) ask. | Él / Ella / Ud. pide. | PEE-deh |
| We ask. | Nosotros -as pedimos. | peh-DEE-mohs |
| You (plural familiar) ask. | Vosotros -as pedís. | PEH-dees |
| They / You (plural formal) ask. | Ellos / Ellas / Uds. piden. | PEE-dehn |

**Note:** Verbs that end in **-cer** such as **conocer** change the **c** to **zc** before an ending that begins with **o** or **a**.

### CONOCER "To Know" (someone)

| English | Spanish | Pronunciation |
|---|---|---|
| I know. | Yo cono*zc*o. | koh-NOHS-koh |
| You (singular familiar) know. | Tú conoc*es*. | koh-NOH-sehs |
| He / She knows. You (singular formal) know. | Él / Ella / Ud. conoc*e*. | koh-NOH-seh |
| We know. | Nosotros -as conoc*emos*. | koh-noh-SEH-mohs |
| You (plural familiar) know. | Vosotros -as conoc*éis*. | koh-noh-SEH-ees |
| They / You (plural formal) know. | Ellos / Ellas / Uds. conoc*en*. | koh-NOH-sehn |

### SABER "to Know" (something)

| English | Spanish | Pronunciation |
|---|---|---|
| I know. | Yo sé. | koh-NOHS-koh |
| You (singular familiar) know. | Tú sab*es*. | koh-NOH-sehs |
| He/ She knows. You (singular formal) know. | Él / Ella / Ud. sab*e*. | koh-NOH-seh |
| We know. | Nosotros -as sab*emos*. | koh-noh-SEH-mohs |
| You (plural familiar) know. | Vosotros -as sab*éis*. | koh-noh-SEH-ees |
| They / You (plural formal) know. | Ellos / Ellas / Uds. sab*en*. | koh-NOH-sehn |

### Gustar

Spanish doesn't have a verb that literally means "to like." Instead, they use *gustar*, which means to please. So rather than say I like chocolate, you say:

**Me gusta el chocolate.** I like chocolate.
(Literally: Chocolate is pleasing to me.)

When what is liked is plural, the verb is plural:

**Me gustan las tortillas.** I like tortillas.
(Literally: Tortillas are pleasing to me.)

The person doing the liking is represented by an indirect object pronoun placed in front of the verb, as illustrated below.

|  | GUSTAR "To Like" |
|---|---|
| I like the tortilla. | *Me* gusta la tortilla. |
| You (informal singular) like the tortilla. | *Te* gusta la tortilla. |
| He / She likes the tortilla. You (formal singular) like the tortilla. | *Le* gusta la tortilla. |
| We like the tortilla. | *Nos* gusta la tortilla. |
| You (informal plural) like the tortilla. | *Os* gusta la tortilla. |
| They / You (formal plural) like the tortilla. | *Les* gusta la tortilla. |

### JUGAR "To Play"

| I play. | Yo j*ue*go. | HWEH-goh |
|---|---|---|
| **You** (singular familiar) **play.** | Tú j*ue*gas. | HWEH-gahs |
| He / She plays. You (singular formal) **play.** | Él / Ella / Ud. j*ue*ga. | HWEH-gah |
| We play. | Nosotros -as jug*a*mos. | hoo-GAH-mohs |
| **You** (plural familiar) play | Vosotros -as jug*ái*s. | hoo-GAYS |
| They / You (plural formal) **play.** | Ellos / Ellas / Uds. j*ue*gan. | HWEH-gahn |

## REFLEXIVE VERBS

Spanish has many reflexive verbs (when subject and object both refer to the same person or thing). The following common verbs are used reflexively: vestirse (to dress oneself), quedarse (to stay), bañarse (to bathe oneself), and levantarse (to wake up).

### VESTIRSE "To Dress"

| I get dressed. | Yo me v*i*sto. | meh VEES-toh |
|---|---|---|
| **You** (singular familiar) **get dressed.** | Tú te v*i*stes. | teh VEES-tehs |
| He / She gets dressed. You (singular formal) get dressed. | Él / Ella / Ud. se v*i*ste. | seh VEES-teh |
| We get dressed. | Nosotros -as nos vest*i*mos. | nohs vehs-TEE-mohs |
| **You** (plural familiar) get dressed | Vosotros -as os vest*i*s | ohs vehs-TEES |
| They / You (plural formal) **get dressed.** | Ellos / Ellas / Uds. se v*i*sten. | seh VEES-tehn |

## ETIQUETTE & CUSTOMS

**Gestures** The language barrier forces travelers to communicate with their hands more frequently than they would normally. (Ignorance of a certain word can produce the most creative form of mime as a substitute.) Some gestures mean the same no matter where you go—such as twisting a flat open hand to mean "so so." Many others are particular to a region.

For instance, a sweeping gesture under the chin means "I don't know" or "I don't care" in Argentina. Hitting your left palm with your right knuckle means "I don't believe you, that's stupid," in Mexico. And the OK sign—the thumb and index finger forming a circle with the remaining three fingers held up—may mean all's well in the U.S., but it's an extremely vulgar gesture in most South American countries. It's best to refrain from using this hand signal during your travels.

**Gift Giving** Exchanging gifts is as popular a custom in South America as anywhere else.

In general, a dinner invitation calls for a token of appreciation; a bunch of flowers or bottle of wine will be well-received. A gift from your home country should delight your South American friends, but women should be careful about buying men gifts, as the gesture may be misconstrued. In business, it's appropriate to cement a relationship with a gift; small, quality items such as leather goods, ball-point pens, or imported bottles of liquor, will make a positive impression. Gifts are almost always opened immediately.

**Greetings** South America is a touchy-feely continent. Both men and women like to hug and kiss when meeting and departing. A more formal handshake and keen eye contact are the norm, however, with strangers—especially foreigners. As you become better acquainted, you can expect bear hugs and cheek kisses, even from the most macho men. This is especially true in Argentina, where it's normal to greet every woman with a kiss on her cheek.

In Peru, Bolivia, Costa Rica, and Ecuador, cheek kisses aren't customary except within families or among old friends. In urban areas, a traditional handshake still reigns supreme.

At social events, it's important to greet everyone individually— a time-consuming but endearing habit. After you shake hands, kiss, or hug a stranger, give your name. When you leave, you must repeat the whole process.

An older person should always be addressed as *Señor* or *Señora*, *Don* or *Doña*. This is also an occasion when the more formal *usted* (you) should be used. Use the same formal address for someone in authority, as in *Señor Policia* or *Señor Medico*. In general, the younger the person, the more informal you can be.

Young people address each other as *amigo* or *chico* (*che* in Argentina), and use the more informal *tu* (*vos* in Argentina). Venezuela is an exception. There, *usted* is used in most instances.

Although it's important to try to use the correct address, people rarely get offended, especially with a foreigner. Ironically, the more formal tense is most often used when people want to insult or argue with each other.

Business cards are commonly exchanged upon first meetings, especially in Argentina. It's a useful way of overcoming the language barrier and exchanging information. It's even more helpful if you print it in English on one side and Spanish on the other.

**Punctuality**   Be aware of the somewhat lax manner of time-keeping in South America. The lack of clocks in public spaces, such as town squares and on church steeples, betrays a relaxed attitude toward time. As a general rule, you can expect to tack a half-hour onto any appointed meeting time. For example, if the time arranged is 11am, don't expect anyone to show up before 11:30am. This applies to both business and social events.

A tactful way of determining a meeting time is to ask, *"¿la hora inglésa o la hora Argentina?"* (or whatever country applies). The first means, "be punctual." The second means, "take your time."

For a business meeting, it's wise to call and confirm an hour or so beforehand. This way you know if the person is going to show up at all.

There are some exceptions to this rule. Chileans are on the whole more punctual than their South American counterparts.

In general, there has been a gradual improvement in "time management," as many South American governments run punctuality campaigns, stressing the importance of being on time in business. This is especially true in the travel industry. Also, multinational companies expect their employees to adapt to the western idea of meeting at the appointed hour.

For a social event, such as a party, it's wise to do as the locals do and be late. If you arrive on time, you'll surprise everyone, including the host, and you may find yourself alone until other guests arrive.

## FUN FACTS

- The world has Latin America to thank for: chocolate, the potato, maize, and chewing gum.
- The world can also thank Latin America for hammocks, rubber, canoes, and tobacco.
- The Andes is the longest mountain chain in the world.
- Colombia is the second-oldest democracy in the Western Hemisphere.
- Butch Cassidy and The Sundance Kid hid out in Argentina and met their end in Bolivia.
- In 1876, a small refrigerator ship called *Le Frigorifique* crossed the Tropics and the beef boom began.
- Spanish and Portuguese are not the only languages spoken in South America. There are over 350 Indian languages, the most important of which are Quechuan and Aymara.

- The monument that marks exactly where the Equator lies in Ecuador is actually 500 ft. (150m) off the mark.
- Chile argues with Peru over who invented *pisco* and *ceviche*. Uruguay and Argentina are at loggerheads over *dulce de leche*.
- Buenos Aires has the highest concentration of psychiatrists in the world.
- Iquitos, Peru, is the largest city in the world without road links.
- Angel Falls, Venezuela, the world's highest waterfall, is just under ²/₃ mile (1km) high.
- Five out of seven of Ecuador's ex-presidents are either in prison or exiled.
- Bolivia has the highest ski slope in the world, at 3 miles (5,345m).
- Mexico is the most populous Spanish-speaking country in the world.
- Mexico City is sinking 6 to 8 inches a year because it's built on top of an underground reservoir. The city is the oldest capital in the Americas and the world's third largest metropolis after Tokyo and New York City.
- Mexico introduced chocolate to the world.
- Costa Ricans have a life expectancy of 76.1 years. Their literacy rate is 96.2%. And 92% have access to phones.
- Avenida 9 de Julio, in Buenos Aires, is the widest street in the world, with 16 lanes.
- The driest place on earth is the Atacama Desert, in Argentina. Virtually no vegetation grows there, and in some parts of the Atacama Desert, it has never rained.
- Colombia supplies 90% of the world's production of emeralds.

## CHAPTER TWO
### GETTING THERE & GETTING AROUND

This section deals with every form of transportation. Whether you've just reached your destination by plane or you're renting a car to tour the countryside, you'll find the phrases you need in the next 30 pages.

### AT THE AIRPORT

| | |
|---|---|
| I am looking for _____ | **Estoy buscando _____** |
| | *ehs-TOY boos-KAHN-doh* |
| a porter. | **un portero.** |
| | *oon pohr-TEH-roh* |
| the check-in counter. | **el mostrador de registro.** |
| | *ehl mohs-trah-DOHR deh reh-HEES-troh* |
| the ticket counter. | **el mostrador de ventas de boletos.** |
| | *ehl mohs-trah-DOHR deh VEHN-tahs deh boh-LEH-tohs* |
| arrivals. | **las llegadas.** |
| | *lahs yeh-GAH-dahs* |
| departures. | **las salidas.** |
| | *lahs sah-LEE-dahs* |
| gate number _____. | **la puerta de salida _____.** |
| | *lah PWEHR-tah de sah-LEE-dah* |

*For full coverage of numbers, see p7.*

| | |
|---|---|
| the waiting area. | **el área de espera.** |
| | *ehl AH-reh-ah deh ehs-PEH-rah* |
| the men's restroom. | **el baño para caballeros.** |
| | *ehl BAH-nyoh PAH-rah kah-bah-YEH-rohs* |
| the women's restroom. | **el baño para damas.** |
| | *ehl BAH-nyoh PAH-rah DAH-mahs* |

the police station.

**la estación de policías.**
*lah ehs-tah-SYOHN deh poh-lee-SEE-ahs*

a security guard.

**un guardia de seguridad.**
*oon GWAHR-dyah deh seh-goo-ree-DAHD*

the smoking area.

**el área de fumar.**
*ehl AH-reh-ah deh foo-MAHR*

the information booth.

**el puesto de información.**
*ehl PWEHS-toh deh een-for-mah-SYOHN*

a public telephone.

**un teléfono público.**
*oon teh-LEH-foh-noh POO-blee-koh*

an ATM.

**un cajero automático.**
*oon kah-HEH-roh ow-toh-MAH-tee-koh*

baggage claim.

**el reclamo de equipaje.**
*ehl reh-KLAH-moh de eh-kee-PAH-heh*

a luggage cart.

**un carrito para equipaje.**
*oon kah-RREE-toh PAH-rah eh-kee-PAH-heh*

a currency exchange.

**un lugar de cambio de moneda.**
*oon loo-GAHR deh KAHM-byoh deh moh-NEH-dah*

a café.

**un café.**
*oon kah-FEH*

a restaurant.

**un restaurante.**
*oon rehs-tow-RAHN-teh*

a bar.

**una cantina.**
*OO-nah kahn-TEE-nah*

| | |
|---|---|
| a bookstore or newsstand. | **una librería o un puesto de periódicos.**<br>*OO-nah lee-breh-REE-ah oh oon PWEHS-toh deh peh-ree-OH-dee-kohs* |
| a duty-free shop. | **una tienda libre de impuestos.**<br>*OO-nah TYEHN-dah LEE-breh deh eem-PWEHS-tohs* |
| Is there Internet access here? | **¿Hay acceso al Internet aquí?**<br>*aye ahk-SEH-soh ahl een-tehr-NEHT ah-KEE* |
| I'd like to page someone. | **Quisiera mandar a llamar a alguien.**<br>*kee-SYEH-rah mahn-DAHR ah yah-MAHR ah AHLG-yehn* |
| Do you accept credit cards? | **¿Aceptan tarjetas de crédito?**<br>*ah-SEHP-tahn tahr-HEH-tahs deh KREH-dee-toh* |

## CHECKING IN

| | |
|---|---|
| I would like a one-way ticket to ____. | **Me gustaría un boleto de ida para ____.**<br>*meh goos-tah-REE-ah oon boh-LEH-toh deh EE-dah PAH-rah* |
| I would like a round trip ticket to ____. | **Me gustaría un boleto de ida y vuelta para ____.**<br>*meh goos-tah-REE-ah oon boh-LEH-toh de EE-dah ee VWEHL-tah PAH-rah* |
| How much are the tickets? | **¿Cuánto cuestan los boletos?**<br>*KWAHN-toh KWEHS-tahn lohs boh-LEH-tohs* |
| Do you have anything less expensive? | **¿Tiene algo más económico?**<br>*TYEH-neh AHL-goh mahs eh-koh-NOH-mee-koh* |
| How long is the flight? | **¿Cuán largo es el vuelo?**<br>*kwahn LAHR-goh ehs ehl VWEH-loh* |

## Common Airport Signs

| | |
|---|---|
| **Llegadas** | Arrivals |
| **Salidas** | Departures |
| **Terminal** | Terminal |
| **Puerto de salida** | Gate |
| **Boletería** | Ticketing |
| **Aduana** | Customs |
| **Reclamo de equipaje** | Baggage Claim |
| **Empuje** | Push |
| **Jale** | Pull |
| **No fumar** | No Smoking |
| **Entrada** | Entrance |
| **Salida** | Exit |
| **Caballeros** | Men's |
| **Damas** | Women's |
| **Autobuses de transporte** | Shuttle Buse |
| **Taxis** | Taxis |

*For full coverage of number terms, see p7.*
*For full coverage of time, see p12.*

| | |
|---|---|
| What time does flight _____ leave? | **¿A qué hora sale el vuelo _____?** *ah keh OH-rah SAH-leh ehl VWEH-loh* |
| What time does flight _____ arrive? | **¿A qué hora llega el vuelo _____?** *ah keh OH-rah YEH-gah ehl VWEH-loh* |
| Do I have a connecting flight? | **¿Tengo un vuelo de conexión?** *TEHNG-goh oon VWEH-loh deh koh-nehk-SYOHN* |
| Do I need to change planes? | **¿Necesito cambiar aviones?** *neh-seh-SEE-toh kahm-BYAHR ah-VYOH-nehs* |
| My flight leaves at __:__. | **Mi vuelo sale a las ___:___.** *mee VWEH-loh SAH-leh ah lahs* |

*For full coverage of numbers, see p7.*

| | |
|---|---|
| What time will the flight arrive? | **¿A qué hora llega el vuelo?** *ah keh OH-rah YEH-gah ehl VWEH-loh* |
| Is the flight on time? | **¿El vuelo está a tiempo?** *ehl VWEH-loh ehs-TAH ah TYEHM-poh* |
| Is the flight delayed? | **¿El vuelo está retrasado?** *ehl VWEH-loh ehs-TAH reh-trah-SAH-doh* |
| From which terminal is flight _____ leaving? | **¿De cuál terminal sale el vuelo _____?** *deh kwahl tehr-mee-NAHL SAH-leh ehl VWEH-loh* |
| From which gate is flight _____ leaving? | **¿De cuál puerta de salida sale el vuelo _____?** *deh kwahl PWEHR-tah deh sah-LEE-dah SAH-leh ehl VWEH-loh* |
| How much time do I need for check-in? | **¿Cuánto tiempo necesito para registrarme?** *KWAHN-toh TYEHM-poh neh-seh-SEE-toh PAH-rah reh-hees-TRAHR-me* |

| | |
|---|---|
| Is there an express check-in line? | **¿Hay una fila expresa?** |
| | *aye OO-nah FEE-lah ehs-PREH-soh* |
| Is there electronic check-in? | **¿Hay registro electrónico?** |
| | *ay reh-HEES-troh eh-lehk-TROH-nee-koh* |

**Seat Preferences**

| | |
|---|---|
| I would like _____ ticket(s) in _____ | **Quisiera _____ boleto(s) en _____** |
| | *kee-SYEH-rah _____ boh-LEH-toh(s) ehn* |
| first class. | **primera clase.** |
| | *pree-MEH-rah KLAH-seh* |
| business class. | **la clase de negocios.** |
| | *lah KLAH-seh deh neh-GOH-syohs* |
| economy class. | **la clase económica.** |
| | *lah KLAH-seh eh-koh-NOH-mee-kah* |
| I would like _____ | **Me gustaría _____** |
| | *meh goos-tah-REE-ah* |
| Please don't give me _____ | **Por favor no me dé _____** |
| | *pohr fah-VOHR noh meh deh* |
| a window seat. | **un asiento de ventana.** |
| | *oon ah-SYEHN-toh deh vehn-TAH-nah* |
| an aisle seat. | **un asiento de pasillo.** |
| | *oon ah-SYEHN-toh deh pah-SEE-yoh* |
| an emergency exit row seat. | **un asiento en la fila de emergencia.** |
| | *oon ah-SYEHN-toh ehn lah FEE-lah deh eh-mehr-HEHN-syah* |
| a bulkhead seat. | **un asiento detrás del tabique.** |
| | *oon ah-SYEHN-toh deh-TRAHS dehl tah-BEE-keh* |
| a seat by the restroom. | **un asiento cerca de los baños.** |
| | *oon ah-SYEHN-toh SEHR-kah deh lohs BAH-nyohs* |

GETTING THERE

| | |
|---|---|
| a seat near the front. | **un asiento cerca del frente.**<br>*oon ah-SYEHN-toh SEHR-kah*<br>*dehl FREHN-teh* |
| a seat near the middle. | **un asiento cerca del centro.**<br>*oon ah-SYEHN-toh SEHR-kah*<br>*dehl SEHN-troh* |
| a seat near the back. | **un asiento cerca de atrás.**<br>*oon ah-SYEHN-toh SEHR-kah*<br>*deh ah-TRAHS* |
| Is there a meal on the flight? | **¿Sirven comida en este vuelo?**<br>*SEER-vehn koh-MEE-dah ehn EHS-teh VWEH-loh* |
| I'd like to order ____ | **Quisiera ordenar ____**<br>*kee-SYEH-rah ohr-deh-NAHR* |
| a vegetarian meal. | **una comida vegetariana.**<br>*OO-nah koh-MEE-dah veh-heh-tah-RYAH-nah* |
| a kosher meal. | **una comida kósher.**<br>*OO-nah koh-MEE-dah KOH-shehr* |
| a diabetic meal. | **una comida para diabéticos.**<br>*OO-nah koh-MEE-dah PAH-rah dyah-BEH-tee-kohs* |
| I am traveling to ____. | **Estoy viajando hacia ____.**<br>*ehs-TOY vyah-HAHN-doh HAH-syah* |
| I am coming from ____. | **Estoy regresando de ____.**<br>*ehs-TOY reh-greh-SAHN-doh de* |
| I arrived from ____. | **Llegué de ____.**<br>*yeh-GEH deh* |

*For full coverage of country terms, see English / Spanish dictionary.*

| | |
|---|---|
| I'd like to change / cancel / confirm my reservation. | **Quisiera cambiar / cancelar / confirmar mi reservación.**<br>*kee-SYEH-rah kahm-BYAHR / kahn-seh-LAHR / kohn-feer-MAHR mee reh-sehr-vah-SYOHN* |

| | |
|---|---|
| I have ____ bags to check. | **Tengo ____ bolsas que registrar.** *TEHNG-goh ____ BOHL-sahs keh reh-hees-TRAHR* |

*For full coverage of numbers, see p7.*

**Passengers with Special Needs**

| | |
|---|---|
| Is that wheelchair accessible? | **¿Eso es accesible para personas con impedimentos?** *EH-soh ehs ahk-seh-SEE-bleh PAH-rah pehr-SOH-nahs kohn eem-peh-dee-MEHN-tohs* |
| May I have a wheelchair / walker please? | **¿Me puede dar una silla de ruedas / un andador, por favor?** *meh PWEH-deh dahr OO-nah SEE-yah deh RWEH-dahs / oon ahn-dah-DOHR pohr fah-VOHR* |
| I need some assistance boarding. | **Necesito un poco de ayuda al abordar.** *neh-seh-SEE-toh oon POH-koh deh ah-YOO-dah ahl ah-bohr-DAHR* |
| I need to bring my service dog. | **Necesito traer a mi perro de servicio.** *neh-seh-SEE-toh trah-EHR ah mee PEH-rroh deh sehr-VEE-syoh* |
| Do you have services for the hearing impaired? | **¿Tienen servicios para las personas con impedimentos auditivos?** *TYEH-nehn sehr-VEE-syohs PAH-rah lahs pehr-SOH-nahs kohn eem-peh-dee-MEHN-tohs ow-dee-TEE-vohs* |
| Do you have services for the visually impaired? | **¿Tienen servicios para las personas con impedimentos visuales?** *TYEH-nehn sehr-VEE-syohs pah-rah lahs pehr-SOH-nahs kohn eem-peh-dee-MEHN-tohs vee-soo-AH-lehs* |

GETTING THERE

**Trouble at Check-In**

| | |
|---|---|
| How long is the delay? | **¿Cuán largo es el retraso?** |
| | *kwahn LAHR-goh ehs ehl reh-TRAH-soh* |
| My flight was late. | **Mi vuelo estuvo tarde.** |
| | *mee VWEH-loh ehs-TOO-voh TAHR-deh* |
| I missed my flight. | **Perdí mi vuelo.** |
| | *pehr-DEE mee VWEH-loh* |
| When is the next flight? | **¿Cuándo es el próximo vuelo?** |
| | *KWAHN-doh ehs ehl PROHK-see-moh VWEH-loh* |
| May I have a meal voucher? | **¿Me puede dar un vale para comida?** |
| | *meh PWEH-deh dahr oon VAH-leh pah-rah koh-MEE-dah* |
| May I have a room voucher? | **¿Me puede dar un vale para hospedaje?** |
| | *meh PWEH-deh dahr oon VAH-leh pah-rah ohs-peh-DAH-heh* |

## AT CUSTOMS / SECURITY CHECKPOINTS

| | |
|---|---|
| I'm traveling with a group. | **Estoy viajando con un grupo.** |
| | *ehs-TOY vyah-HAHN-doh kohn oon GROO-poh* |
| I'm on my own. | **Estoy viajando solo -a.** |
| | *ehs-TOY vyah-HAHN-doh SOH-loh -lah* |
| I'm traveling on business. | **Estoy viajando por negocios.** |
| | *ehs-TOY vyah-HAHN-doh pohr neh-GOH-syohs* |
| I'm on vacation. | **Estoy de vacaciones.** |
| | *ehs-TOY deh vah-kah-SYOH-nehs* |
| I have nothing to declare. | **No tengo nada que declarar.** |
| | *noh TEHNG-goh NAH-dah keh deh-klah-RAHR* |

| | |
|---|---|
| I would like to declare ____. | **Quisiera declarar ____.**<br>*kee-SYEH-rah deh-klah-RAHR* |
| I have some liquor. | **Tengo un poco de licor.**<br>*TEHNG-goh oon POH-koh deh lee-KOHR* |
| I have some cigars. | **Tengo unos cigarros.**<br>*TENHG-goh oo-nohs see-GAH-rrohs* |
| They are gifts. | **Son regalos.**<br>*sohn reh-GAH-lohs* |
| They are for personal use. | **Son para uso personal.**<br>*sohn PAH-rah OO-soh pehr-soh-NAHL* |
| That is my medicine. | **Esa es mi medicina.**<br>*EH-sah ehs mee meh-dee-SEE-nah* |
| I have my prescription. | **Tengo mi receta.**<br>*TEHNG-goh mee rreh-SEH-tah* |
| My children are traveling on the same passport. | **Mis niños están viajando bajo el mismo pasaporte.**<br>*mees NEE-nyohs ehs-TAHN vyah-HAHN-doh BAH-hoh ehl MEES-moh pah-sah-POHR-teh* |
| I'd like a male / female officer to conduct the search. | **Quisiera que un oficial varón / mujer haga el registro.**<br>*kee-SYEH-rah keh oon oh-fees-YAHL vah-ROHN / moo-HEHR AH-gah ehl reh-HEES-trohx* |

**Trouble at Security**

| | |
|---|---|
| Help me. I've lost ____ | **Ayúdeme. Perdí ____**<br>*ah-YOO-dah-meh pehr-DEE* |
| my passport. | **mi pasaporte.**<br>*mee pah-sah-POHR-teh* |
| my boarding pass. | **mi boleta de abordaje.**<br>*mee boh-LEH-tah deh bohr-DAH-heh* |

### Listen Up: Security Lingo

| | |
|---|---|
| **Por favor, quítese los zapatos.** | Please remove your shoes. |
| **Quítese la chaqueta / el suéter.** | Remove your jacket / sweater. |
| **Quítese las joyas.** | Remove your jewelry. |
| **Coloque su equipaje sobre el cinturón.** | Place your bags on the conveyor belt. |
| **Por favor hágase a un lado.** | Step to the side. |
| **Debemos realizar una inspección manual.** | We have to do a hand search. |

| | |
|---|---|
| my identification. | **mi identificación.** |
| | *mee ee-dehn-tee-fee-kah-SYOHN* |
| my wallet. | **mi cartera.** |
| | *mee kahr-TEH-rah* |
| my purse. | **mi bolso.** |
| | *mee BOHL-soh* |
| Someone stole my purse / wallet! | **¡Alguien me robó mi bolso / cartera!** |
| | *ah-YOO-dah AHLG-yehn meh roh-BOH mee BOHL-soh / kahr-TEH-rah* |

### IN-FLIGHT

It's unlikely you'll need much Spanish on the plane, but these phrases will help if a bilingual flight attendant is unavailable or if you need to talk to a Spanish-speaking neighbor.

| | |
|---|---|
| I think that's my seat. | **Creo que ese es mi asiento.** |
| | *KREH-oh keh EH-seh ehs mee ah-SYEHN-toh* |
| May I have ____ | **¿Me puede dar ____** |
| | *meh PWEH-deh dahr* |
| water? | **agua?** |
| | *AH-wah* |

| | |
|---|---|
| sparkling water? | **agua carbonatada?** |
| | *AH-wah kahr-boh-nah-TAH-dah* |
| orange juice? | **jugo de naranja?** |
| | *HOO-goh deh nah-RAHN-hah* |
| soda? | **soda / refresco / gaseosa?** |
| | *SOH-dah / reh-FREHS-koh / gah-seh-OH-sah* |
| diet soda? | **soda / refresco / gaseosa de dieta?** |
| | *SOH-dah / reh-FREHS-koh / gah-seh-OH-sah deh DYEH-tah* |
| a beer? | **una cerveza?** |
| | *OO-nah sehr-VEH-sah* |
| wine? | **vino?** |
| | *VEE-noh* |

*For a complete list of drinks, see p100.*

| | |
|---|---|
| a pillow? | **una almohada?** |
| | *OO-nah ahl-moh-AH-dah* |
| a blanket? | **una frazada?** |
| | *OO-nah frah-SAH-dah* |
| a hand wipe? | **una toallita húmeda?** |
| | *OO-nah toh-ah-YEE-tah OO-meh-dah* |
| headphones? | **audífonos?** |
| | *ow-DEE-foh-nohs* |
| a magazine or newspaper? | **una revista o un periódico?** |
| | *OO-nah reh-VEES-tah oh oon pehr-YOH-dee-koh* |
| When will the meal be served? | **¿Cuándo servirán la comida?** |
| | *KWAHN-doh sehr-vee-RAHN lah koh-MEE-dah* |
| How long until we land? | **¿Cuánto falta para llegar?** |
| | *KWAHN-toh FAHL-tah pah-rah yeh-GAHR* |

GETTING THERE

| | |
|---|---|
| May I move to another seat? | **¿Me puedo mover a otro asiento?** *meh PWEH-doh moh-VEHR ah OH-troh ah-SYEHN-toh* |
| How do I turn the light on / off? | **¿Cómo enciendo / apago la luz?** *KOH-moh ehn-SYEHN-doh / ah-PAH-go lah loos* |

**Trouble In-Flight**

| | |
|---|---|
| These headphones are broken. | **Estos audífonos están rotos.** *EHS-tohs ow-DEE-foh-nohs ehs-TAHN ROH-tohs* |
| I spilled. | **Tuve un derrame.** *TOO-veh oon deh-RRAH-meh* |
| My child spilled. | **Mi niño -a tuvo un derrame.** *mee NEE-nyoh -nyah TOO-veh oon deh-RRAH-me* |
| My child is sick. | **Mi niño -a está enfermo -a.** *mee NEE-nyoh -nyah ehs-TAH ehn-FEHR-moh -mah* |
| I need an airsickness bag. | **Necesito una bolsa para mareos.** *neh-seh-SEE-toh OO-nah BOHL-sah pah-rah mah-REH-ohs* |
| I smell something strange. | **Huelo algo extraño.** *WEH-loh AHL-goh ehs-TRAH-nyoh* |
| That passenger is behaving suspiciously. | **Ese pasajero se está comportando sospechosamente.** *EH-seh pah-sah-HEH-roh seh ehs-TAH kohm-pohr-TAHN-doh sohs-peh-choh-sah-MEHN-teh* |

**BAGGAGE CLAIM**

| | |
|---|---|
| Where is baggage claim for flight ____? | **¿Dónde está el reclamo de equipaje para el vuelo ____?** *DOHN-deh ehs-TAH ehl reh-KLAH-moh deh eh-kee-PAH-heh pah-rah ehl VWEH-loh* |

| | |
|---|---|
| Would you please help with my bags? | **¿Me puede ayudar con mis bolsas?**<br>*meh PWEH-deh ah-yoo-DAHR kohn mees BOHL-sahs* |
| I am missing ____ bags. | **Me faltan ____ bolsas.**<br>*meh FAHL-tahn ____ BOHL-sahs* |

*For full coverage of numbers, see p7.*

| | |
|---|---|
| My bag is ____ | **Mi bolsa ____**<br>*mee BOHL-sah* |
| lost. | **está perdida.**<br>*ehs-TAH pehr-DEE-dah* |
| damaged. | **está dañada.**<br>*ehs-TAH dah-NYAH-dah* |
| stolen. | **fue robada.**<br>*fweh roh-BAH-dah* |
| a suitcase. | **es una maleta.**<br>*ehs OO-nah mah-LEH-ta* |
| a briefcase. | **es un maletín.**<br>*ehs oon mah-leh-TEEN* |
| a carry-on. | **es una maleta de mano.**<br>*ehs OO-nah mah-LEH-tah deh MAH-noh* |
| a suit bag. | **es una bolsa para trajes.**<br>*ehs OO-nah BOHL-sah PAH-rah TRAH-hehs* |
| a trunk. | **es un baúl.**<br>*ees oon bah-OOL* |
| golf clubs. | **son palos de golf.**<br>*sohn PAH-lohs deh gohlf* |

*For full coverage of color terms, see English / Spanish Dictionary.*

| | |
|---|---|
| hard. | **es dura.**<br>*ehs DOO-rah* |
| made out of ____ | **está hecha de ____**<br>*ehs-TAH EH-chah deh ____* |
| canvas. | **lona.**<br>*LOH-nah* |

| vinyl. | **vinilo.** |
| | *vee-NEE-loh* |
| leather. | **cuero.** |
| | *KWEH-roh* |
| hard plastic. | **plástico duro.** |
| | *PLAH-stee-koh DOO-roh* |
| aluminum. | **aluminio.** |
| | *ah-loo-MEE-nyoh* |

## RENTING A VEHICLE

| Is there a car rental agency in the airport? | **¿Hay una agencia de alquiler de autos en el aeropuerto?** |
| | *aye OO-nah ah-HEN-syah deh ahl-kee-LEHR deh OW-tohs ehn ehl ah-eh-roh-PWEHR-toh* |
| I have a reservation. | **Tengo una reservación.** |
| | *TEHNG-goh OO-nah reh-sehr-vah-SYOHN* |

### Vehicle Preferences

| I would like to rent ____ | **Quisiera alquilar ____** |
| | *kee-SYEH-rah ahl-kee-LAHR* |
| an economy car. | **un auto económico.** |
| | *oon OW-toh eh-koh-NOH-mee-koh* |
| a midsize car. | **un auto mediano.** |
| | *oon OW-toh meh-DYAH-noh* |
| a sedan | **un sedán.** |
| | *oon seh-DAHN* |
| a convertible. | **un convertible.** |
| | *oon kohn-vehr-TEE-bleh* |
| a van. | **una furgoneta.** |
| | *OO-nah foor-goh-NEH-tah* |
| a sports car. | **un auto deportivo.** |
| | *oon OW-toh deh-pohr-TEE-voh* |

| | |
|---|---|
| a 4-wheel-drive vehicle. | **un auto de tracción en las cuatro ruedas.** |
| | *oon OW-toh deh trahk-SYOHN ehn lahs KWAH-troh RWEH-dahs* |
| a motorcycle. | **una motocicleta.** |
| | *OO-nah moh-toh-see-KLEH-tah* |
| a scooter. | **una motoneta.** |
| | *OO-nah mo-toh-NEH-tah* |
| Do you have one with _____ | **¿Tiene uno con _____** |
| | *TYEH-neh OO-noh kohn* |
| air conditioning? | **aire acondicionado?** |
| | *AYEE-reh ah-kohn-dee-syoh-NAH-doh* |
| a sunroof? | **techo corredizo?** |
| | *TEH-choh koh-rreh-DEE-soh* |
| a CD player? | **un lector de discos compactos?** |
| | *oon lehk-TOHR deh DEES-kohs kohm-PAHK-tohs* |
| satellite radio? | **radio satélite?** |
| | *RAH-dyoh sah-TEH-lee-teh* |
| satellite tracking? | **navegación por satélite?** |
| | *nah-veh-gah-SYOHN pohr sah-TEH-lee-teh* |
| an onboard map? | **un mapa a bordo?** |
| | *oon MAH-pah ah-BOHR-doh* |
| a DVD player? | **un lector de DVD?** |
| | *oon lehk-TOHR deh deh-veh-DEH* |
| child seats? | **asientos infantiles?** |
| | *ah-SYEHN-tohs een-fahn-TEE-lehs* |
| Do you have a _____ | **¿Tiene un auto _____** |
| | *TYEH-neh oon OW-toh* |
| smaller car? | **más pequeño?** |
| | *mahs peh-KEH-nyoh* |
| bigger car? | **más grande?** |
| | *mahs GRAHN-deh* |

| | |
|---|---|
| cheaper car? | **más barato?**<br>*mahs bah-RAH-toh* |
| Do you have a non-smoking car? | **¿Tiene un auto de no fumar?**<br>*TYEH-neh oon OW-toh deh noh foo-MAHR* |
| I need an automatic transmission. | **Necesito una transmisión automática.**<br>*neh-seh-SEE-toh OO-nah trahns-mee-SYOHN ow-toh-MAH-tee-kah* |
| A standard transmission is okay. | **Una transmisión manual está bien.**<br>*OO-nah trahns-mee-SYOHN mah-NWAHL eh-STAH BYEHN* |
| May I have an upgrade? | **¿Puedo recibir una mejora de categoría?**<br>*PWEH-doh reh-see-BEER OO-nah meh-HO-rah deh kah-teh-goh-REE-ah* |

## Money Matters

| | |
|---|---|
| What's the daily / weekly / monthly rate? | **¿Cuál es la tarifa diaria / semanal / mensual?**<br>*kwahl ehs lah tah-REE-fah DYAHR-yah / seh-mah-NAHL / mehn-SWAHL* |
| What is the mileage rate? | **¿Cuál es la tarifa por milla / kilómetro?**<br>*kwahl ehs lah tah-REE-fah pohr MEE-yah / kee-LOH-meh-troh* |
| How much is insurance? | **¿Cuánto cuesta el seguro?**<br>*KWAHN-toh KWEHS-tah ehl seh-GOO-roh* |
| Are there other fees? | **¿Hay otros honorarios?**<br>*aye OH-trohs oh-noh-RAHR-yohs* |
| Is there a weekend rate? | **¿Hay una tarifa de fin de semana?**<br>*aye OO-nah tah-REE-fah deh feen deh seh-MAH-nah* |

## Technical Questions

What kind of fuel does it take?
**¿Qué tipo de combustible usa?**
*keh TEE-poh deh kohm-boos-TEE-bleh OO-sah*

Do you have the manual in English?
**¿Tiene el manual en inglés?**
*TYEH-neh ehl mah-NWAHL ehn eeng-GLEHS*

Do you have a booklet in English with the local traffic laws?
**¿Tiene un folleto en inglés con las leyes de tráfico locales?**
*TYEH-neh oon foh-YEH-toh ehn eeng-GLEHS kohn lahs LEH-yehs deh TRAH-fee-koh loh-KAH-lehs*

## Car Troubles

The _____ doesn't work.
**_____ no funciona.**
*noh foon-SYOH-nah*

*See diagram on p58 for car parts.*

It is already dented.
**Ya está abollado.**
*YAH ehs-TAH ah-boh-YAH-doh*

It is scratched.
**Está rayado.**
*ehs-TAH rah-YAH-doh*

The windshield is cracked.
**El parabrisas está agrietado.**
*ehl pah-rah-BREE-sahs ehs-TAH ahg-ryeh-TAH-doh*

The tires look low.
**Las llantas se ven un poco vacías.**
*lahs YAHN-tahs seh vehn oon POH-koh VAH-syahs*

It has a flat tire.
**Tiene una llanta vacía.**
*TYEH-neh OO-nah YAHN-tah VAH-syah*

Whom do I call for service?
**¿A quién llamo para servicio?**
*ah KYEHN YAH-moh pah-rah sehr-VEE-syoh*

It won't start.
**No enciende.**
*noh ehn-SYEHN-deh*

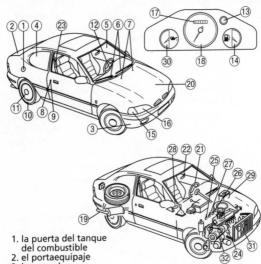

1. la puerta del tanque
   del combustible
2. el portaequipaje
3. los parachoques
4. la ventana
5. el parabrisas
6. el limpiaparabrisas
7. el lavador
   de parabrisas
8. el seguro
9. los seguros
   automáticos
10. las llantas
11. las ruedas
12. la ignición
13. la luz de advertencia
14. el indicador del
    combustible
15. las luces de giro
16. los focos delanteros

17. el odómetro
18. el velocímetro
19. el silenciador
20. el capó
21. el volante
22. el espejo
23. el cinturón de seguridad
24. el motor
25. el acelarador
26. el embrague
27. los frenos
28. el freno de mano
29. el acumulador
30. el indicador de aceite
31. el radiador
32. la manguera del ventilador

It's out of gas.

**No tiene combustible.**
*noh TYEH-neh kohm-boos-TEEB-leh*

The Check Engine light is on.

**La luz de examinar el motor está encendida.**
*lah loos dee ehk-sah-mee-NAHR ehl moh-TOHR ehs-TAH ehn-sehn-DEE-dah*

The oil light is on.

**La luz del aceite está encendida.**
*lah loos dehl ah-SEH-ee-teh ehs-TAH ehn-sehn-DEE-dah*

The brake light is on.

**La luz del freno está encendida.**
*lah loos dehl FREH-noh ehs-TAH ehn-sehn-DEE-dah*

It runs rough.

**Corre un poco áspero.**
*KOH-rreh oon POH-koh AHS-peh-roh*

The car is over-heating.

**El auto se sobrecalienta.**
*ehl OW-toh seh soh-breh-kah-LYEHN-tah*

**Asking for Directions**

Excuse me, please.

**Perdóneme.**
*pehr-DOH-neh-meh*

How do I get to ____?

**¿Cómo llego a ____?**
*KOH-moh YEH-goh ah*

Go straight.

**Siga directo.**
*SEE-gah dee-REHK-toh*

Turn left.

**Vire a la izquierda.**
*VEE-reh ah lah ees-KYEHR-dah*

Continue right.

**Continúe a mano derecha.**
*kohn-tee-NOO-eh ah MAH-noh dee-REH-chah*

It's on the right.

**Está a mano derecha.**
*ehs-TAH ah MAH-noh dee-REH-chah*

| | |
|---|---|
| Can you show me on the map? | **¿Puede mostrarme en el mapa?** *PWEH-deh mohs-TRAHR-meh ehn ehl MAH-pah* |
| How far is it from here? | **¿Cuán lejos está de aquí?** *kwahn LEH-hohs ehs-TAH deh ah-KEE* |
| Is this the right road for ____? | **¿Es ésta la carretera correcta para ____?** *ehs EHS-tah lah kah-rreh-TEH-rah koh-RREHK-tah PAH-rah* |
| I've lost my way. | **Estoy perdido -a.** *ehs-TOY pehr-DEE-doh -dah* |
| Would you repeat that? | **¿Puede repetir eso?** *PWEH-deh reh-peh-TEER EH-so* |
| Thanks for your help. | **Gracias por su ayuda.** *GRAH-syahs pohr soo ah-YOO-dah* |

*For full coverage of direction-related terms, see p5.*

**Sorry, Officer**

| | |
|---|---|
| What is the speed limit? | **¿Cuál es el límite de velocidad?** *kwahl ehs ehl LEE-mee-teh deh veh-loh-see-DAHD* |

## Road Signs

| | |
|---|---|
| Límite de velocidad | Speed Limit |
| Pare | Stop |
| Ceda el paso | Yield |
| Peligro | Danger |
| Calle sin salida | No Exit |
| Tránsito en una dirección | One Way |
| No entre | Do Not Enter |
| Carretera cerrada | Road Closed |
| Peaje | Toll |
| Efectivo solamente | Cash Only |
| No estacione | No Parking |
| Tarifa de estacionamiento | Parking Fee |
| Estacionamiento | Parking Garage |

| | |
|---|---|
| I wasn't going that fast. | **Yo no iba tan rápido.** |
| | *yoh noh EE-bah tahn RAH-pee-doh* |
| How much is the fine? | **¿De cuánto es la multa?** |
| | *deh KWAHN-toh ehs lah* |
| | *MOOL-tah* |
| Where do I pay the fine? | **¿Dónde pago la multa?** |
| | *DOHN-deh PAH-goh lah MOOL-tah* |
| Do I have to go to court? | **¿Tengo que ir a corte?** |
| | *TEHNG-goh keh eer ah KOHR-teh* |
| I had an accident. | **Tuve un accidente.** |
| | *TOO-veh oon ahk-see-DEHN-teh* |
| The other driver hit me. | **El otro chofer me dio.** |
| | *ehl OH-troh choh-FEHR meh* |
| | *DEE-oh* |
| I'm at fault. | **Es mi culpa.** |
| | *ehs mee KOOL-pah* |

## BY TAXI

| | |
|---|---|
| Where is the taxi stand? | **¿Dónde está el puesto de taxis?** |
| | *DOHN-deh ehs-TAH ehl PWEHS-toh deh TAHK-sees* |
| Is there a limo / bus / van for my hotel? | **¿Hay una limosina / un autobús / una furgoneta para mi hotel?** |
| | *ay OO-nah lee-moh-SEE-nah / oon ow-toh-BOOS / OO-nah foor-goh-NEH-tah PAH-rah mee oh-TEHL* |

### Listen Up: Taxi Lingo

| | |
|---|---|
| **¡Súbanse!** | Get in! |
| **Deje su equipaje. Lo tengo.** | Leave your luggage. I got it. |
| **Sale 100 pesos por cada maleta.** | It's 100 pesos for each bag. |
| **¿Cuántos pasajeros?** | How many passengers? |
| **¿Tiene prisa?** | Are you in a hurry? |

| | |
|---|---|
| I need to get to ____. | **Necesito ir a ____.** |
| | *neh-seh-SEE-toh eer ah* |
| How much will that cost? | **¿Cuánto costará eso?** |
| | *KWAHN-toh kohs-tah-RAH EH-soh* |
| How long will it take? | **¿Cuánto tomará?** |
| | *KWAHN-toh toh-mah-RAH* |
| Can you take me / us to the train / bus station? | **¿Puede llevarme / llevarnos a la estación del tren / autobús?** |
| | *PWEH-deh yeh-VAHR-meh / yeh-VAHR-nohs ah lah ehs-tah-SYOHN dehl trehn / ow-toh-BOOS* |
| I am in a hurry. | **Tengo prisa.** |
| | *TEHNG-goh PREE-sah* |
| Slow down. | **Reduzca la velocidad.** |
| | *rreh-DOOS-kah lah veh-loh-see-DAHD* |
| Am I close enough to walk? | **¿Estoy suficientemente cerca como para caminar?** |
| | *ehs-TOY soo-fee-syehn-teh-MEHN-teh SEHR-kah koh-moh pah-rah kah-mee-NAHR* |
| Let me out here. | **Déjeme salir de aquí.** |
| | *DEH-heh-meh sah-LEER deh ah-KEE* |
| That's not the correct change. | **Ese no es el cambio correcto.** |
| | *EH-seh noh ehs ehl KAM-byoh koh-REHK-toh* |

## BY TRAIN

| | |
|---|---|
| How do I get to the train station? | **¿Cómo llego a la estación del tren?** |
| | *KOH-moh YEH-goh ah lah ehs-tah-SYOHN dehl trehn* |
| Would you take me to the train station? | **¿Puede llevarme a la estación del tren?** |
| | *PWEH-deh yeh-VAHR-meh ah lah ehs-tah-SYOHN dehl trehn* |

| | |
|---|---|
| How long is the trip to ____? | **¿Cuán largo es el viaje a ____?** *kwahn LAHR-goh ehs ehl VYAH-heh ah* |
| When is the next train? | **¿Cuándo sale el próximo tren?** *KWAHN-doh SAH-leh ehl PROHK-see-moh trehn* |
| Do you have a schedule / timetable? | **¿Tiene un itinerario?** *TYEH-neh oon ee-tee-neh-RAH-ryoh* |
| Do I have to change trains? | **¿Tengo que cambiar trenes?** *TEHNG-goh keh kahm-BYAHR TREH-nehs* |
| a one-way ticket | **un boleto de ida** *oon boh-LEH-toh deh EE-dah* |
| a round-trip ticket | **un boleto de ida y vuelta** *oon boh-LEH-toh deh EE-dah ee VWEHL-tah* |
| Which platform does it leave from? | **¿De cuál plataforma sale?** *deh kwahl plah-tah-FOHR-mah SAH-leh* |
| Is there a bar car? | **¿Hay un vagón cantina?** *aye oon vah-GOHN kahn-TEE-nah* |
| Is there a dining car? | **¿Hay un vagón para cenar?** *aye oon vah-GOHN pah-rah seh-NAHR* |
| Which car is my seat in? | **¿En cuál vagón está mi asiento?** *ehn kwahl vah-GOHN ehs-TAH mee ah-SYEHN-toh* |
| Is this seat taken? | **¿Este asiento está ocupado?** *EHS-teh ah-SYEHN-toh ehs-TAH oh-koo-PAH-doh* |
| Where is the next stop? | **¿Dónde es la próxima parada?** *DOHN-deh ehs lah PROHK-see-mah pah-RAH-dah* |
| How many stops to ____? | **¿Cuántas paradas hasta ____?** *KWAHN-tahs pah-RAH-dahs AHS-tah* |

| What's the train number and destination? | ¿Cuál es el número del tren y su destino? |
| | *kwahl ehs ehl NOO-meh-roh dehl trehn ee soo dehs-TEE-noh* |

## BY BUS

| How do I get to the bus station? | ¿Cómo llego a la estación de autobuses? |
| | *KOH-moh YEH-go ah lah ehs-tah-SYOHN deh ow-toh-BOO-sehs* |
| Would you take me to the bus station? | ¿Me puede llevar a la estación de autobuses? |
| | *meh PWEH-deh yeh-VAHR ah lah ehs-tah-SYOHN deh ow-toh-BOO-sehs* |
| May I have a bus schedule? | ¿Me puede dar un itinerario? |
| | *meh PWEH-deh dahr oon ee-tee-neh-RAH-ryoh* |
| Which bus goes to ____? | ¿Cuál autobús va para ____? |
| | *kwahl ow-toh-BOOS vah pah-rah* |
| Where does it leave from? | ¿De dónde sale? |
| | *deh DOHN-deh SAH-leh* |
| How long does the bus take? | ¿Cuánto se tarda el autobús? |
| | *KWAHN-toh seh TAHR-dah ehl ow-toh-BOOS* |
| How much is it? | ¿Cuánto cuesta? |
| | *KWAHN-to KWEH-stah* |
| Is there an express bus? | ¿Hay un autobús expreso? |
| | *ay oon ow-toh-BOOS ehs-PREH-soh* |
| Does it make local stops? | ¿Hace paradas locales? |
| | *AH-seh pah-RAH-dahs loh-KAH-lehs* |

| | |
|---|---|
| Does it run at night? | **¿El autobús corre de noche?** |
| | *ehl ow-toh-BOOS KOH-rreh deh NOH-che* |
| When does the next bus leave? | **¿Cuándo parte el próximo autobús?** |
| | *KWAHN-doh PAHR-teh ehl PROHK-see-moh ow-toh-BOOS* |
| a one-way ticket | **un boleto de ida** |
| | *oon boh-LEH-toh deh EE-dah* |
| a round-trip ticket | **un boleto de ida y vuelta** |
| | *oon boh-LEH-toh deh EE-dah ee VWEHL-tah* |
| How long will the bus be stopped? | **¿Por cuánto tiempo estará detenido el autobús?** |
| | *pohr KWAHN-toh TYEHM-poh ehs-tah-RAH deh-teh-NEE-doh ehl ow-toh-BOOS* |
| Is there an air conditioned bus? | **¿Hay un autobús con aire acondicionado?** |
| | *aye oon ow-toh-BOOS kohn AYE-reh ah-kohn-dee-syoh-NAH-doh* |
| Is this seat taken? | **¿Este asiento está ocupado?** |
| | *EHS-teh ah-SYEHN-toh ehs-TAH oh-koo-PAH-doh* |
| Where is the next stop? | **¿Dónde es la próxima parada?** |
| | *DOHN-deh ehs lah PROHK-see-mah pah-RAH-dah* |

GETTING THERE

### Humping the Bus?!

Be very careful with the verb *coger*. In Spain, it means to catch or grab—as in, I'm going to catch the bus. But in much of Latin America, coger is an obscenity—the equivalent of "fuck" in English. If all you want to do is *ride* the bus (in the literal sense), it's best to say **Voy a tomar el autobús** in Latin America.

Please tell me when we reach ____.

**Por favor dígame cuando lleguamos a ____.**
*pohr fah-VOHR DEE-gah-meh KWAHN-doh yeh-GAH-mohs ah*

Let me off here.

**Déjeme aquí.**
*DEH-heh-meh ah-KEE*

## BY BOAT OR SHIP

Would you take me to the port?

**¿Me puede llevar al puerto?**
*meh PWEH-deh yeh-VAHR ahl PWEHR-toh*

When does the ship sail?

**¿Cuándo zarpa el barco?**
*KWAHN-doh SAHR-pah ehl BAHR-koh*

How long is the trip?

**¿Cuán largo es el viaje?**
*kwahn LAHR-goh ehs ehl VYAH-heh*

Where are the life preservers?

**¿Dónde están los salvavidas?**
*DOHN-deh ehs-TAHN lohs sahl-vah-VEE-dahs*

I would like a private cabin.

**Quisiera un camarote privado.**
*kee-SYEH-rah oon kah-mah-ROH-teh pree-VAH-doh*

Is the trip rough?

**¿El viaje es difícil?**
*ehl VYAH-heh ehs dee-FEE-seel*

I feel seasick.

**Me siento mareado -a.**
*meh SYEHN-toh mah-reh-AH-doh -dah*

I need some seasick pills.

**Necesito unas píldoras para los mareos.**
*neh-seh-SEE-toh OO-nahs peel-DOH-rahs pah-rah lohs mah-REH-ohs*

Where is the bathroom?

**¿Dónde está el baño?**
*DOHN-deh ehs-TAH ehl BAH-nyoh*

Does the ship have a casino?

¿El barco tiene un casino?
*ehl BAHR-koh TYEH-neh oon kah-SEE-noh*

Will the ship stop at ports along the way?

¿El barco se detendrá en puertos a lo largo del camino?
*ehl BAHR-koh seh deh-tehnd-RAH ehn PWEHR-tohs ah loh LAHR-goh dehl kah-MEE-noh*

## BY SUBWAY

Where's the subway station?

¿Dónde está la estación de metro?
*DOHN-deh ehs-TAH lah ehs-tah-SYOHN deh MEH-troh*

Where can I buy a ticket?

¿Dónde puedo comprar un boleto?
*DOHN-deh PWEH-doh kohm-PRAHR oon boh-LEH-toh*

# SUBWAY TICKETS

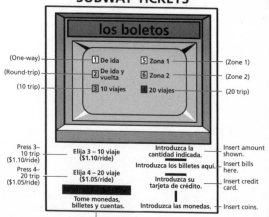

los boletos

(One-way) — 1 De ida — 5 Zona 1 — (Zone 1)
(Round-trip) — 2 De ida y vuelta — 6 Zona 2 — (Zone 2)
(10 trip) — 3 10 viajes — 20 viajes — (20 trip)

Press 3–10 trip ($1.10/ride) — Elija 3 – 10 viaje ($1.10/ride) — Introduzca la cantidad indicada. — Insert amount shown.

Press 4–20 trip ($1.05/ride) — Elija 4 – 20 viaje ($1.05/ride) — Introduzca los billetes aquí. — Insert bills here.

Introduzca su tarjeta de crédito. — Insert credit card.

Tome monedas, billetes y cuentas. — Introduzca las monedas. — Insert coins.

(Take change, tickets, receipt)

| | |
|---|---|
| Could I have a map of the subway? | **¿Puede darme un mapa del metro?** <br> *PWEH-deh DAHR-meh oon MAH-pah dehl MEH-troh* |
| Which line should I take for ____? | **¿Cuál línea debo tomar para ____?** <br> *kwahl LEE-neh-ah DEH-boh toh-MAHR PAH-rah* |
| Is this the right line for ____? | **¿Es ésta la línea correcta para ____?** <br> *ehs EHS-tah lah LEE-neh-ah koh-RREHK-tah PAH-rah* |
| Which stop is it for ____? | **¿Cuál es la parada para ____?** <br> *kwahl ehs lah pah-RAH-dah PAH-rah* |
| How many stops is it to ____? | **¿Cuántas paradas faltan para ____?** <br> *KWAHN-tahs pah-RAH-dahs FAHL-tahn PAH-rah* |
| Is the next stop ____? | **¿La próxima parada es ____?** <br> *lah PROHK-see-mah pah-RAH-dah ehs* |
| Where are we? | **¿Dónde estamos?** <br> *DOHN-deh ehs-TAH-mohs* |
| Where do I change to ____? | **¿Adónde me cambio para ____?** <br> *ah-DOHN-deh meh KAHM-byoh PAH-rah* |
| What time is the last train to ____? | **¿A qué hora pasa el último tren para ____?** <br> *ah keh OH-rah PAH-sah ehl OOL-tee-moh trehn PAH-rah* |

## TRAVELERS WITH SPECIAL NEEDS

| | |
|---|---|
| Do you have wheelchair access? | **¿Tienen acceso para sillas de ruedas?** <br> *TYEH-nehn ahk-SEH-soh PAH-rah SEE-yahs deh RWEH-dahs* |
| Do you have elevators? Where? | **¿Tienen elevadores? ¿Dónde?** <br> *TYEH-nehn eh-leh-vah-DOH-rehs DOHN-deh* |

Do you have ramps? Where?

¿Tienen rampas? ¿Dónde?
*TYEH-nehn RRAHM-pahs DOHN-deh*

Are the restrooms wheelchair accessible?

¿Los baños son accesibles para sillas de ruedas?
*lohs BAH-nyohs sohn ahk-seh-SEE-blehs pah-rah SEE-yahs deh RWEH-dahs*

Do you have audio assistance for the hearing impaired?

¿Ustedes tienen asistencia auditiva para las personas con impedimentos auditivos?
*oos-TEH-dehs TYEH-nehn ah-sees-TEHN-syah ow-dee-TEE-vah PAH-rah lahs pehr-SOH-nahs kohn eem-peh-dee-MEHN-tohs ow-dee-TEE-vohs*

I am deaf.

Yo tengo impedimentos auditivos.
*yoh TEHN-goh eem-peh-dee-MEHN-tohs ow-dee-TEE-vohs*

May I bring my service dog?

¿Puedo traer a mi perro de servicio?
*PWEH-doh trah-EHR ah mee PEH-rroh deh sehr-VEE-syoh*

I am blind.

Yo tengo impedimentos visuales.
*yoh TEHN-goh eem-peh-dee-MEHN-tohs vee-SWAH-lehs*

I need to charge my power chair.

Necesito recargar mi silla de ruedas eléctrica.
*neh-seh-SEE-toh reh-kahr-GAHR mee SEE-yah deh RWEH-dahs eh-LEHK-tree-kah*

## PASSPORTS & VISAS

Remember, your passport must be valid for longer than your length of stay abroad. Nearly all Latin American countries do not require a visa for American and Canadian tourists for visits of up to 90 days. Brazil and Panama are exceptions to this rule, and require all visitors to obtain a visa or tourist card before entering the country.

Be sure to check the State Department's **Foreign Entry Requirements** (http://travel.state.gov/foreignentryreqs.html) for up-to-date information on entry requirements and consulate locations before you go.

Allow plenty of time before your trip to apply for a passport; processing normally takes 3 weeks but can take longer during busy periods, especially in the spring. Residents of the U.S. can download passport applications from the U.S. State Department website (www.travel.state.gov). For general information, contact the **National Passport Agency** at © **877/487-6868.** For faster service, check **www.passportsandvisas.com**.

## HOW TO GET THE BEST PLANE TICKETS

Join frequent flyer clubs, even if you never get a free ticket; membership entitles you to a better selection of seats and other perks. Call the airline once you've booked online to confirm your seat assignments. Avoid seats in the rear of the plane, which can be noisy and offer less wiggle room. Seats near pantries and toilets are noisy too.

If two of you are traveling together, book the aisle and window seat in a three-seat row; the middle seat is the last to go, so you may have it to yourselves (and if the middle seat is taken, the passenger will likely be happy to switch with you).

As a rule, it's best to ask for a seat as far forward as possible. Bulkhead seats have the most leg room, but you may end up next to a baby.

Compare prices on major online booking sites (such as Expedia) with prices on specific airlines sites; the airline site may offer a better deal. To save the fee airlines charge for booking with an operator, ask a live airline operator as many questions as you'd like first, but then book online.

Check prices offered by consolidators (or bucket shops), which advertise in travel sections of Sunday papers. Beware, however, that these tickets are usually nonrefundable or rigged with stiff cancellation penalties, often as high as 50% to 75% of the ticket price. Also be aware that some consolidators will put you on charter airlines, which may depart at inconvenient times or experience delays.

Several reliable consolidators are worldwide and available on the Internet. **STA Travel** (www.sta.com) is now the world's leading consolidator specializing in student travel, thanks to their purchase of Council Travel, but they offer good fares for travelers of all ages.

**FlyCheap** ( © **800/FLY-CHEAP**; www.flycheap.com), owned by package-holiday megalith MyTravel, has especially good access to fares for sunny destinations. **Air Tickets Direct** ( © **800/778-3447**; www.airticketsdirect.com) is based in Montreal and leverages the currently weak Canadian dollar for low fares; it will also book trips to places that U.S. travel agents won't touch, such as Cuba.

## GETTING THROUGH THE AIRPORT

With the federalization of airport security, screening procedures at U.S. airports are more stable and consistent than ever. Generally, you'll be fine if you arrive at the airport **2 hours before** an international flight; if you show up late, tell an airline employee and they'll probably whisk you to the front of the line.

Bring a **current, government-issued photo ID** such as a driver's license or passport. The Transportation Security Administration (TSA) has phased out gate check-in at all U.S. airports, and **e-tickets** have made paper tickets nearly obsolete.

Federalization in the U.S. has stabilized **what you can carry on** and **what you can't**. The general rule is that sharp things are out, nail clippers are okay, and food and beverages must be passed through the X-ray machine. But security screeners can't make you drink from your coffee cup.

Bring food in your carry-on rather than checking it, because explosive-detection machines used on checked luggage have been known to mistake food (especially chocolate) for bombs. Travelers in the U.S. are allowed one carry-on bag, plus a "personal item" such as a purse, briefcase, or laptop bag. Carry-on hoarders can stuff all sorts of things into a laptop bag; as long as it has a laptop in it, it's still considered a personal item. The **Transportation Security Administration** (TSA) has issued a list of restricted items; check its website (www.tsa.gov) for details.

Airport screeners may decide that your checked luggage needs to be searched by hand. You can now purchase luggage locks that allow screeners to open and re-lock a checked bag if hand-searching is necessary. Look for **Travel Sentry certified locks** at luggage or travel shops and Brookstone stores (you can buy them online at www.brookstone.com). These locks, approved by the TSA, can be opened by luggage inspectors with a special code or key. For more information on the locks, visit www.travelsentry.org. If you use something other than TSA-approved locks, your lock will be cut off your suitcase if a TSA agent needs to hand-search your luggage.

## GETTING AROUND BY PLANE

**LanChile** offers the most comprehensive service in South America. Besides flying to most major cities in Chile and Peru, the airline also offers flights between Argentina, Brazil, Bolivia, Ecuador, Uruguay, and Venezuela. **Grupo Taca**, **Aerolíneas Argentinas**, and **Varig** also have several international routes.

If you plan on traveling among Chile, Argentina, Uruguay, and Brazil, you should consider buying a **Mercosur Air Pass**. The pass allows you to make three stopovers in each country, with a total maximum of 10 stopovers. The pass is good for 7 to 30 days. Prices are based on mileage covered. You must buy the air pass outside of South America, and your initial flight must be on Aerolíneas Argentinas, Aerolíneas del Sur, Pluna, or Varig. For more information, contact **Globotur Travel** at © 800/998-5521 or visit www.globotur.com.

LanChile and American Airlines have joined forces to create the **Visit South America** Airpass, which allows you to travel between Argentina, Bolivia, Brazil, Colombia, Chile, Ecuador, Peru, Venezuela, and Uruguay. You must purchase a minimum of three flight segments, but you can only travel for 60 days or fewer. Again, fares are based on distance traveled, and you must buy the pass in your home country. Contact **LanChile** ( © 866/435-9526; www.lanchile.com) or **American Airlines** ( © 800/433-7300; www.aa.com) for more information.

## TRAVEL IN THE AGE OF BANKRUPTCY

Airlines go bankrupt, so protect yourself by purchasing your ticket with a credit card. The Fair Credit Billing Act guarantees that you can get your money back from the credit card company if a travel supplier goes under (and if you request the refund within 60 days of the bankruptcy). Travel insurance can also help, but make sure it covers against "carrier default" for your specific travel provider. Be aware that if a U.S. airline goes belly up, a 2001 federal law requires other carriers to take you to your destination (albeit on a space-availability basis) for a fee of no more than $25, provided you rebook within 60 days of the cancellation.

GETTING THERE

## CHAPTER THREE

### LODGING

This chapter will help you find the right accommodations, at the right price, and the amenities you might need during your stay.

### ROOM PREFERENCES

| | |
|---|---|
| Please recommend ____ | **Por favor recomiende ____** |
| | *pohr fah-VOHR reh-koh-MYEHN-deh* |
| a clean hostel. | **una hospedería limpia.** |
| | *OO-nah ohs-peh-deh-REE-ah LEEM-pyah* |
| a moderately priced hotel. | **un hotel de precio módico.** |
| | *oon oh-TEHL deh PREH-syoh MOH-dee-koh* |
| a moderately priced B&B. | **una hospedería con cama y desayuno de precio módico.** |
| | *OO-nah ohs-peh-deh-REE-ah kohn KAH-mah ee deh-sah-YOO-noh deh PREH-syoh MOH-dee-ko* |
| a good hotel / motel. | **un buen hotel / motel.** |
| | *oon bwehn oh-TEHL / moh-TEHL* |
| Does the hotel have ____ | **¿El hotel tiene ____** |
| | *ehl oh-TEHL TYEH-neh* |
| a pool? | **una piscina?** |
| | *OO-nah pee-SEE-nah* |
| a casino? | **un casino?** |
| | *oon kah-SEE-noh* |
| suites? | **suites?** |
| | *soo-EE-tehs* |
| a balcony? | **un balcón?** |
| | *oon bahl-KOHN* |
| a fitness center? | **un centro de gimnasia?** |
| | *oon SEHN-troh deh heem-NAH-syah* |

74

| | |
|---|---|
| a spa? | **un balneario?** |
| | *oon bahl-neh-AH-ryoh* |
| a private beach? | **una playa privada?** |
| | *OO-nah PLAH-yah pree-VAH-dah* |
| a tennis court? | **una cancha de tenis?** |
| | *OO-nah KAHN-chah deh TEH-nees* |
| I would like a room for ____. | **Quisiera una habitación para ____.** |
| | *kee-SYEH-rah OO-nah ah-bee-tah-SYOHN pah-rah* |

*For full coverage of number terms, see p7.*

| | |
|---|---|
| I would like ____ | **Quisiera ____** |
| | *kee-SYEH-rah* |
| a king-sized bed. | **una cama king.** |
| | *OO-nah KAH-mah keeng* |
| a double bed. | **una cama doble.** |
| | *OO-nah KAH-mah DOH-bleh* |
| twin beds. | **dos camas individuales.** |
| | *dohs KAH-mahs een-dee-vee-DWAHL-ehs* |
| adjoining rooms. | **habitaciones adjuntas.** |
| | *ah-bee-tah-SYOH-nehs ad-HOON-tahs* |
| a smoking room. | **una habitación de fumar.** |
| | *OO-nah ah-bee-tah-SYOHN deh foo-MAHR* |

LODGING

## Listen Up: Reservations Lingo

| | |
|---|---|
| **No tenemos vacantes.** | We have no vacancies. |
| **¿Hasta cuándo se queda?** | How long will you be staying? |
| **¿Sección de fumar o de no fumar?** | Smoking or non smoking? |

| | |
|---|---|
| a non-smoking room. | **una habitación de no fumar.** |
| | *OO-nah ah-bee-tah-SYOHN deh* |
| | *noh foo-MAHR* |
| a private bathroom. | **un baño privado.** |
| | *oon BAH-nyoh pree-VAH-doh* |
| a shower. | **una ducha.** |
| | *OO-nah DOO-cha* |
| a bathtub. | **una bañera.** |
| | *OO-nah bah-NYEH-rah* |
| air conditioning. | **aire acondicionado.** |
| | *AYE-reh ah-cohn-dee-syoh-* |
| | *NAH-doh* |
| televisión. | **un televisor.** |
| | *oon teh-leh-vee-SOHR* |
| cable. | **televisión por cable.** |
| | *teh-leh-vee-SYOHN pohr* |
| | *KAH-bleh* |
| satellite TV. | **televisión por satélite.** |
| | *teh-leh-vee-SYOHN pohr* |
| | *sah-TEH-lee-teh* |
| a telephone. | **un teléfono.** |
| | *oon teh-LEH-foh-noh* |
| Internet access. | **acceso al Internet.** |
| | *ahk-SEH-soh ahl een-tehr-NEHT* |
| high-speed Internet access. | **acceso al Internet de alta velocidad.** |
| | *ahk-SEH-soh ahl een-tehr-NEHT* |
| | *deh AHL-tah veh-loh-see-DAHD* |
| a refrigerator. | **un refrigerador.** |
| | *oon reh-free-heh-rah-DOHR* |
| a beach view. | **vista a la playa.** |
| | *VEES-tah ah lah PLAH-yah* |
| a city view. | **vista a la ciudad.** |
| | *VEES-tah ah lah see-oo-DAHD* |

| | |
|---|---|
| a kitchenette. | **una cocina pequeña.**<br>*OO-nah koh-SEE-nah*<br>*peh-KEH-nyah* |
| a balcony. | **un balcón.**<br>*oon bahl-KOHN* |
| a suite. | **una suite.**<br>*OO-nah SWEE-teh* |
| a penthouse. | **un ático de lujo.**<br>*oon AH-tee-koh deh LOO-ho* |
| I would like a room ____ | **Quisiera una habitación ____**<br>*kee-SYEH-rah OO-nah ah-bee-*<br>*tah-SYOHN* |
| on the ground floor. | **en el primer piso.**<br>*ehn ehl pree-MEHR PEE-soh* |
| near the elevator. | **cerca del elevador.**<br>*SEHR-kah dehl eh-leh-vah-DOHR* |
| near the stairs. | **cerca de las escaleras.**<br>*SEHR-kah deh lahs ehs-kah-*<br>*LEH-rahs* |
| near the pool. | **cerca de la piscina.**<br>*SEHR-kah deh lah pee-SEE-nah* |
| away from the street. | **lejos de la calle.**<br>*LEH-hohs deh lah KAH-yeh* |
| I would like a corner room. | **Quisiera una habitación de esquina.**<br>*kee-SYEH-rah OO-na ah-bee-tah-*<br>*SYOHN deh ehs-KEE-nah* |
| Do you have ____ | **¿Tiene ____**<br>*TYEH-neh* |
| a crib? | **una cuna?**<br>*OO-nah KOO-nah* |
| a foldout bed? | **una cama desplegable?**<br>*OO-nah KAH-mah dehs-pleh-*<br>*GAH-bleh* |

## FOR GUESTS WITH SPECIAL NEEDS

| | |
|---|---|
| I need a room with ____ | **Necesito una habitación con ____**<br>*neh-seh-SEE-toh OO-nah ah-bee-tah-SYOHN kohn* |
| wheelchair access. | **acceso para silla de ruedas.**<br>*ahk-SEH-soh pah-rah SEE-yah deh RWEH-dahs* |
| services for the visually impaired. | **servicios para las personas con impedimentos visuales.**<br>*sehr-VEE-syohs pah-rah lahs pehr-SOH-nahs kohn eem-peh-dee-MEHN-tohs vee-SWAH-lehs* |
| services for the hearing impaired. | **servicios para las personas con impedimentos auditivos.**<br>*sehr-VEE-syohs pah-rah lahs pehr-SOH-nahs kohn eem-peh-dee-MEHN-tohs ow-dee-TEE-vohs* |
| I am traveling with a service dog. | **Estoy viajando con un perro de servicio.**<br>*ehs-TOY vyah-HAHN-doh kohn oon PEH-rroh deh sehr-VEE-syoh* |

## MONEY MATTERS

| | |
|---|---|
| I would like to make a reservation. | **Quisiera hacer una reservación.**<br>*kee-SYEH-rah ah-SEHR OO-nah reh-sehr-vah-SYOHN* |
| How much per night? | **¿Cuánto cuesta por noche?**<br>*KWAHN-toh KWEHS-tah pohr NOH-cheh* |
| Do you have a ____ | **¿Tiene una tarifa ____?**<br>*TYEH-neh OO-nah tah-REE-fah* |
| weekly / monthly rate? | **semanal / mensual?**<br>*seh-mah-NAHL / mehn-SWAHL* |
| a weekend rate? | **una tarifa de fin de semana?**<br>*OO-nah tah-REE-fah deh feen deh seh-MAH-nah* |

We will be staying for ____ days / weeks.

**¿Nos quedaremos por ____ días / semanas.**

*nohs keh-dah-REH-mohs pohr ____ DEE-ahs / seh-MAH-nahs.*

*For full coverage of number terms, see p7.*

When is checkout time?

**¿Cuál es la hora de salida?**

*kwahl ehs lah OH-rah deh sah-LEE-dah*

*For full coverage of time-related terms, see p12.*

Do you accept credit cards / travelers checks?

**¿Aceptan tarjetas de crédito / cheques de viajero?**

*ah-SEHP-tahn tahr-HEH-tahs deh KREH-dee-toh / CHEH-kehs deh vyah-HEH-roh*

May I see a room?

**¿Puedo ver una habitación?**

*PWEH-doh vehr OO-nah ah-bee-tah-SYOHN*

la ventana
el baño
el espejo
la luz
la lámpara
la ducha
el escritorio
las cortinas
el cielo
el televisor
la pared
la bañera
el lavabo
la almohada
el inodoro
el cubrecama/
la colcha
la silla
la mesa
la cama
el mini-bar
el piso

| | |
|---|---|
| How much are taxes? | **¿Cuántos son los impuestos?** *KWAHN-tohs sohn lohs eem-PWEHS-tohs* |
| Is there a service charge? | **¿Hay un cargo por servicio?** *aye oon KAHR-goh pohr sehr-VEE-syoh* |
| I'd like to speak with the manager. | **Quisiera hablar con el gerente.** *kee-SYEH-rah ah-BLAHR kohn ehl heh-REHN-teh* |

## IN-ROOM AMENITIES

| | |
|---|---|
| I'd like ____ | **Quisiera ____** *kee-SYEH-rah* |
| to place an international call. | **hacer una llamada internacional.** *ah-SEHR OO-nah yah-MAH-dah een-tehr-nah-syoh-NAHL* |
| to place a long-distance call. | **hacer una llamada de larga distancia.** *ah-SEHR OO-nah yah-MAH-dah deh LAHR-gah dees-TAHN-syah* |
| directory assistance in English. | **asistencia en inglés.** *ah-sees-TEHN-syah ehn een-GLEHS* |

### Instructions for dialing the hotel phone

| | |
|---|---|
| **Para llamar a otra habitación, marque el número de la habitación.** | To call another room, dial the room number. |
| **Para llamadas locales, marque primero el 9.** | To make a local call, first dial 9. |
| **Para la operadora, marque el 0.** | To call the operator, dial 0. |

| | |
|---|---|
| room service. | **servicio de habitaciones.** |
| | *sehr-VEE-syoh deh ah-bee-tah-* |
| | *SYOH-nehs* |
| maid service. | **servicio de camarera.** |
| | *sehr-VEE-syoh deh kah-mah-* |
| | *REH-rah* |
| the front desk ATT operator. | **la operadora de ATT de la** |
| | **recepción.** |
| | *lah oh-peh-rah-DOH-rah deh ah* |
| | *teh tee deh lah reh-* |
| | *sehp-SYOHN* |
| Do you have room service? | **¿Tienen servicio de habitaciones?** |
| | *TYEH-nehn sehr-VEE-syoh deh* |
| | *ah-bee-tah-SYOH-nehs* |
| When is the kitchen open? | **¿Cuándo abre la cocina?** |
| | *KWAHN-doh AH-breh lah* |
| | *koh-SEE-nah* |
| When is breakfast served? | **¿Cuándo se servirá el desayuno?** |
| | *KWAHN-doh seh sehr-vee-RAH* |
| | *ehl deh-sah-YOO-noh* |

*For full coverage of time-related terms, see p12.*

| | |
|---|---|
| Do you offer massages? | **¿Ustedes ofrecen masajes?** |
| | *oo-STEH-dehs oh-FREH-sehn mah-* |
| | *SAH-hehs* |
| Do you have a lounge? | **¿Tienen un salón público?** |
| | *TYEH-nehn oon sah-LOHN POO-* |
| | *blee-koh* |
| Do you have a business center? | **¿Tienen un centro de negocios?** |
| | *TYEH-nehn oon SEHN-troh deh* |
| | *neh-GOH-syohs* |
| Do you serve breakfast? | **¿Sirven desayuno?** |
| | *SEER-vehn deh-sah-YOO-noh* |
| Do you have Wi-Fi? | **¿Ustedes ofrecen red inalámbrica?** |
| | *oos-TEH-dehs oh-FREH-sehn rehd* |
| | *ee-nah-LAHM-bree-kah* |

LODGING

| | |
|---|---|
| May I have a newspaper in the morning? | **¿Puedo recibir un periódico en la mañana?** |
| | *PWEH-deh reh-see-BEER oon pehr-YOH-dee-koh ehn lah mah-NYAH-nah* |
| Do you offer a tailor service? | **¿Ustedes ofrecen un servicio de sastre?** |
| | *oos-TEH-dehs oh-FREH-sehn oon sehr-VEE-syoh deh SAHS-treh* |
| Do you offer laundry service? | **¿Ustedes ofrecen servicio de lavandería?** |
| | *oos-TEH-dehs oh-FREH-sehn sehr-VEE-syoh deh lah-vahn-deh-REE-ah* |
| Do you offer dry cleaning? | **¿Ustedes ofrecen servicio de limpieza en seco?** |
| | *oos-TEH-dehs oh-FREH-sehn sehr-VEE-syoh deh leem-PYEH-sah ehn SEH-koh* |
| May we have ____ | **¿Podemos tener ____** |
| | *poh-DEH-mohs teh-NEHR* |
| clean sheets today? | **sábanas limpias hoy?** |
| | *SAH-bah-nahs LEEM-pee-ahs oy* |
| more towels? | **más toallas?** |
| | *mahs toh-AH-yahs* |
| more toilet paper? | **más papel sanitario?** |
| | *mahs pah-PEHL sah-nee-TAH-ryoh* |
| extra pillows? | **almohadas adicionales?** |
| | *ahl-moh-AH-dahs ah-dees-yoh-NAH-lehs* |
| Do you have an ice machine? | **¿Tienen una máquina de hielo?** |
| | *TYEH-nehn OO-nah MAH-kee-nah deh YEH-loh* |

| | |
|---|---|
| Did I receive any ____ | **¿Recibí ____** |
| | *reh-see-BEE* |
| messages? | **algún mensaje?** |
| | *ahl-GOON mehn-SAH-heh* |
| mail? | **alguna correspondencia?** |
| | *ahl-GOO-nah koh-rrehs-pohn-DEHN-syah* |
| faxes? | **algún fax?** |
| | *ahl-GOON fahks* |
| A spare key, please. | **Una llave adicional, por favor.** |
| | *OO-nah YAH-veh ah-dees-yoh-NAHL, pohr fah-VOHR* |
| More hangers, please. | **Más perchas, por favor.** |
| | *mahs PEHR-chahs pohr fah-VOHR* |
| I am allergic to down pillows | **Soy alérgico -a a las almohadas de plumas.** |
| | *soy ah-LEHR-hee-koh -kah ah lahs ahl-moh-AH-dahs deh PLOO-mahs* |
| I'd like a wake up call. | **Quisiera una llamada para despertar.** |
| | *kee-SYEH-rah OO-nah yah-MAH-dah pah-rah dehs-pehr-TAHR* |

*For full coverage of how to tell time, see p12.*

| | |
|---|---|
| Do you have alarm clocks? | **¿Tiene relojes despertadores?** |
| | *TYEH-neh reh-LOH-hehs dehs-pehr-tah-DOH-rehs* |
| Is there a safe in the room? | **¿Hay una caja fuerte en la habitación?** |
| | *aye OO-nah KAH-hah FWEHR-teh ehn lah ah-bee-tah-SYOHN* |
| Does the room have a hair dryer? | **¿La habitación tiene un secador de pelo?** |
| | *lah ah-bee-tah-SYOHN TYEH-neh oon seh-kah-DOHR deh PEH-loh* |

## HOTEL ROOM TROUBLE

May I speak with the manager?
**¿Puedo hablar con el gerente?**
*PWEH-doh ah-BLAHR kohn ehl heh-REHN-teh*

The _____ does not work.
**_____ no funciona.**
*noh foon-SYOH-nah*

television
**El televisor**
*ehl teh-leh-vee-SOHR*

telephone
**El teléfono**
*ehl teh-LEH-foh-noh*

air conditioning
**El aire acondicionado**
*ehl AYE-reh ah-kohn-dee-syoh-NAH-doh*

Internet access
**El acceso al Internet**
*ehl ahk-SEH-soh ahl een-tehr-NET*

cable TV
**El servicio de cable TV**
*ehl sehr-VEE-syoh deh KAH-bleh teh VEH*

There is no hot water.
**No hay agua caliente.**
*noh ay AH-wah kah-LYEHN-teh*

The toilet is over-flowing!
**¡El inodoro se está desbordando!**
*ehl ee-noh-DOH-roh seh ehs-TAH dehs-bohr-DAHN-doh*

| This room is _____ | **Esta habitación _____** |
| | *EHS-tah ah-bee-tah-SYOHN* |
| too noisy. | **es muy ruidosa.** |
| | *ehs MOO-ee roo-ee-DOH-sah* |
| too cold. | **está muy fría.** |
| | *ehs-TAH MOO-ee FREE-ah* |
| too warm. | **está muy cálida.** |
| | *ehs-TAH MOO-ee KAH-lee-dah* |
| This room has _____ | **Esta habitación tiene _____** |
| | *EHS-tah ah-bee-tah-SYOHN* |
| | *TYEH-neh* |
| bugs. | **insectos.** |
| | *een-SEHK-tohs* |
| mice. | **ratones.** |
| | *rah-TOH-nehs* |
| I'd like a different room. | **Quisiera una habitación diferente.** |
| | *kee-SYEH-rah OO-nah ah-bee-tah-SYOHN dee-feh-REHN-teh* |
| Do you have a bigger room? | **¿Tiene una habitación más grande?** |
| | *TYEH-neh OO-nah ah-bee-tah-SYOHN mahs GRAHN-deh* |
| I locked myself out of my room. | **Me quedé fuera de mi habitación.** |
| | *meh keh-DEH FWEH-rah deh mee ah-bee-tah-SYOHN* |
| Do you have any fans? | **¿Tiene abanicos?** |
| | *TYEH-ne ah-bah-NEE-kohs* |
| The sheets are not clean. | **Las sábanas no están limpias.** |
| | *lahs SAH-bah-nahs noh ehs-TAHN LEEM-pyahs* |
| The towels are not clean. | **Las toallas no están limpias.** |
| | *lahs to-AH-yahs noh ehs-TAHN LEEM-pyahs* |
| The room is not clean. | **La habitación no está limpia.** |
| | *lah ah-bee-tah-SYOHN noh ehs-TAH LEEM-pyah* |

LODGING

The guests next door / above / below are being very loud.

**Los huéspedes al lado / arriba / abajo son muy ruidosos.**
*lohs WEHS-peh-dehs ahl LAH-doh / ah-RREE-bah / ah-BAH-hoh sohn MOO-ee roo-ee-DOH-sohs*

## CHECKING OUT

I think this charge is a mistake.

**Creo que este cargo es un error.**
*KREH-oh keh EHS-teh KAHR-goh ehs oon eh-RROHR*

Please explain this charge to me.

**Por favor explíqueme este cargo.**
*pohr fah-VOHR ehs-PLEE-keh-meh EHS-teh KAHR-goh*

Thank you, we enjoyed our stay.

**Gracias, disfrutamos nuestra estadía.**
*GRAH-syahs dees-froo-TAH-mohs NWEHS-trah ehs-tah-DEE-ah*

The service was excellent.

**El servicio fue excelente.**
*ehl sehr-VEE-syoh fweh ehk-seh-LEHN-teh*

The staff is very professional and courteous.

**El personal es muy profesional y cortés.**
*ehl pehr-soh-NAHL ehs MOO-ee proh-feh-syoh-NAHL ee kohr-TEHS*

Please call a cab for me.

**Por favor, llame a un taxi para mí.**
*pohr fah-VOHR YAH-meh ah oon TAHK-see PAH-rah mee*

Would someone please get my bags?

**¿Alguien puede ayudarme con mis bolsas?**
*AHLG-yehn PWEH-deh ah-yoo-DAHR-meh kohn mees BOHL-sahs*

## HAPPY CAMPING

| | |
|---|---|
| I'd like a site for ____ | **Quisiera un lugar para ____**<br>*kee-SYEH-rah oon loo-GAHR*<br>*pah-rah* |
| a tent. | **una tienda de campaña.**<br>*OO-nah TYEHN-dah deh kahm-*<br>*PAH-nyah* |
| a camper. | **un carro de acampar.**<br>*oon KAH-rroh deh ah-*<br>*kahm-PAHR* |
| Are there ____ | **¿Hay ____**<br>*ay* |
| bathrooms? | **baños?**<br>*BAH-nyohs* |
| showers? | **duchas?**<br>*DOOH-chahs* |
| Is there running water? | **¿Hay agua de llave?**<br>*ay AH-wah deh YAH-veh* |
| Is the water drinkable? | **¿El agua es potable?**<br>*ehl AH-wah ehs poh-TAH-bleh* |
| Where is the electrical hookup? | **¿Dónde está la conexión eléctrica?**<br>*DOHN-deh ehs-TAH lah koh-nehk-*<br>*SYOHN eh-LEHK-tree-kah* |

LODGING

## ACCOMMODATIONS

**Government Ratings**   Most Latin American governments rate hotels from one to five stars, based on a number of objective criteria, such as facilities and hygiene (elevators, swimming pools, private baths, and so on). The more stars, the better and more expensive the hotel *as a rule*; but it's important to keep in mind that government stars do not rate intangibles such as comfort or charm, and that a three-star hotel can be preferable to a four- or five-star property. That's why holistic guidebook ratings, based on a traveler's firsthand experience, are so important to review.

**Five-star** hotels meet the highest standards. Beds are comfortable, bathrooms should be in excellent working order (usually with a wall-mounted shower and tub), and services and hygiene should meet the highest international standards. **Four-star** hotels are only slightly below, with perhaps less luxurious linens or room service with limited hours. Four-star hotels are usually less expensive but always offer basic services such as hot water and minibars with bottled drinking water (in Mexico, four-star hotels have bathroom taps that dispense purified drinking water). **Three-star** hotels generally have private bathrooms and cable TVs. **Two-star** hotels most always offer hot water in tiny, basic bathrooms. **One-star** hotels may offer just a bed and use of a bathroom down the hall. Don't expect a TV in most one- and two-star hotels, though there are exceptions.

## MAJOR HOTEL CHAINS IN LATIN AMERICA

Mexico is the premier destination for travelers on package tours and, not surprisingly, it has the largest number of vacation-oriented chain hotels. Here's a list of Latin America's major chains:

**Amerian Hotels** (www.amerianhoteles.com)   This Argentine-owned chain offers upscale accommodations catering to the business traveler in larger cities. Little known outside the country, the Amerian chain offers reasonable prices for superior accommodations.

**Brisas Hotels & Resorts** (www.brisas.com.mx)   These were the hotels that originally attracted jet-set travelers to Mexico. Spectacular in a retro way, they offer the laid-back luxury that distinguishes a Mexican vacation.

**Fiesta Americana and Fiesta Inn** (www.posadas.com)   Part of the Mexican-owned Grupo Posadas company, these hotels set the country's standard for midrange facilities and services. They generally offer comfortable, spacious rooms and have excellent beach-resort packages. Fiesta Inn hotels are usually business-oriented.

**Hoteles Camino Real** (www.caminoreal.com)   The premier Mexican hotel chain maintains a high standard for service at its properties, all of which carry five stars. Its beach hotels are traditionally located on the best beaches. The hotels are famous for their vivid and contrasting colors.

**Hoteles Dann** (www.hotelesdann.com)   This chain of modern, four-star hotels can be found all over Colombia and Ecuador. Catering to business travelers, they're usually conveniently located near convention centers.

**NH Hotels** (www.nh-hotels.com)   These are owned by a Spanish company with a growing number of hotels in Argentina, Brazil, and Chile. The four-star properties are modern and cater mostly to business travelers and those seeking upscale amenities such as a health club, 24-hour room service, and a business center. What sets NH Hotels apart is their focus on contemporary decor and superior customer service.

**Presidente Hotels** (www.presidente.cl)   Also known as Club Presidente hotels, these can be found in almost every large city in Chile. Business-oriented, they offer most of the amenities of luxury hotels at a more reasonable price.

**Quinta Real Grand Class Hotels and Resorts** (www.quinta real.com)   Owned by Summit Hotels and Resorts, these are

LODGING

noted for architectural and cultural details that reflect the regions in which they're located. Attention to detail and excellent service are the rule.

## HOW TO GET THE BEST ROOMS & PRICES

**Somebody has to get the best room, and it might as well be you.**    You can start by joining the hotel's frequent-guest program, which may make you eligible for upgrades. It's free.

**Ask for everything.**    When you make your reservation, ask if the hotel is renovating; if it is, request a room away from the construction. Ask about nonsmoking rooms, rooms with views, rooms with twin, queen- or king-size beds. If you're a light sleeper, ask for a quiet room away from vending machines, elevators, bars, restaurants, and swimming pools. Ask for a room that has been recently renovated or redecorated. If you aren't happy with your room when you arrive, ask for another one. Hotels will often accommodate you. Always ask about corner rooms—they're often larger and quieter, with more windows and light, and they often cost the same as standard rooms.

**Ask about special rates or other discounts.**    Once you're quoted a price, ask whether a less expensive room is available, or whether any special rates apply to you. You may qualify for corporate, student, military, senior, or other discounts. Find out the hotel policy on children: Do kids stay free, or is there a special rate? Will a suite cost less than two separate rooms?

**Remember the law of supply and demand.**    Resort hotels are most crowded and therefore most expensive on weekends, so discounts are usually available for midweek stays. Business hotels in downtown locations are busiest during the week, so you can score big discounts over the weekend. Many hotels have high-season and low-season prices; booking the day after high season ends can mean big discounts.

**Look into group or long-stay discounts.**    If you're traveling with a large group (10 or more people), you should be able to negotiate a bargain rate. Likewise, if you're planning a long stay (at least 5 days), you might qualify for a discount. As a general rule, expect 1 night free after a 7-night stay.

**Avoid excess charges and hidden costs.**    When you book a room, inquire whether the hotel charges for parking. Ask about local taxes and service charges, which can increase the cost of a room by 15% or more. If a hotel insists upon tacking on a surprise "resort fee" for amenities you didn't use, you can often make a case for getting it removed.

**Consider the pros and cons of all-inclusive resorts and hotels.**    If you're heading to a resort destination, this option may save you money, but beware that "all-inclusive" means different things at different hotels. Many all-inclusive hotels will include three meals daily, sports equipment, spa entry, and other amenities; others may include all or most drinks. In general, you'll save money going the "all-inclusive" way—so long as you use the facilities provided. The downside is that your choices are limited, and you're stuck eating and playing in one place for the duration of your vacation.

**Book an efficiency or studio unit.**    A room with a kitchenette allows you to shop for groceries and cook your own meals. This is a big money saver, especially for families or groups on long stays.

**Book online.**    When booking a room in a chain hotel, you may get a better deal by emailing the individual hotel's reservation desk, rather than the chain's central web address or toll-free number. This way, you can make special requests, such as a king-size bed or a quiet room. Even if you book online, however, it's a good idea to email the hotel directly to spell out your requirements and confirm your reservation. If you're thinking about booking through an online travel agency such as Expedia, keep in mind that hotels sometimes offer special rates only on their own websites. Shop around.

LODGING

# CHAPTER FOUR

## DINING

This chapter includes a menu reader and the language you need to communicate in a range of dining establishments and food markets.

### FINDING A RESTAURANT

| | |
|---|---|
| Would you recommend a good ____ restaurant? | ¿Podría recomendar un buen restaurante ____ *poh-DREE-ah reh-koh-mehn-DAHR oon bwehn reh-stow-RAHN-teh* |
| local | local? *loh-KAHL* |
| Italian | italiano? *ee-tah-LYAH-noh* |
| French | francés? *frahn-SEHS* |
| German | alemán? *ah-leh-MAHN* |
| Spanish | español? *ehs-pah-NYOHL* |
| Chinese | chino? *CHEE-noh* |
| Japanese | japonés? *hah-poh-NEHS* |
| Asian | asiático? *ah-SYAH-tee-koh* |
| pizza | de pizza? *deh PEET-sah* |
| steakhouse | de parrilla? *deh pah-RREE-yah* |
| family | familiar? *fah-mee-LYAHR* |

| | |
|---|---|
| seafood | **de mariscos?** |
| | *deh mah-REES-kohs* |
| vegetarian | **vegetariano?** |
| | *veh-heh-tah-RYAH-noh* |
| buffet-style | **estilo buffet?** |
| | *ehs-TEE-loh boo-FEH* |
| Greek | **griego?** |
| | *GRYEH-goh* |
| budget | **económico?** |
| | *eh-koh-NOH-mee-koh* |
| Which is the best restaurant in town? | **¿Cuál es el mejor restaurante en el pueblo?** |
| | *kwahl ehs ehl meh-HOHR reh-stoh-RAHN-teh ehn ehl PWEH-bloh* |
| Is there a late-night restaurant nearby? | **¿Hay un restaurante cercano abierto hasta tarde en la noche?** |
| | *aye oon reh-stoh-RAHN-teh SEHR-kah-noh ah-BYEHR-toh AHS-tah TAHR-deh ehn lah NOH-cheh* |
| Is there a restaurant that serves breakfast nearby? | **¿Hay un restaurante cercano que sirva desayuno?** |
| | *aye oon reh-stoh-RAHN-teh SEHR-ka-noh keh SEER-vah deh-sah-YOO-noh* |
| Is it very expensive? | **¿Es muy caro?** |
| | *ehs MOO-ee KAH-roh* |
| Do I need a reservation? | **¿Necesito una reservación?** |
| | *neh-seh-SEE-toh OO-nah reh-sehr-vah-SYOHN* |
| Do I have to dress up? | **¿Necesito vestirme elegante-mente?** |
| | *neh-seh-SEE-toh veh-STEER-meh eh-leh-gahn-teh-MEHN-teh* |

| | |
|---|---|
| Do they serve lunch? | **¿Sirven almuerzo?** |
| | *SEER-vehn ahl-MWEHR-soh* |
| What time do they open for dinner? | **¿A qué hora abren para la cena?** |
| | *ah KEH OH-rah AHB-rehn PAH-rah lah SEH-nah* |
| For lunch? | **¿Para almuerzo?** |
| | *PAH-rah ahl-MWEHR-soh* |
| What time do they close? | **¿A qué hora cierran?** |
| | *ah KEH OH-rah SYEH-rrahn* |
| Do you have a take out menu? | **¿Tienen un menú para llevar?** |
| | *TYEH-nehn oon meh-NOO PAH-rah yeh-VAHR* |
| Do you have a bar? | **¿Tienen un bar?** |
| | *TYEH-nehn oon bahr* |
| Is there a café nearby? | **¿Hay un café cerca?** |
| | *aye oon kah-FEH SEHR-kah* |

## GETTING SEATED

| | |
|---|---|
| Are you still serving? | **¿Todavía están sirviendo?** |
| | *toh-dah-VEE-ah ehs-TAHN seer-VYEHN-doh* |
| How long is the wait? | **¿Cuán larga es la espera?** |
| | *kwahn LAHR-gah ehs lah ehs-PEH-rah* |
| Do you have a nonsmoking section? | **¿Tienen una sección de no fumar?** |
| | *TYEH-nehn OO-nah sehk-SYOHN deh noh foo-MAHR* |
| A table for ____, please. | **Una mesa para ____, por favor.** |
| | *OO-nah MEH-sah PAH-rah ____ pohr fah-VOHR* |

*For a full list of numbers, see p7.*

| | |
|---|---|
| Do you have a quiet, table? | **¿Tienen una mesa tranquila?** |
| | *TYEH-nehn OO-nah MEH-sah trahn-KEE-lah* |

## Listen Up: Restaurant Lingo

¿Sección de fumar o de no fumar?
*sehk-SYOHN deh foo-MAHR*
*oh deh noh foo-MAHR*

Smoking or nonsmoking?

Necesita una corbata y una chaqueta.
*neh-seh-SEE-tah OO-nah kohr-BAH-tah ee OO-na chah-KEH-tah*

You'll need a tie and jacket.

Lo siento, no se permite pantalones cortos.
*loh SYEHN-toh noh seh pehr-MEE-tehn pahn-tah-LOH-nehs KOHR-tohs*

I'm sorry, no shorts are allowed.

¿Le puedo traer algo de tomar?
*leh PWEH-doh trah-EHR AHL-goh deh toh-MAHR*

May I bring you something to drink?

¿Le gustaría ver una lista de vinos?
*leh goos-tah-REE-ah vehr OO-nah LEES-tah deh VEE-nohs*

Would you like to see a wine list?

¿Le gustaría saber cuáles son nuestros platos especiales?
*leh goos-tah-REE-ah sah-BEHR KWAH-lehs sohn NWEHS-trohs PLAH-tohs ehs-peh-SYAH-lehs*

Would you like to hear our specials?

¿Está listo para ordenar?
*ehs-TAH LEES-toh PAH-rah ohr-deh-NAHR*

Are you ready to order?

Lo siento. Su tarjeta de crédito ha sido rechazada.
*loh SYEHN-toh soo tahr-HEH-tah deh KREH-dee-toh hah SEE-doh reh-chah-SAH-dah*

I'm sorry. Your credit card was declined.

| | |
|---|---|
| May we sit outside / inside please? | **¿Podemos sentarnos afuera / adentro por favor?**<br>*poh-DEH-mohs sehn-TAHR-nohs*<br>*ah-FWEH-rah / ah-DEHN-troh pohr*<br>*fah-VOHR* |
| May we sit at the counter? | **¿Podemos sentarnos en el mostrador?**<br>*poh-DEH-mohs sehn-TAHR-nohs*<br>*ehn ehl mohs-trah-DOHR* |
| A menu please? | **¿Un menú por favor?**<br>*oon meh-NOO pohr fah-VOHR* |

## ORDERING

| | |
|---|---|
| Do you have a special tonight? | **¿Tienen un especial esta noche?**<br>*TYEH-nehn oon ehs-peh-SYAHL*<br>*EHS-tah NOH-cheh* |
| What do you recommend? | **¿Qué recomienda usted?**<br>*KEH reh-koh-MYEHN-dah oos-TEHD* |
| May I see a wine list? | **¿Puedo ver una lista de vinos?**<br>*PWEH-doh vehr OO-nah LEES-tah*<br>*deh VEE-nohs* |
| Do you serve wine by the glass? | **¿Ustedes sirven vino por la copa?**<br>*oos-TEH-dehs SEER-vehn VEE-noh*<br>*pohr lah KOH-pah* |
| May I see a drink list? | **¿Puedo ver una lista de bebidas?**<br>*PWEH-doh vehr OO-nah LEES-tah*<br>*deh beh-BEE-dahs* |
| I would like it cooked ____ | **Me gustaría ____**<br>*meh goos-tah-REE-ah* |
| rare. | **crudo.**<br>*KROO-doh* |
| medium rare. | **a medio cocer.**<br>*ah MEH-dyoh koh-SEHR* |
| medium. | **término medio.**<br>*TEHR-mee-noh MEH-dyoh* |

| | |
|---|---|
| medium well. | **medio bien cocido.** |
| | *MEH-dyoh byehn koh-SEE-doh* |
| well. | **bien cocido.** |
| | *byehn koh-SEE-doh* |
| charred. | **achicharrado.** |
| | *ah-chee-chah-RRAH-doh* |
| Do you have a _____ menu? | **¿Tiene un menú _____** |
| | *TYEH-neh oon meh-NOO* |
| diabetic | **diabético?** |
| | *dee-ah-BEH-tee-koh* |
| kosher | **kósher?** |
| | *KOH-shehr* |
| vegetarian | **vegetariano?** |
| | *veh-heh-tah-RYAH-noh* |
| children's | **para niños?** |
| | *PAH-rah NEE-nyohs* |
| What is in this dish? | **¿Qué hay en este plato?** |
| | *keh aye ehn EHS-teh PLAH-toh* |
| How is it prepared? | **¿Cómo está preparado?** |
| | *KOH-moh eh-STAH preh-PAH-rah-do* |
| What kind of oil is that cooked in? | **¿En qué tipo de aceite está cocido?** |
| | *ehn keh TEE-poh deh ah-SEH-ee-teh eh-STAH koh-SEE-doh* |
| Do you have any low-salt dishes? | **¿Tiene platos bajos en sal?** |
| | *TYEH-neh PLAH-tohs BAH-hohs ehn sahl* |
| On the side, please. | **Al lado, por favor.** |
| | *ahl LAH-doh pohr fah-VOHR* |
| May I make a substitution? | **¿Puedo hacer una sustitución?** |
| | *PWEH-doh ah-SEHR OO-nah soos-tee-too-SYOHN* |

| | |
|---|---|
| I'd like to try that. | **Me gustaría probar eso.**<br>*meh goos-tah-REE-ah proh-BAHR*<br>*EH-soh* |
| Is that fresh? | **¿Eso es fresco?**<br>*EH-so ehs FREHS-koh* |
| Waiter! | **¡Mozo! ¡Mesero!** (Colombia)<br>*MOH-soh / meh-SEH-roh* |
| Extra butter, please. | **Mantequilla adicional, por favor.**<br>*mahn-teh-KEE-yah ah-dee-syoh-*<br>*NAHL pohr fah-VOHR* |
| No butter, thanks. | **Sin mantequilla, por favor.**<br>*seen mahn-teh-KEE-yah pohr fah-*<br>*VOHR* |
| No cream, thanks. | **Sin crema, por favor.**<br>*seen KREH-mah pohr fah-VOHR* |
| Dressing on the side, please. | **El aderezo por el lado, por favor.**<br>*ehl ah-deh-REH-soh pohr ehl LAH-*<br>*doh pohr fah-VOHR* |
| No salt, please. | **Sin sal, por favor.**<br>*seen sahl pohr fah-VOHR* |
| May I have some oil, please? | **¿Me puede dar un poco de aceite,**<br>**por favor?**<br>*meh PWEH-deh dahr oon POH-*<br>*koh deh ah-SEH-ee-teh pohr fah-*<br>*VOHR* |
| More bread, please. | **Más pan, por favor.**<br>*mahs pahn pohr fah-VOHR* |
| I am lactose intolerant. | **Soy intolerante a la lactosa.**<br>*soy een-toh-loh-RAHN-teh ah lah*<br>*lahk-TOH-sah* |
| Would you recommend something without milk? | **¿Podría recomendar algo sin**<br>**leche?**<br>*poh-DREE-ah reh-koh-mehn-*<br>*DAHR AHL-goh seen LEH-cheh* |

| | |
|---|---|
| I am allergic to ____ | **Soy alérgico -a a ____** |
| | *soy ah-LEHR-hee-koh -kah ah* |
| seafood. | **los mariscos.** |
| | *lohs mah-REES-kohs* |
| shellfish. | **los crustáceos.** |
| | *lohs kroos-TAH-seh-ohs* |
| nuts. | **las nueces.** |
| | *lahs-NWEH-sehs* |
| peanuts. | **los cacahuates, los manís (Puerto Rico, S.Am.)** |
| | *lohs kah-kah-WAH-tehs, lohs mah-NEES* |
| Water ____, please. | **Agua ____, por favor.** |
| | *AH-wah ____ pohr fah-VOHR* |
| with ice | **con hielo** |
| | *kohn YEH-loh* |
| without ice | **sin hielo** |
| | *seen YEH-loh* |
| I'm sorry, I don't think this is what I ordered. | **Lo siento, no creo que esto sea lo que ordené.** |
| | *loh SYEHN-toh noh KREH-oh keh EHS-toh SEH-ah loh keh ohr-deh-NEH* |
| My meat is a little over / under cooked. | **Mi carne está un poco recocida / cruda.** |
| | *mee KAHR-neh ehs-TAH oon POH-koh reh-koh-SEE-dah / KROO-dah* |
| My vegetables are a little over / under cooked. | **Mis vegetales están un poco recocidos / crudos.** |
| | *mees veh-he-TAH-lehs ehs-TAHN oon POH-koh reh-koh-SEE-dohs / KROO-dohs* |
| There's a bug in my food! | **¡Hay un insecto en mi comida!** |
| | *aye oon een-SEHK-toh ehn mee koh-MEE-dah* |

DINING

| | |
|---|---|
| May I have a refill? | **¿Puede rellenar mi bebida?** |
| | *PWEH-deh reh-yeh-NAHR mee* |
| | *beh-BEE-dah* |
| A dessert menu, please. | **Un menú de postres, por favor.** |
| | *oon meh-NOO deh POHS-trehs* |
| | *pohr fah-VOHR* |

## DRINKS

| | |
|---|---|
| alcoholic | **con alcohol** |
| | *kohn ahl-koh-OHL* |
|   neat / straight | **sencillo** |
| | *sehn-SEE-yoh* |
|   on the rocks | **en las rocas** |
| | *ehn lahs ROH-kahs* |
|   with (seltzer or soda) | **con agua (de seltzer o de soda)** |
|   water | *kohn AH-wah (deh sehlt-SEHR* |
| | *oh deh SOH-dah)* |
| beer | **cerveza** |
| | *sehr-VEH-sah* |
| brandy | **brandy** |
| | *BRAHN-dee* |
| coffee | **café** |
| | *kah-FEH* |
|   cappuccino | **cappuccino** |
| | *kah-poo-CHEE-noh* |
|   iced coffee | **café helado** |
| | *kah-FEH heh-LAH-doh* |
| cognac | **coñac** |
| | *koh-NYAHK* |
| espresso | **café expreso** |
| | *kah-FEH ehs-PREH-soh* |
| fruit juice | **jugo de fruta** |
| | *HOO-goh deh FROO-tah* |

*For a full list of fruits, see p115.*

### How Do You Take It?

*Tomar* means to take. But if a bartender asks, *¿Quiere tomar algo?*, he's not inviting you to steal his fancy corkscrew. He's asking what you'd like to drink.

| | |
|---|---|
| gin | **ginebra** |
| | *hee-NEH-brah* |
| hot chocolate | **chocolate caliente** |
| | *cho-koh-LAH-teh kah-LYEHN-teh* |
| lemonade | **limonada** |
| | *lee-moh-NAH-dah* |
| liqueur | **licor** |
| | *lee-KOHR* |
| milk | **leche** |
| | *LEH-cheh* |
| milkshake | **batido de leche** |
| | *bah-TEE-doh deh LEH-cheh* |
| nonalcoholic | **sin alcohol** |
| | *seen ahl-koh-OHL* |
| rum | **ron** |
| | *rohn* |
| tea | **té** |
| | *teh* |
| vodka | **vodka** |
| | *VOHD-kah* |
| wine | **vino** |
| | *VEE-noh* |
| dry white wine | **vino blanco seco** |
| | *VEE-noh BLAHN-koh SEH-koh* |
| full-bodied wine | **vino de cuerpo entero** |
| | *VEE-noh deh KWEHR-poh ehn-TEH-roh* |

| house wine | **vino de la casa** |
| | *VEE-noh deh lah KAH-sah* |
| light-bodied wine | **vino de cuerpo liviano** |
| | *VEE-noh deh KWEHR-poh lee-* |
| | *VYAH-noh* |
| red wine | **vino tinto** |
| | *VEE-noh TEEN-toh* |
| rosé | **vino rosado** |
| | *VEE-noh roh-SAH-doh* |
| sparkling sweet wine | **vino dulce burbujeante** |
| | *VEE-noh DOOL-seh boor-boo-* |
| | *heh-AHN-teh* |
| sweet wine | **vino dulce** |
| | *VEE-noh DOOL-seh* |

## SETTLING UP

| I'm stuffed. | **Estoy lleno -a.** |
| | *ehs-TOY YEH-noh -nah* |
| The meal was excellent. | **La comida estuvo excelente.** |
| | *lah koh-MEE-dah ehs-TOO-voh* |
| | *ehk-seh-LEHN-teh* |
| There's a problem with my bill. | **Hay un problema con mi factura.** |
| | *aye oon proh-BLEH-mah kohn mee* |
| | *fahk-TOO-rah* |
| Is the tip included? | **¿La propina está incluida?** |
| | *lah proh-PEE-nah ehs-TAH* |
| | *een-kloo-EE-dah* |
| My compliments to the chef! | **¡Mis felicitaciones para el chef!** |
| | *mees feh-lee-see-tah-SYOH-nehs* |
| | *PAH-rah ehl chef* |
| Check, please. | **El cheque, por favor.** |
| | *ehl CHEH-keh pohr fah-VOHR* |

## MENU READER

Latin American cuisine varies broadly from region to region, but we've tried to make our list of classic dishes as encompassing as possible.

### APPETIZERS / TAPAS

**aceitunas:** olives
*ah-seh-ee-TOO-nahs*

**albóndigas:** meatballs in sauce
*ahl-BOHN-dee-gahs*

**bacalao:** dried salt cod
*bah-kah-LAH-oh*

**conejo:** braised rabbit
*koh-NEH-ho*

**croquetas:** croquettes
*kroh-KEH-tahs*

**gambas:** broiled shrimp with garlic
*GAHM-bahs*

**jamón:** ham
*hah-MOHN*

  **jamón de bellota:** free-range, acorn-fed ham
  *hah-MOHN deh beh-YOH-tah*

  **jamón ibérico:** aged Iberian ham
  *hah-MOHN ee-BEH-ree-koh*

  **jamón serrano:** dry-cured serrano ham
  *hah-MOHN seh-RRAH-noh*

**pescados fritos:** fried fish
*pehs-KAH-dohs FREE-tohs*

**quesos:** cheeses
*KEH-sohs*

  **de leche de cabra:** goat's milk
  *deh LEH-cheh deh KAH-brah*

  **mozzarella:** mozzarella
  *moht-sah-REH-yah*

  **parmesano:** Parmesan
  *pahr-meh-SAH-noh*

**rallado:** grated
*rah-YAH-doh*
**requesón:** cottage
*reh-keh-SOHN*
**suave:** mild
*soo-AH-veh*
**tortilla española:** omelet with potato
*tohr-TEE-yah ehs-pah-NYOH-lah*

## SALADS

**chonta:** hearts-of-palm salad
*CHOHN-tah*
**ensalada mixta:** salad with lettuce, tomatoes, olives, tuna
*ehn-sah-LAH-dah MEES-tah*
**ensalada de verduras:** green salad
*ehn-sah-LAH-dah deh vehr-DOO-rahs*
**ensalada de espinacas:** spinach salad
*ehn-sah-LAH-dah deh ehs-pee-NAH-kahs*
**ensalada de arúgula:** arugula salad
*ehn-sah-LAH-dah deh ah-ROO-goo-lah*
**ensalada de tomates:** tomato salad
*ehn-sah-LAH-dah deh toh-MAH-tehs*
**ensalada de berro:** watercress salad
*ehn-sah-LAH-dah deh BEH-rroh*
**ensalada de lechuga romaine:** romaine salad
*ehn-sah-LAH-dah deh leh-CHOO-gah rroh-MEHN*

## SAUCES / SEASONING BASES

**adobo:** mixture of crushed peppercorns, salt, oregano,
  garlic, olive oil, and lime juice or vinegar
*ah-DOH-boh*
**mole:** sauce of unsweetened chocolate, chiles, and spices
*MOH-leh*
**romesco:** tomato / almond sauce with olive oil and garlic
*rroh-MEHS-koh*
**sofrito:** mixture of onions, cilantro, garlic, and chiles
*soh-FREE-tohs*

## SOUPS AND STEWS

**asopao:** Puerto Rican gumbo made with chicken or shellfish
*ah-soh-PAH-oh*

**buseca:** stew with sausages
*boo-SEH-kah*

**caldo gallego:** soup with salt pork, white beans, chorizo, ham, and turnip / collard greens
*KAHL-doh gah-YEH-goh*

**gazpacho:** cold vegetable soup
*gahs-PAH-cho*

**locro de papas:** creamy potato soup
*LOH-kroh deh PAH-pahs*

**manchamantel:** chicken or pork stew with mixed vegetables and fruit
*mahn-chah-mahn-TEHL*

**menudo:** tripe stew
*meh-NOO-doh*

**mondongo:** beef tripe and vegetable soup
*mohn-DOHN-goh*

**sancocho, sancochado:** thick soup with meats, vegetables, and corn on the cob, served with rice
*sahn-KOH-choh, sahn-koh-CHAH-doh*

**sancocho de gallina:** chicken soup
*sahn-KOH-choh deh gah-YEE-nah*

**sopa de ajo:** garlic soup
*SOH-pah deh AH-hoh*

**sopa de chiles poblanos:** green chili soup
*SOH-pah deh CHEE-lehs poh-BLAH-nohs*

**sopa negra / frijoles negros:** black bean soup
*SOH-pah NEH-grah / free-HOH-lehs NEH-grohs*

## RICE DISHES

**arroz con gandules:** yellow rice with pigeon peas
*ah-RROHS kohn gahn-DOO-lehs*

**arroz negro:** rice stew with octopus in its own ink
*ah-RROHS NEH-groh*

**paella:** festive seafood / meat rice stew with vegetables, seasoned with saffron
*pah-EH-yah*

## SIDE / VEGETABLE DISHES

**aguacate relleno, palta rellena (S.Am):** stuffed avocado
*ah-wah-KAH-teh rreh-YEH-noh*

**calabacitas en crema:** squash in cream sauce
*kah-lah-bah-SEE-tahs ehn KREH-mah*

**chiles rellenos:** poblano peppers stuffed with cheese or ground meat, battered and fried
*CHEE-lehs rreh-YEH-nohs*

**patacones, chifles (Peru, Ecuador):** fried plantains
*pah-tah-KOH-nehs, CHEE-flehs*

**pristinos:** pumpkin fritters
*prees-TEE-nohs*

**rocoto relleno:** stuffed pepper
*rroh-KOH-toh rreh-YEH-noh*

**tostones:** fried breadfruit or plantain slices
*tohs-TOH-nehs*

**yuca frita:** fried yucca
*YOO-kah FREE-tah*

*For a full list of vegetables, see p117.*

## SAUSAGES

**butifarra:** spiced pork breakfast sausage
*boo-tee-FAH-rrah*

**chorizo:** spicy pork sausage
*cho-REE-soh*

**morcilla:** black pudding
*mohr-SEE-yah*

**salchichón:** Puerto Rican salami-style sausage
*sahl-chee-CHOHN*

## BEEF

**bife de lomo:** filet mignon
*BEE-feh deh LOH-moh*

**carne en polvo:** seasoned ground beef
*KAHR-neh ehn POHL-voh*

**carne mechada:** Cuban-style stuffed beef
*KAHR-neh meh-CHAH-dah*

**locro criollo:** beef stew with potatoes
*LOH-kroh kree-OH-yoh*

**lomo fino:** beef tenderloin in port sauce
*LOH-moh FEE-noh*

**lomo salteado, loma saltado (S.Am):** beef strips with mixed
  vegetables and rice
*LOH-moh sahl-teh-AH-doh, LOH-moh sahl-TAH-do*

**olla de carne:** beef stew with yucca, squash, and pumpkin
*OH-yah deh KAHR-neh*

**ropa vieja:** stewed shredded beef
*ROH-pah VYEH-hah*

## ORGAN MEATS

**guisado de riñones:** kidney stew
*gee-SAH-doh deh ree-NYOH-nehs*

**menudo:** tripe stew
*meh-NOO-doh*

**pastelón de menudencias:** tripe pie
*pahs-teh-LOHN deh meh-noo-DEHN-syahs*

**riñoncitos al vino:** chicken kidneys stewed in a wine sauce.
*rreh-nyohn-SEE-tohs ahl VEE-noh*

## GOAT

**cabrito asado:** oven-roasted kid
*kah-BREE-toh ah-SAH-doh*

**seco de chivo:** goat stew in wine sauce
*SEH-koh deh CHEE-voh*

## PORK

**carnitas:** slow-cooked pork served with corn tortillas
*kahr-NEE-tahs*

**chicharrón:** deep-fried pork skin
*chee-chah-RROHN*

**cochinillo / lechón asado:** roast suckling pig
*koh-chee-NEE-yoh / leh-CHOHN ah-SAH-doh*
**costillas:** pork ribs
*kohs-TEE-yahs*
**puerco en adobo:** pork in chili sauce
*PWEHR-koh ehn ah-DOH-boh*
**seco de chancho:** pork stew
*SEH-koh deh CHAHN-cho*

## POULTRY

**ají de gallina:** creamed chicken with green chilis
*ah-HEE deh gah-YEE-nah*
**arroz con pollo:** rice with chicken and vegetables
*ah-RROHS kohn POH-yoh*
**chilaquiles:** chicken / cheese / tortilla casserole
*chee-lah-KEE-lehs*
**empanadas de pavo:** turkey individual meat pies
*ehm-pah-NAH-dahs deh PAH-voh*
**mole poblano:** chicken with bitter chocolate / chile sauce
*MOH-leh poh-BLAH-noh*
**patas de pavo rellenas:** stuffed turkey legs
*PAH-tahs deh PAH-voh reh-YEH-nahs*
**pollo a la brasa:** spit-roasted chicken
*POH-yoh ah lah BRAH-sah*
**pollo al jerez:** chicken in sherry
*POH-yoh ahl heh-REHS*
**pollo frito:** fried chicken
*POH-yoh FREE-toh*
**sopa de pavo:** turkey soup
*SOH-pah deh PAH-voh*

## FISH AND SEAFOOD

**ceviche:** seafood marinated with lemon or lime, along with
  cilantro, garlic, red pepper, and onion; served cold
*seh-VEE-cheh*

**bacalao guisado:** cod marinated in herbs
*bah-kah-LAH-oh gee-SAH-doh*
**camarones al ajillo:** garlic shrimp stew
*kah-mah-ROH-nehs ahl ah-HEE-yoh*
**camarones en cerveza:** shrimp in beer
*kah-mah-ROH-nehs ehn sehr-VEH-sah*
**chupin de camarones:** spicy shrimp stew
*CHOO-peen deh kah-mah-ROH-nehs*
**escabeche:** spicy fish stew
*ehs-kah-BEH-cheh*
**guiso de róbalo:** Cuban style sea bass stew.
*GEE-soh deh ROH-bah-loh*
**jueyes hervidos:** boiled crab
*HWEH-yehs ehr-VEE-dohs*
**salmorejo de jueyes:** crab in tomato and garlic sauce.
*sahl-moh-REH-hoh deh HWEH-yehs*
**taquitos de pescado:** grilled shark in tomato sauce on tacos.
*tah-KEE-tohs deh pehs-KAH-doh*
**zarzuela:** mixed fish and seafood soup with tomatoes,
  saffron, garlic, and wine served over bread
*sahr-SWEH-lah*
*For a full list of fish, see p114.*

## DESSERTS

**arroz con leche / arroz con dulce:** rice pudding
*ah-RROHS kohn LEH-cheh / ah-RROHS kohn DOOL-seh*
**buñuelos:** round, thin fritters dipped in sugar (may also be
  savory)
*boon-yoo-EH-lohs*
**dulce de plátano:** ripe yellow plantains cooked in wine and
  spices
*DOOL-seh deh PLAH-tah-noh*
**flan:** custard
*flahn*
**helado:** ice cream
*eh-LAH-doh*

DINING

**panqueques:** dessert crepes with caramel and whipped
  cream
*pahn-KEH-kehs*

**pastel tres leches:** three-milk cake
*pahs-TEHL trehs LEH-chehs*

**sopapillas:** puffed up crisps of a pie crust like dough,
  drizzled with honey and sprinkled with powdered sugar
*soh-pah-PEE-yahs*

**tembleque:** coconut milk custard
*tehm-BLEH-keh*

## STREET FOOD

**arepas:** savory stuffed cornmeal patties
*ah-REH-pahs*

**caña:** raw sugar cane
*KAH-nyah*

**chalupas:** corn tortillas filled with meat and cheese
*chah-LOO-pahs*

**chicha:** juice, punch
*CHEE-chah*

**chorreados:** corn pancakes with sour cream
*choh-rreh-AH-dohs*

**churros:** breakfast / dessert fritters
*CHOO-rrohs*

**coco verde:** green coconut
*KOH-koh VEHR-deh*

**cuchifrito:** deep-fried pork pieces (ears, tail, etc.)
*koo-chee-FREE-toh*

### Eating out of Pocket

Street food is generally inexpensive. Keep a supply of
small-denomination bills and change on you because
treat vendors generally won't be able to change large
bills.

**empañadas / empanadas:** turnovers filled with meat and / or cheese, beans, potatoes
*ehm-pah-NYAH-dahs / ehm-pah-NAH-dahs*

**empanadas chilenas:** turnovers filled with meat, boiled onion and raisins, an olive, and part of a hard-boiled egg
*ehm-pah-NAH-dahs chee-LEH-nahs*

**enchiladas:** pastries stuffed with cheese, meat, or potatoes
*ehn-chee-LAH-dahs*

**gorditas:** thick, fried corn tortillas stuffed with cheese, beans, and / or meat
*gohr-DEE-tahs*

**juanes:** rice tamales with chicken or fish
*HWAH-nehs*

**piraguas, raspadillas (Peru):** shaved ice with fruit syrup
*pee-RAH-wahs, rahs-pad-DEE-yahs*

**pupusas:** corn pancakes with cheese
*poo-POO-sahs*

**quesadillas:** tortillas with cheese
*keh-sah-DEE-yahs*

**rellenos:** bits of meat or cheese breaded with yucca or potato paste and deep fried
*rreh-YEH-nohs*

**salteñas (aka empanadas chilenas):** chicken or beef with onions and raisins wrapped in pastry
*sahl-TEH-nyahs*

**tacos:** traditional Mexican are made with ground tongue
*TAH-kohs*

**tamales:** chicken, pork, or potatoes with chiles in cornmeal steamed inside a banana leaf or corn husk
*tah-MAH-lehs*

**tortas:** sandwiches with meat and/or cheese, garnished with vegetables (frosted cake in S.Am)
*TOHR-tahs*

## BUYING GROCERIES

In most Latin American countries, groceries can be bought at open-air "farmers' markets," neighborhood stores, or large supermarkets.

### AT THE SUPERMARKET

| Which aisle has ____ | ¿En cuál pasillo se encuentran ___ |
|---|---|
| | *ehn kwahl pah-SEE-yoh seh ehn-KWEHN-trahn* |
| baby food? | **la comida de bebés?** |
| | *lah koh-MEE-dah deh beh-BEHS* |
| bread? | **el pan?** |
| | *ehl pahn* |
| canned goods? | **los artículos enlatados?** |
| | *lohs ahr-TEE-koo-lohs ehn-lah TAH-dohs* |
| cheese? | **el queso?** |
| | *ehl KEH-soh* |
| cookies? | **las galletas?** |
| | *lahs gah-YEH-tahs* |
| fruit? | **las frutas?** |
| | *lahs FROO-tahs* |
| juice? | **el jugo?** |
| | *ehl HOO-goh* |
| paper plates and napkins? | **los platos de papel y las servilletas?** |
| | *lohs PLAH-tohs deh pah-PEHL ee lahs sehr-vee-YEH-tahs* |
| snack food? | **los bocadillos?** |
| | *lohs boh-kah-DEE-yohs* |
| spices? | **las especias?** |
| | *lahs ehs-PEH-syahs* |

| toiletries? | **los artículos de tocador?** |
| | *lohs ahr-TEE-koo-lohs deh toh-* |
| | *kah-DOHR* |
| water? | **el agua?** |
| | *ehl AH-wah* |

## AT THE BUTCHER SHOP

| Is the meat fresh? | **¿La carne es fresca?** |
| | *lah KAHR-neh ehs FREHS-kah* |
| Do you sell fresh ____ | **¿Ustedes venden ____** |
| | *oos-TEH-dehs VEHN-dehn* |
| beef? | **carne de res fresca?** |
| | *KAHR-neh deh rrehs FREHS-cah* |
| goat? | **cabra fresca?** |
| | *KAH-brah FREHS-kah* |
| lamb? | **cordero fresco?** |
| | *kohr-DEH-roh FREHS-koh* |
| pork? | **cerdo fresco?** |
| | *SEHR-doh FREHS-koh* |
| I would like a cut of ____ | **Quisiera un corte de ____** |
| | *kee-SYEH-rah oon KOHR-teh deh* |
| brisket. | **pecho.** |
| | *PEH-cho* |
| chops. | **chuletas.** |
| | *choo-LEH-tahs* |
| filet. | **filete.** |
| | *fee-LEH-teh* |
| rump roast. | **cuadril / solomillo.** |
| | *kwah-DREEL / soh-loh-MEE-yoh* |
| T-bone. | **chuletón.** |
| | *choo-leh-TOHN* |
| tenderloin. | **lomo / filete.** |
| | *LOH-moh / fee-LEH-teh* |
| Thick / Thin cuts, please. | **Cortes finos / gruesos, por favor.** |
| | *KOHR-tehs FEE-nohs / GRWEH-* |
| | *sohs pohr fah-VOHR* |

DINING

| | |
|---|---|
| Please trim the fat. | **Por favor, córtele la grasa.** |
| | *pohr fah-VOHR KOHR-teh-leh lah* |
| | *GRAH-sah* |
| Do you have any sausage? | **¿Tiene salchichas?** |
| | *TYEH-neh sahl-CHEE-chas* |
| Is / Are the ____ fresh? | **¿Es / Son fresco -a -os -as ____** |
| | *ehs / sohn FREHS-koh -kah -kohs* |
| | *-kahs* |
| clams | **las almejas?** |
| | *lahs ahl-MEH-hahs* |
| fish | **el pescado?** |
| | *ehl pehs-KAH-doh* |
| flounder | **la platija?** |
| | *lah plah-TEE-hah* |
| octopus | **el pulpo?** |
| | *ehl POOL-poh* |
| oysters | **las ostras?** |
| | *lahs OHS-trahs* |
| sea bass | **el róbalo?** |
| | *ehl ROH-bah-loh* |
| seafood | **los mariscos?** |
| | *lohs mah-REES-kohs* |
| shark | **el tiburón?** |
| | *ehl tee-boo-ROHN* |
| shrimp | **los camarones?** |
| | *lohs kah-mah-ROH-nehs* |
| squid | **el calamar?** |
| | *ehl kahl-ah-MAHR* |
| turtle | **la tortuga?** |
| | *lah tohr-TOO-gah* |
| May I smell it? | **¿Puedo olerlo -a?** |
| | *PWEH-doh oh-LEHR-loh -lah* |

| | |
|---|---|
| Would you please ____ | ¿Por favor, puede ____ |
| | *pohr fah-VOHR PWEH-deh* |
| filet it? | **cortarlo -a en filetes?** |
| | *kohr-TAHR-loh -lah ehn* |
| | *fee-LEH-tehs* |
| debone it? | **deshuesarlo -a?** |
| | *dehs-weh-SAHR-loh -lah* |
| remove the head and | **quitarle la cabeza y la cola?** |
| tail? | *kee-TAHR-leh lah* |
| | *kah-BEH-sah ee lah KOH-lah* |

## AT THE PRODUCE STAND / MARKET
**Fruits**

| | |
|---|---|
| apple | **manzana** |
| | *mahn-ZAH-nah* |
| apricot | **albaricoque** |
| | *ahl-bah-ree-KOH-keh* |
| banana | **plátano, banana** |
| | *PLAH-tah-noh, bah-NAH-nah* |
| blackberries | **zarzamora, mora negra** |
| | *sahr-sah-MOH-rah, MOH-rah* |
| | *NEH-grah* |
| blueberry | **arándano azul, mora azul** |
| | *ah-RAHN-dah-noh ah-SOOL,* |
| | *MOH-rah ah-SOOL* |
| breadfruit | **fruta de pan, panapén, pana** |
| | *FROO-tah deh pahn, pah-nah-* |
| | *PEHN, PAH-nah* |
| cantaloupe | **cantalupo, melón** |
| | *kahn-tah-LOO-poh, meh-LOHN* |
| carambola, star fruit | **carambola** |
| | *kah-rahm-BOH-lah* |
| cherry | **cereza** |
| | *seh-REH-sah* |
| citron | **cidra** |
| | *SEE-drah* |

| | |
|---|---|
| coconut | **coco** |
| | *KOH-koh* |
| cranberry | **arándano rojo** |
| | *ah-RAHN-dah-noh ROH-hoh* |
| gooseberry | **grosella** |
| | *groh-SEH-yah* |
| grapefruit | **toronja** |
| | *toh-ROHN-hah* |
| grapes (green, red) | **uvas (verdes, rojas)** |
| | *OO-vahs (VEHR-dehs, RROH-hahs)* |
| guava | **guayaba** |
| | *wah-YAH-bah* |
| honeydew | **melón** |
| | *meh-LOHN* |
| kiwi | **kiwi** |
| | *KEE-wee* |
| lemon | **limón, limón amarillo (Mexico)** |
| | *lee-MOHN, lee-MOHN ah-mah-REE-yoh* |
| lime | **lima, limoncillo, limón verde (Mexico)** |
| | *LEE-mah, lee-mohn-SEE-yoh, lee-mohn VEHR-de* |
| mango | **mango** |
| | *MAHNG-goh* |
| melon | **melón** |
| | *meh-LOHN* |
| orange | **naranja** |
| | *nah-RAHN-hah* |
| palm fruit | **fruta de palma** |
| | *FROO-tah deh PAHL-mah* |
| papaya | **papaya** |
| | *pah-PAH-yah* |

| | |
|---|---|
| peach | **melocotón, durazno**<br>*meh-loh-koh-TOHN,*<br>*doo-RAHS-noh* |
| pear | **pera**<br>*PEH-rah* |
| pineapple | **piña**<br>*PEE-nyah* |
| plum | **ciruela**<br>*seer-WEH-lah* |
| soursop (spiny, yellow-green fruit with tart pulp) | **guanábana**<br>*wah-NAH-bah-nah* |
| strawberry | **fresa, frutilla (Chile)**<br>*FREH-sah, froo-TEE-yah* |
| tamarind | **tamarindo**<br>*tah-mah-REEN-doh* |
| tangerine | **mandarina**<br>*mahn-dah-REE-nah* |
| watermelon | **sandía, melón de agua**<br>*sahn-DEE-ah, meh-LOHN deh*<br>*AH-wah* |

**Vegetables**

| | |
|---|---|
| artichoke | **alcachofa**<br>*ahl-kah-CHOH-fah* |
| avocado | **aguacate, palta (S.Am)**<br>*ah-wah-KAH-teh, PAHL-tah* |
| bamboo shoots | **retoños de bambú**<br>*reh-TOH-nyohs deh bahm-BOO* |
| bean sprouts | **brotes de soja**<br>*BROH-tehs deh SOH-ha* |
| breadnut | **panapén**<br>*pah-nah-PEHN* |
| broccoli | **brócoli**<br>*BROH-koh-lee* |

| | |
|---|---|
| beans | **frijoles**<br>*free-HOH-lehs* |
| carrot | **zanahoria**<br>*sah-nah-OH-ryah* |
| cauliflower | **coliflor**<br>*koh-lee-FLOHR* |
| celery | **apio**<br>*AH-pyoh* |
| corn | **maíz**<br>*mah-EES* |
| cucumber | **pepino**<br>*peh-PEE-noh* |
| eggplant | **berenjena**<br>*beh-rehn-HEH-nah* |
| green beans | **frijoles verdes, vainitas (S.Am)**<br>*free-HOH-lehs VEHR-dehs, vahee-NEE-tahs* |
| lettuce | **lechuga**<br>*leh-CHOO-gah* |
| ñame (white yam) | **ñame (batata blanca)**<br>*NYAH-meh (bah-TAH-tah BLAHN-kah)* |
| okra | **quimbombo**<br>*keem-BOHM-boh* |
| olives | **aceitunas**<br>*ah-sehee-TOO-nahs* |
| onion | **cebolla**<br>*seh-BOH-yah* |
| peppers | **pimiento, chile**<br>*pee-MYEHN-toh, CHEE-leh* |
| bell | **cascabeles**<br>*kahs-kah-BEH-lehs* |
| cayenne | **pimienta de Cayena**<br>*pee-MYEHN-tah deh kah-YEH-nah* |

| | |
|---|---|
| chipotle | **chipotle** |
| | *chee-POHT-leh* |
| habanero | **habanero, habañero** |
| | *ah-bah-NEH-roh, ah-bah-* |
| | *NYEH-roh* |
| hot | **picante** |
| | *pee-KAHN-teh* |
| jalapeno | **jalapeño** |
| | *hah-lah-PEH-nyoh* |
| mild | **suave** |
| | *soo-AH-veh* |
| poblano | **poblano** |
| | *poh-BLAH-noh* |
| plantain | **plátano verde, plantaina, llantén** |
| | *PLAH-tah-noh VEHR-deh, plahn-* |
| | *TAHEE-nah, yahn-TEHN* |
| regular | **regular** |
| | *reh-goo-LAHR* |
| ripe | **maduro** |
| | *mah-DOO-roh* |
| potato | **papa, patata** |
| | *PAH-pah, pah-TAH-tah* |
| sorrel | **acedera** |
| | *ah-seh-DEH-rah* |
| spinach | **espinaca** |
| | *ehs-pee-NAH-kah* |
| sweet corn | **maíz dulce** |
| | *mah-EES DOOL-seh* |
| squash | **zapallo** |
| | *sah-PAH-yoh* |
| tomato | **tomate, jitomate (Mexico)** |
| | *toh-MAH-teh, hee-toh-MAH-teh* |
| yam | **batata, camote (S.Am)** |
| | *bah-TAH-tah, kah-MOH-teh* |

## Fresh Herbs and Spices

| allspice | **pimienta inglesa** |
| | *pee-MYEHN-tah eeng-GLEH-sah* |
| anise | **anís** |
| | *AH-nees* |
| basil | **albahaca** |
| | *ahl-bah-AH-kah* |
| bay leaf | **hoja de laurel seca** |
| | *OH-hah deh low-REHL SEH-kah* |
| black pepper | **pimienta negra** |
| | *pee-MYEHN-tah NEH-grah* |
| cacao | **cacao** |
| | *kah-KAH-oh* |
|   dried | **seco** |
| | *SEH-koh* |
|   fresh | **fresco** |
| | *FREHS-koh* |
|   seed | **en semilla** |
| | *ehn seh-MEE-yah* |
| caraway | **alcaravea** |
| | *ahl-kah-rah-VEH-ah* |
| cilantro | **cilantro** |
| | *see-LAHN-troh* |
| clove | **clavo** |
| | *KLAH-voh* |
| coriander | **culantro** |
| | *kooh-LAHN-troh* |
| cumin | **comino** |
| | *koh-MEE-noh* |
| dill | **eneldo** |
| | *eh-NEHL-doh* |
| garlic | **ajo** |
| | *AH-hoh* |
| marjoram | **mejorana** |
| | *meh-hoh-RAH-nah* |

| | |
|---|---|
| oregano | **orégano** |
| | *oh-REH-gah-noh* |
| paprika | **paprika** |
| | *pah-PREE-kah* |
| parsley | **perejil** |
| | *peh-reh-HEEL* |
| rosemary | **romero** |
| | *rroh-MEH-roh* |
| saffron | **azafrán** |
| | *ah-sah-FRAHN* |
| sage | **salvia** |
| | *SAHL-vyah* |
| salt | **sal** |
| | *sahl* |
| sugar | **azúcar** |
| | *ah-SOO-kahr* |
| thyme | **tomillo** |
| | *toh-MEE-yoh* |

## AT THE DELI

| | |
|---|---|
| What kind of salad is that? | **¿Qué tipo de ensalada es ésa?** |
| | *keh TEE-poh deh ehn-sah-LAH-dah ehs EH-sah* |
| What type of cheese is that? | **¿Qué tipo de queso es ese?** |
| | *keh TEE-poh deh KEH-soh ehs EH-seh* |
| What type of bread is that? | **¿Qué tipo de pan es ese?** |
| | *keh TEE-poh deh pahn ehs EH-seh* |
| Some of that, please. | **Un poco de eso, por favor.** |
| | *oon POH-koh deh EH-soh pohr fah-VOHR* |
| Is the salad fresh? | **¿La ensalada está fresca?** |
| | *lah ehn-sah-LAH-dah ehs-TAH FREHS-kah* |

I'd like ____

Quisiera ____
*kee-SYEH-rah*

that cheese.

**ese queso.**
*EH-seh KEH-soh*

chicken salad.

**ensalada de pollo.**
*ehn-sah-LAH-dah deh POH-yoh*

cole slaw.

**ensalada de col.**
*ehn-sah-LAH-dah deh KOHL*

ham.

**jamón.**
*hah-MOHN*

mayonaisse.

**mayonesa.**
*mah-yoh-NEH-sah*

mustard.

**mostaza.**
*mohs-TAH-sah*

a package of tofu.

**un paquete de tofu.**
*oon pah-KEH-teh deh TOH-foo*

a pickle.

**un pepinillo.**
*oon peh-pee-NEE-yoh*

roast beef.

**asado de res.**
*ah-SAH-doh deh rehs*

a salad.

**una ensalada.**
*OO-nah ehn-sah-LAH-dah*

a sandwich.

**un sándwich.**
*oon SAHND-weech*

tuna salad.

**ensalada de atún.**
*ehn-sah-LAH-dah deh ah-TOON*

Is that smoked?

**¿Eso es ahumado?**
*EH-soh ehs ah-oo-MAH-doh*

a pound (in kgs)

**una libra (0.454 kg)**
*OO-nah LEE-brah*

a quarter-pound (in kgs)

**un cuarto de libra (0.113 kg)**
*ooh KWAHR-toh deh LEE-brah*

a half-pound (in kgs)

**media libra (0.227 kg)**
*MEH-dyah LEE-brah*

## DINING OUT

**Dining Times**   In some regions of Latin America, restaurants do not get going until very late. In Argentina and Uruguay, many restaurants don't open before 9pm, and they remain open with large groups of families, including children, until the early hours.

The rest of Latin America follows a more conventional schedule, with restaurants opening at 7pm and taking orders until 11pm. The Sunday midday meal is sacred in most countries, sometimes stretching from noon to 5 or 6pm. In Quito (Ecuador) and the Andean highlands, locals consume a large lunch and almost never meet socially for dinner.

**Tipping**   Tipping varies from country to country, but it's usually 5% to 10% of the bill. Throughout Latin America, if you pay by credit card, it's a good idea to leave the tip in cash so the waiter actually receives it. Beware that some countries add a whopping sales tax to the listed price. This is particularly true in Uruguay (23%) and Ecuador (22%). Uruguayan restaurants also add a table cover charge (called *cubierto*) of about $1.

## BEERS & SPECIALTY DRINKS

South America is not a continent for great beers. *Cerveza* is generally light and cold and nothing else—adequate to quench a thirst but nothing to write home about. Every country has its own brands, but you may see some familiar names such as Budweiser and Carlsberg. Draft beer is known as *chopp*.

The good news is that there are plenty of alternatives to beer. Here are some of the most popular alcoholic drinks:

**Aguardiente**   As the name implies, this "hot water" leaves a warm feeling inside. A cheap and popular liquor in Colombia and Ecuador, it's made from a mix of natural and industrial ingredients. The best is made from aniseed.

**Fernet**    An Italian *digestif* that's the party drink in Argentina. It tastes like a cheap Jagermeister with a hint of herb and mint. It's delicious with lots of cola and ice.

**Manzanilla**    This liquor, made from chamomile, is a popular *digestif* in Chile.

**Pisco**    Popular in Chile and Peru, this grape brandy is powerful straight. Mix it with cola (known as *piscola*) or in a *pisco sour* (egg white, lemon juice, and sugar).

**Rum (*ron*)**    No beach experience in Venezuela is complete without a *Cuba Libre* in the hand. Brands to watch for are Cacique and Ron Añejo Aniversario.

**Tequila**    Mexico's signature drink, this potent brew is made from the fermented juice of the indigenous agave plant.

## VINTAGE WINE

Only a few countries produce quality wines in Latin America. The best of them are produced in Argentina and Chile.

### Argentina

**Malbec**    Red. Rich, soft, and easy to drink, with hints of black currant and oak. Pairs well with all cuts of red meat. *Best Labels*: Achaval ferrer, Alta Vista, Enrique Foster, Renacer, Doña Paula.

**Torrontes**    Fruity white, very floral on the nose, with hints of peach, musk, and spice. Great as an aperitif or with seafood dishes. *Best Labels*: Etchart, Alta Vista, Michel Torino, Crios, Zuccardi.

**Tempranillo**    Red. Soft and full bodied. Pairs well with cream-based sauces and goat cheese. *Best Labels*: O.Fournier, Zuccardi, Viniterra Tittarelli, Santa Faustina.

**Best year for Argentinean wines:** 2002. Worst year: 1998.

### Bolivia

**Cabernet Sauvignon**    Red. Smooth and silky with a good dose of oak and hints of black currant. Goes well with all grilled meats. *Best Labels*: Cenavit, La Concepcion, Campos de Solana, Milcast.

### Chile
**Cabernet Sauvignon:** Deep, earthy red wine with lots of texture and hints of oak. Very easy to drink. Goes well with all meat dishes. *Best Labels:* Casa Silva, J&F Lurton, Montes, Santa Laura, Concha Y Toro.

**Carmenere:** Red. Unusual varietal with hints of cassis, coffee beans, and a smooth, long finish. Pairs perfectly with hearty Chilean stews. *Best Labels:* Carmen, Casa Rivas, Los Robles.

**Best Year for Chilean wines:** 2002. Worst year: 1998

### Uruguay
**Tannat:** Red. Tannic, jet black with hints of violets and black cherry. Wonderful to drink with aged cheeses or with a spicy pasta sauce. *Best Labels:* Ariano, Bruzzone y Sciutti, Filguera, Moizo, Santa Rosa.

**Best Year for Uruguayan wines:** 2002

## POPULAR NON-ALCOHOLIC DRINKS
**Fruit Juice**  On every street corner in the tropical north, you'll find fresh fruit juice stands serving the most exotic beverages, some from fruits you've never heard of, blended with crushed ice. These are known as *jugos* in Colombia and Venezuela. With milk, you can also turn them into shakes known as *batidos* or *vitaminas*.

**Inca Cola**  Peru`s most popular soft drink is a cola with a radioactive yellow color and the taste of chewing gum.

***Mate***  Every Argentine or Uruguayan seems to possess a thermos or *mate* gourd, which many take with them wherever they go. These are used to hold a bitter beverage made of *yerba* (tea leaf) and hot water. This medicinal drink is of ancient origins, introduced to the world by the Guarani Indians of South America. It's said to aid weight loss, increase longevity, energize the body, and so on. Curiously, it's rare that you'll find *mate* for sale in cafes or bars.

**DINING**

*Mate de Coca*   Bolivia's answer to espresso is a tea made from the coca leaf—a tonic recommended for mild altitude sickness.

## COFFEE

Ecuador makes tons of good coffee, but little of the good stuff stays in the country. When you ask for a coffee you'll most likely get a cup of hot water and a spoonful of Nescafe—or worse. In Argentina, a *cortado mediana* is most similar to what coffee with milk should be.

## DINING ESTABLISHMENTS

*Bodegon*   This is a traditional local restaurant in Buenos Aires, with a menu limited to meat. Waiters serve with good-humored rudeness.

*Cevicheria*   These Peruvian restaurants specialize in *ceviche* (marinated raw fish).

*Churrascarias*   These grill houses use charcoal on every kind of meat, especially chicken and beef.

*Marisquerias*   Fresh fish restaurants in Chile.

*Parilla or Parillada*   Popular steakhouses in Argentina, Paraguay, and Uruguay.

*Restobar*   A hybrid restaurant-bar where you can eat, drink, or both.

*Tenedor Libre*   All-you-can-eat restaurants in Argentina.

## HOTEL MEAL PLANS

Carefully consider your hotel's meal plan. If you enjoy eating out and sampling local cuisine, choose a **Continental Plan** (CP) with breakfast only, or a **European Plan** (EP), which doesn't include any meals, for maximum flexibility.

# CHAPTER FIVE

## SOCIALIZING

Whether you're meeting people in a bar or a park, you'll find the language you need, in this chapter, to make new friends.

### GREETINGS

| | |
|---|---|
| Hello. | **Hola.** |
| | *OH-lah* |
| How are you? | **¿Cómo estás?** |
| | *KOH-moh ehs-TAHS* |
| Fine, thanks. | **Bien, gracias.** |
| | *byehn GRAH-syahs* |
| And you? | **¿Y usted?** |
| | *ee oos-TEHD* |
| I'm exhausted from the trip. | **Estoy cansado -a del viaje.** |
| | *ehs-TOY kahn-SAH-doh -dah dehl VYAH-heh* |
| I have a headache. | **Tengo dolor de cabeza.** |
| | *TEHNG-goh doh-LOHR deh kah-BEH-sah* |
| I'm terrible. | **Estoy terrible.** |
| | *ehs-TOY teh-RREE-bleh* |
| I have a cold. | **Tengo un resfriado.** |
| | *TEHNG-goh oon rehs-free-AH-doh* |
| Good morning. | **Buenos días.** |
| | *BWEH-nohs DEE-ahs* |
| Good evening. | **Buenas noches.** |
| | *BWEH-nahs NOH-chehs* |
| Good afternoon. | **Buenas tardes.** |
| | *BWEH-nahs TAHR-dehs* |
| Good night. | **Buenas noches.** |
| | *BWEH-nahs NOH-chehs* |

## Listen Up: Common Greetings

| | |
|---|---|
| **Es un placer.**<br>*ehs oon plah-SEHR* | It's a pleasure. |
| **Mucho gusto.**<br>*MOO-choh GOOS-toh* | Delighted. |
| **A la orden.**<br>*ah lah OHR-dehn* | At your service. / As you wish. |
| **Encantado -a.**<br>*ehn-kahn-TAH-do -dah* | Charmed. |
| **Buenas.**<br>*BWEH-nahs* | Good day. (shortened) |
| **Hola.**<br>*OH-lah* | Hello. |
| **¿Qué tal?**<br>*keh TAHL* | How's it going? |
| **¿Cómo anda?**<br>*KOH-moh AHN-dah* | How's it going? |
| **¿Qué hubo?**<br>*keh OO-boh* | What's up? |
| **¿Qué pasa?**<br>*keh PAH-sah* | What's going on? |
| **¡Venga!**<br>*VEHN-gah* | Bye! (Spain) |
| **Adiós.**<br>*ah-DYOHS* | Goodbye. |
| **Nos vemos.**<br>*nohs VEH-mohs* | See you later. |

## THE LANGUAGE BARRIER

| | |
|---|---|
| I don't understand. | **No entiendo.**<br>*noh ehn-TYEHN-doh* |
| Please speak more slowly. | **Por favor hable más lento.**<br>*pohr fah-VOHR AH-bleh mahs LEHN-toh* |

| | |
|---|---|
| Please speak louder. | **Por favor hable más alto.** |
| | *pohr fah-VOHR AH-bleh mahs* |
| | *AHL-toh* |
| Do you speak English? | **¿Usted habla inglés?** |
| | *oos-TEHD AH-blah eeng-GLEHS* |
| I speak ____ better than Spanish. | **Yo hablo ____ mejor que español.** |
| | *yoh AH-bloh ____ meh-HOHR keh* |
| | *ehs-pah-NYOHL* |

## Curse Words

Here are some common curse words, used across Latin America and Spain.

| | |
|---|---|
| **mierda / cagada** | shit |
| *MYEHR-dah / kah-GAH-dah* | |
| **hijo de puta** | son of a bitch (literally, son |
| *EE-hoh deh POO-tah* | of a whore) |
| **huevón** | jerk |
| *weh-VOHN* | |
| **carajo** | damn |
| *kah-RAH-hoh* | |
| **culón** | ass |
| *koo-LOHN* | |
| **jodido / jodienda** | screwed up |
| *hoh-DEE-doh /* | |
| *hoh-DYEHN-dah* | |
| **cabrón** | bastard |
| *kah-BROHN* | |
| **chingada** | fucked up (Mexican) |
| *cheeng-GAH-dah* | |
| **follar / coger / joder** | to fuck |
| *foh-YAHR / koh-HEHR /* | |
| *hoh-DEHR* | |
| *See p22, 23 for conjugations.* | |

| | |
|---|---|
| Please spell that. | **Por favor deletree eso.** |
| | *pohr fah-VOHR deh-leh-TREH-eh* |
| | *EH-soh* |
| Please repeat that? | **¿Por favor repita eso?** |
| | *pohr fah-VOHR reh-PEE-tah* |
| | *EH-soh* |
| How do you say ____? | **¿Cómo usted dice ____?** |
| | *KOH-moh oos-TEHD DEE-seh* |
| Would you show me that in this dictionary? | **¿Me puede mostrar eso en este diccionario?** |
| | *meh PWEH-deh mohs-TRAHR EH-soh ehn EHS-teh deek-syoh-NAH-ryoh* |

## GETTING PERSONAL

People in Latin America are generally friendly, but more formal than Americans or Europeans. Remember to use the *usted* form of address, until given permission to employ the more familiar *tú*.

### INTRODUCTIONS

| | |
|---|---|
| What is your name? | **¿Cuál es su nombre?** |
| | *kwahl ehs soo NOHM-breh* |
| My name is ____. | **Me llamo ____.** |
| | *meh YAH-moh* |
| I'm very pleased to meet you. | **Es un placer conocerle.** |
| | *ehs oon plah-SEHR koh-noh-SEHR-leh* |
| May I introduce my ____ | **¿Puedo presentarle a mi ____** |
| | *PWEH-doh preh-sehn-TAHR-leh ah mee* |
| How is your ____ | **¿Cómo está su / están sus ____** |
| | *KOH-moh ehs-TAH soo / ehs-TAHN soos* |
| aunt / uncle? | **tía -o?** |
| | *TEE-ah -oh* |
| boss? | **jefe?** |
| | *HEH-feh* |

| | |
|---|---|
| boyfriend / girlfriend? | **novio -a?** |
| | *NOH-vyoh -vyah* |
| brother / sister? | **hermano -a?** |
| | *ehr-MAH-noh -nah* |
| child? | **hijo -a?** |
| | *EE-hoh -hah* |
| cousin? | **primo -a?** |
| | *PREE-moh -mah?* |
| family? | **familia?** |
| | *fah-MEE-lyah* |
| father? | **padre?** |
| | *PAH-dreh* |
| friend / friends? | **amigo -a? / amigos -gas?** |
| | *ah-MEE-goh -gah /* |
| | *ah-MEE-gohs -gahs* |
| fiancée / fiancé? | **prometido -a?** |
| | *proh-meh-TEE-doh -dah* |
| grandparents? | **abuelos?** |
| | *ah-BWEH-lohs* |
| husband? | **esposo?** |
| | *ehs-POH-soh* |
| mother? | **madre?** |
| | *MAH-dreh?* |
| neighbor? | **vecino?** |
| | *veh-SEE-noh* |
| niece/nephew? | **sobrino -a?** |
| | *soh-BREE-noh -nah* |
| parents? | **padres?** |
| | *PAH-drehs* |
| partner? | **socio -a?** |
| | *SOH-syoh -syah* |
| wife? | **esposa?** |
| | *ehs-POH-sah* |
| Are you married / single? | **¿Usted es casado -a / soltero -a?** |
| | *oos-TEHD ehs kah-SAH-doh -dah /* |
| | *sohl-TEH-roh -rah* |

### Dos and Don'ts

Don't refer to your parents as *los parientes*, which means relatives. Do call them *los padres* (even though *el padre* means father).

| | |
|---|---|
| I'm married. | **Soy casado -a.** |
| | *soy kah-SAH-doh -dah* |
| I'm single. | **Soy soltero -a.** |
| | *soy sohl-TEH-roh -rah* |
| I'm divorced. | **Soy divorciado -a.** |
| | *soy dee-vohr-SYAH-doh -dah* |
| I'm a widow / widower. | **Soy viudo -a.** |
| | *soy VYOO-doh -dah* |
| We're separated. | **Estamos separados.** |
| | *ehs-TAH-mohs seh-pah-RAH-dohs* |
| I live with my boyfriend / girlfriend. | **Vivo con mi novio -a.** |
| | *VEE-voh kohn mee NOH-vyoh -vyah* |
| How old are you? | **¿Qué edad usted tiene?** |
| | *keh eh-DAHD oo-STEHD TYEH-neh* |
| How old are your children? | **¿Qué edad tienen sus hijos?** |
| | *keh eh-DAHD TYEH-nehn soos EE-hos* |
| Wow! That's very young. | **¡Caramba! Eso es muy joven.** |
| | *kah-RAHM-bah! EH-soh ehs MOO-ee HOH-vehn* |
| No you're not! You're much younger. | **¡No lo es! Usted es mucho más joven.** |
| | *noh loh ehs oos-TEHD ehs MOO-choh mahs HOH-vehn* |
| Your wife / daughter is beautiful. | **Su esposa / hija es bella.** |
| | *soo ehs-POH-sah / EE-hah ehs BEH-yah* |

| | |
|---|---|
| Your husband / son is handsome. | **Su esposo / hijo es guapo.**<br>*soo ehs-POH-soh / EE-hoh ehs WAH-poh* |
| What a beautiful baby! | **¡Que bebé tan lindo!**<br>*keh beh-BEH tahn LEEN-doh* |
| Are you here on business? | **¿Usted está aquí por negocios?**<br>*oos-TEHD ehs-TAH ah-KEE pohr neh-GOH-syohs* |
| I am vacationing. | **Estoy de vacaciones.**<br>*ehs-TOY deh vah-kah-SYOH-nehs* |
| I'm attending a conference. | **Estoy asistiendo a una conferencia.**<br>*ehs-TOY ah-sees-TYEHN-doh ah OO-nah kohn-feh-REHN-syah* |
| How long are you staying? | **¿Por cuánto tiempo se va a quedar?**<br>*pohr KWAHN-toh TYEHM-poh seh vah ah keh-DAHR* |
| What are you studying? | **¿Qué estudia?**<br>*keh ehs-TOO-dyah* |
| I'm a student. | **Soy estudiante.**<br>*soy ehs-too-DYAHN-teh* |
| Where are you from? | **¿De dónde es?**<br>*deh DOHN-deh ehs* |

## PERSONAL DESCRIPTIONS

| | |
|---|---|
| Asian | **Asiático -a**<br>*ah-see-AH-tee-koh -kah* |
| African-American | **Africano-americano -a**<br>*ah-free-KAH-noh-ah-meh-ree-KAH-noh -nah* |
| black | **negro -a**<br>*NEH-groh -grah* |
| blond(e) | **rubio -a**<br>*ROO-byoh -byah* |

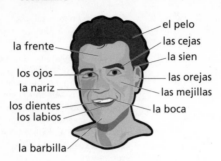

el pelo
las cejas
la sien
la frente
las orejas
los ojos
las mejillas
la nariz
los dientes
los labios
la boca
la barbilla

| biracial | **birracial** |
| | *bee-rrah-SYAHL* |
| blue eyes | **los ojos azules** |
| | *lohs OH-hohs ah-SOO-lehs* |
| brown eyes | **los ojos marrones** |
| | *lohs OH-hohs mah-RROH-nehs* |
| brunette | **moreno -a** |
| | *moh-REH-noh -nah* |
| caucasian | **caucásico -a** |
| | *kow-KAH-see-koh -kah* |
| curly hair | **pelo rizo / crespo** |
| | *PEH-loh REE-soh / KREH-spoh* |
| eyebrows | **las cejas** |
| | *lahs SEH-hahs* |
| eyelashes | **las pestañas** |
| | *lahs pehs-TAH-nyahs* |
| face | **la cara** |
| | *lah KAH-rah* |
| fat | **gordo -a** |
| | *GOHR-doh -dah* |

| | |
|---|---|
| freckles | **las pecas** |
| | *lahs PEH-kahs* |
| green eyes | **los ojos verdes** |
| | *lohs OH-hohs VEHR-dehs* |
| hazel eyes | **los ojos cafés** |
| | *OH-hohs kah-FEHS* |
| kinky hair | **pelo rizo** |
| | *PEH-loh REE-soh* |
| long hair | **pelo largo** |
| | *PEH-loh LAHR-goh* |
| mocha-skinned | **moreno -a** |
| | *moh-REH-noh -nah* |
| moles | **los lunares** |
| | *lohs looh-NAH-rehs* |
| pale | **pálido -a** |
| | *PAH-lee-doh* |
| redhead | **pelirrojo -a** |
| | *peh-lee-RRO-hoh -hah* |
| short | **bajo -a** |
| | *BAH-hoh -hah* |
| short hair | **pelo corto** |
| | *PEH-loh KOHR-toh* |
| straight hair | **pelo lacio** |
| | *PEH-loh LAH-syoh* |
| tall | **alto -a** |
| | *AHL-toh -tah* |
| tanned | **bronceado -a** |
| | *brohn-seh-AH-doh -dah* |
| thin | **delgado -a** |
| | *dehl-GAH-doh -dah* |
| white | **blanco -a** |
| | *BLAHN-koh -kah* |

## Listen Up: Nationalities

| | |
|---|---|
| **Soy alemán -a.**<br>*soy ah-leh-MAHN -nah* | I'm German. |
| **Soy argentino -a.**<br>*soy ahr-hehn-TEE-noh -nah* | I'm Argentinean. |
| **Soy boliviano -a.**<br>*soy boh-lee-VYAH-noh -nah* | I'm Bolivian. |
| **Soy brazileño -a.**<br>*soy brah-see-LEH-nyoh -nyah* | I'm Brazilian. |
| **Soy chino -a.**<br>*soy CHEE-noh -nah* | I'm Chinese. |
| **Soy colombiano -a.**<br>*soy koh-lohm-BYAH-noh -nah* | I'm Colombian. |
| **Soy costarricense.**<br>*soy kohs-tah-rree-SEHN-seh* | I'm Costa Rican. |
| **Soy ecuatoriano -a.**<br>*soy eh-kwah-toh-RYAH-noh -nah* | I'm Ecuadorian. |
| **Soy español -a.**<br>*soy ehs-pah-NYOHL -lah* | I'm Spanish. |
| **Soy francés.**<br>*soy frahn-SEHS* | I'm French. |
| **Soy guatemalteco -a.**<br>*soy wah-teh-mahl-TEH-koh -kah* | I'm Guatemalan. |
| **Soy hindú.**<br>*soy een-DOO* | I'm Hindu. |
| **Soy hondureño -a.**<br>*soy ohn-doo-REH-nyoh -nyah* | I'm Honduran |
| **Soy italiano -a.**<br>*soy ee-tah-LYAH-noh -nah* | I'm Italian. |
| **Soy japonés / japonesa.**<br>*soy hah-poh-NEHS -NEH-sah* | I'm Japanese. |
| **Soy mexicano -a.**<br>*soy meh-hee-KAH-noh -nah* | I'm Mexican. |
| **Soy nicaragüense.**<br>*soy nee-kah-rah-WEHN-seh* | I'm Nicaraguan. |

| | |
|---|---|
| **Soy panameño -a.**<br>*soy pah-nah-MEH-nyoh -nyah* | I'm Panamanian. |
| **Soy paraguayo -a.**<br>*soy pah-rah-WAH-yoh -yah* | I'm Paraguayan. |
| **Soy peruano -a.**<br>*soy peh-roo-AH-noh -nah* | I'm Peruvian. |
| **Soy puertorriqueño -a.**<br>*soy pwehr-toh-rree-KEH-nyoh -nyah* | I'm Puerto Rican. |
| **Soy ruso -a.**<br>*soy ROO-soh -sah* | I'm Russian. |
| **Soy salvadoreño -a.**<br>*soy sahl-vah-doh-REH-nyoh -nyah* | I'm Salvadorian. |
| **Soy uruguayo -a.**<br>*soy oo-roo-WAH-yoh -yah* | I'm Uruguayan. |
| **Soy venezolano -a.**<br>*soy veh-neh-soh-LAH-noh -nah* | I'm Venezuelan. |

*For more nationalities, see p232 and English / Spanish dictionary.*

## DISPOSITIONS AND MOODS

| | |
|---|---|
| angry | **enojado -a**<br>*eh-noh-HAH-doh -dah* |
| anxious | **ansioso -a**<br>*ahn-SYOH-soh -sah* |
| confused | **confundido -a**<br>*kohn-foon-DEE-doh -dah* |
| depressed | **deprimido -a**<br>*deh-pree-MEE-doh -dah* |
| enthusiastic | **entusiasmado -a**<br>*ehn-too-syahs-MAH-doh -dah* |
| happy | **feliz / alegre**<br>*feh-LEES / ah-LEH-greh* |
| sad | **triste**<br>*TREES-teh* |
| stressed | **estresado -a**<br>*ehs-treh-SAH-doh -dah* |
| tired | **cansado -a**<br>*kahn-SAH-doh -dah* |

## PROFESSIONS

What do you do for a living?

**¿En qué trabaja usted?**
*ehn keh trah-BAH-hah oo-STEHD*

Here is my business card.

**Aquí tiene mi tarjeta de presentación.**
*ah-KEE TYEH-neh mee tahr-HEH-tah deh preh-sehn-tah-SYOHN*

I am \_\_\_\_

**Soy \_\_\_\_**
*soy*

an accountant.

**contable.**
*kohn-TAH-bleh*

an artist.

**artista.**
*ahr-TEES-tah*

a craftsperson.

**artesano -a.**
*ahr-teh-SAH-noh -nah*

a designer.

**diseñador -a.**
*dee-seh-nyah-DOHR -DOH-rah*

a doctor.

**doctor.**
*dohk-TOHR*

an editor.

**editor -a.**
*eh-dee-TOHR -TOH-rah*

an educator.

**educador**
*eh-doo-kah-DOHR*

an engineer.

**ingeniero -a.**
*een-heh-NYEH-roh -rah*

a government employee.

**empleado gubernamental.**
*ehm-pleh-AH-doh goo-behr-nah-mehn-TAHL*

a homemaker.

**ama de casa.**
*AH-mah deh KAH-sah*

a lawyer.

**abogado -a.**
*ah-boh-GAH-doh -dah*

| | |
|---|---|
| a military professional. | **profesional militar.** |
| | *proh-feh-syoh-NAHL mee-lee-TAHR* |
| a musician. | **músico -a.** |
| | *MOO-see-koh -kah* |
| a nurse. | **enfermero -a** |
| | *ehn-fehr-MEH-roh -rah* |
| a salesperson. | **vendedor -a.** |
| | *vehn-deh-DOHR -DOH-rah* |
| a writer. | **escritor -a.** |
| | *ehs-kree-TOHR -TOH-rah* |

SOCIALIZING

## DOING BUSINESS

| | |
|---|---|
| I'd like an appointment. | **Quisiera hacer una cita.** |
| | *kee-SYEH-rah ah-SEHR OO-nah SEE-tah* |
| I'm here to see ____. | **Estoy aquí para ver a ____.** |
| | *ehs-TOY ah-KEE pa-rah vehr ah* |
| May I photocopy this? | **¿Puedo fotocopiar esto?** |
| | *PWEH-doh foh-toh-koh-PYAHR EHS-toh* |
| May I use a computer here? | **¿Puedo usar la computadora aquí?** |
| | *PWEH-doh oo-SAHR lah kohm-poo-tah-DOH-rah ah-KEE* |
| What's the password? | **¿Cuál es la contraseña?** |
| | *kwahl ehs lah kohn-trah-SEH-nyah* |
| May I access the Internet? | **¿Puedo acceder el Internet?** |
| | *PWEH-doh ahk-seh-DEHR ahl een-tehr-NEHT* |
| May I send a fax? | **¿Puedo enviar un fax?** |
| | *PWEH-doh ehn-vee-AHR oon fahks* |
| May I use the phone? | **¿Puedo usar el teléfono?** |
| | *PWEH-doh oo-SAHR ehl teh-LEH-foh-noh* |

## PARTING WAYS

| | |
|---|---|
| Keep in touch. | **Manténgase en contacto.**<br>*mahn-TEHNG-gah-seh ehn kohn-TAHK-toh* |
| Please write or email. | **Por favor escríbame o envíeme un e-mail.**<br>*pohr fah-VOHR ehs-KREE-bah-meh oh ehn-VEE-eh-meh oon EE-mehl* |
| Here's my phone number. Call me. | **Aquí tiene mi número de teléfono. Llámeme.**<br>*ah-KEE TYEH-neh mee NOO-meh-roh deh teh-LEH-foh-noh. YAH-meh-meh* |
| May I have your phone number / e-mail please? | **¿Me puede dar su número de teléfono / dirección de e-mail, por favor?**<br>*meh PWEH-deh dahr soo NOO-meh-roh deh teh-LEH-foh-noh / dee-rehk-SYOHN deh EE-mehl pohr fah-VOHR* |
| May I have your card? | **¿Me puede dar su tarjeta?**<br>*meh PWEH-deh dahr soo tahr-HEH-tah* |
| Give me your address and I'll write you. | **Déme su dirección y le escribiré.**<br>*DEH-meh soo dee-rehk-SYOHN ee leh ehs-kree-bee-REH* |

## TOPICS OF CONVERSATION

As in the United States or Europe, the weather and current affairs are common conversation topics.

### THE WEATHER

| | |
|---|---|
| It's so _____ | **Es tan _____**<br>*Ehs tahn* |

| Is it always so ___ ? | ¿Siempre es tan ___ ?<br>*SYEHM-preh ehs tahn* |
|---|---|
| cool. | **frío.**<br>*FREE-oh* |
| cloudy. | **nublado.**<br>*noo-BLAH-doh* |
| humid. | **húmedo.**<br>*OO-meh-doh* |
| rainy. | **lluvioso.**<br>*yoo-vee-OH-soh* |
| sunny. | **soleado.**<br>*soh-leh-AH-doh* |
| warm. | **caliente.**<br>*kah-LYEHN-teh* |
| windy. | **ventoso.**<br>*vehn-TOH-soh* |
| Do you know the weather forecast for tomorrow? | ¿Usted sabe el pronóstico del tiempo para mañana?<br>*oo-STEHD SAH-beh ehl proh-NOHS-tee-koh dehl TYEHM-poh PAH-rah mah-NYAH-nah* |

## THE ISSUES

| What do you think about ___ | ¿Qué usted opina de ___<br>*keh oos-TEHD oh-PEE-nah deh* |
|---|---|
| democracy? | **la democracia?**<br>*lah deh-moh-KRAH-syah* |
| socialism? | **el socialismo?**<br>*ehl soh-syah-LEES-moh* |
| American Democrats? | **los americanos demócratas?**<br>*lohs ah-meh-ree-KAH-nohs deh MOH-krah-tahs* |
| American Republicans? | **los americanos republicanos?**<br>*lohs ah-meh-ree-KAH-nohs reh-poo-blee-KAH-nohs* |

| | |
|---|---|
| the environment? | **el medio ambiente?**<br>*ehl MEH-dyoh ahm-BYEHN-teh* |
| women's rights? | **los derechos de las mujeres?**<br>*lohs deh-REH-chohs deh lahs moo-HEH-rehs* |
| gay rights? | **los derechos de los homo-sexuales?**<br>*lohs deh-reh-chos deh lohs oh-moh-sehk-SWAH-lehs* |
| the economy? | **la economía?**<br>*lah eh-koh-noh-MEE-ah* |
| What political party do you belong to? | **¿A qué partido político usted pertenece?**<br>*ah keh pahr-TEE-doh poh-LEE-tee-koh oos-TEHD pehr-teh-NEH-seh* |
| What did you think of the American election? | **¿Qué usted opina de las elecciones americanas?**<br>*keh oos-TEHD oh-PEE-nah deh lahs eh-lehk-SYOH-nehs ah-meh-ree-KAH-nahs* |
| What do you think of the war in ____? | **¿Qué usted opina de la guerra en ____?**<br>*keh oos-TEHD oh-PEE-nah deh lah GEH-rrah ehn* |

## RELIGION

| | |
|---|---|
| Do you go to church / temple / mosque? | **¿Usted asiste a una iglesia / un templo / una mezquita?**<br>*oos-TEHD ah-SEES-teh ah OO-nah ee-GLEH-syah / oon TEHM-ploh / OO-nah mehs-KEE-tah* |
| Are you religious? | **¿Usted es religioso?**<br>*ooh-STEHD ehs reh-lee-HYOH-soh* |

| | |
|---|---|
| I'm ____ / I was raised ____ | **Soy ____ / Fui criado ____**<br>*soy / FOO-ee kree-AH-doh* |
| agnostic. | **agnóstico.**<br>*ahg-NOHS-tee-koh* |
| atheist. | **ateo -a.**<br>*ah-TEH-oh -ah* |
| Buddhist. | **budista.**<br>*boo-DEES-tah* |
| Catholic. | **católico.**<br>*kah-TOH-lee-koh* |
| Greek Orthodox. | **ortodoxo griego.**<br>*orh-toh-DOHK-soh GRYEH-goh* |
| Hindu. | **hindú.**<br>*een-DOO* |
| Jewish. | **judío.**<br>*hoo-DEE-oh* |
| Muslim. | **musulmán.**<br>*moo-sool-MAHN* |
| Protestant. | **protestante.**<br>*proh-tehs-TAHN-teh* |
| I'm spiritual but I don't attend services. | **Soy espiritual pero no asisto a los servicios.**<br>*soy ehs-pee-ree-TWAHL peh-roh noh ah-SEES-toh ah lohs sehr-VEE-syohs* |
| I don't believe in that. | **Yo no creo en eso.**<br>*yoh noh KREH-oh ehn EH-soh* |
| That's against my beliefs. | **Eso va en contra de mis creencias.**<br>*EH-soh vah ehn KOHN-trah deh mees kreh-EHN-syahs* |
| I'd rather not talk about it. | **Preferiría no hablar de ello.**<br>*preh-feh-ree-REE-ah noh ah-BLAHR deh EH-yoh* |

## GETTING TO KNOW SOMEONE

Following are some conversation starters.

## MUSICAL TASTES

| | |
|---|---|
| What kind of music do you like? | **¿Qué tipo de música le gusta?**<br>*keh TEE-poh deh MOO-see-kah leh GOOS-tah* |
| I like _____ | **Me gusta _____**<br>*meh GOOS-tah* |
| calypso. | **el calipso.**<br>*ehl kah-LEEP-soh* |
| classical. | **la música clásica.**<br>*lah MOO-see-kah KLAH-see-kah* |
| country and western. | **la música country.**<br>*lah MOO-see-kah KOHN-tree* |
| disco. | **el disco.**<br>*ehl DEES-koh* |
| hip hop. | **el hip hop, el jip jop.**<br>*ehl eep ohp, ehl heep HOHP* |
| jazz. | **el jazz.**<br>*ehl jahs* |
| New Age. | **la nueva era.**<br>*lah NWEH-vah EH-rah* |
| opera. | **la ópera.**<br>*lah OH-peh-rah* |
| pop. | **la música pop.**<br>*lah MOO-see-kah pohp* |
| reggae. | **el reggae.**<br>*ehl REH-geh* |
| rock 'n' roll. | **el rock and roll.**<br>*ehl rroh-kahnd-ROHL* |
| show-tunes / musicals. | **los musicales.**<br>*lohs moo-see-KAH-lehs* |
| techno. | **el techno.**<br>*ehl TEHK-noh* |

## HOBBIES

| | |
|---|---|
| What do you like to do in your spare time? | **¿Qué hace usted en su tiempo libre?** <br> *keh AH-seh oos-TEHD ehn soo TYEHM-poh LEE-breh* |
| I like ____ | **Me gusta ____** <br> *meh GOOS-tah* |
| camping. | **acampar.** <br> *ah-kahm-PAHR* |
| cooking. | **cocinar.** <br> *koh-see-NAHR* |
| dancing. | **bailar.** <br> *bah-ee-LAHR* |
| drawing. | **dibujar.** <br> *dee-boo-HAHR* |
| eating out. | **comer fuera.** <br> *koh-MEHR FWEH-rah* |
| going to the movies. | **ir al cine.** <br> *eer ahl SEE-neh* |
| hanging out. | **pasar el rato.** <br> *pah-SAHR ehl RAH-toh* |
| hiking. | **excursionismo.** <br> *ehs-koor-syoh-NEES-moh* |
| painting. | **pintar.** <br> *peen-TAHR* |
| piano. | **el piano.** <br> *ehl PYAH-noh* |
| playing guitar. | **tocar la guitarra.** <br> *toh-KAHR lah gee-TAH-rrah* |

*For other instruments, see the English / Spanish dictionary.*

| | |
|---|---|
| reading. | **leer.** <br> *leh-EHR* |
| sewing. | **coser.** <br> *koh-SEHR* |
| shopping. | **ir de comprar.** <br> *eer deh kohm-PRAHR* |

| | |
|---|---|
| sports. | **los deportes.** |
| | *lohs deh-POHR-tehs* |
| traveling. | **viajar.** |
| | *vyah-HAR* |
| watching TV. | **ver televisión.** |
| | *vehr teh-leh-vee-SYOHN* |
| Do you like to dance? | **¿A usted le gusta bailar?** |
| | *ah oos-TEHD leh GOOS-tah bah-ee-LAHR* |
| Would you like to go out? | **¿Le gustaría salir?** |
| | *leh goos-tah-REE-ah sah-LEER* |
| May I buy you dinner sometime? | **¿Le puedo invitar a cenar alguna vez?** |
| | *leh PWEH-doh een-vee-TAHR ah SEH-nahr ahl-GOO-nah vehs* |
| What kind of food do you like? | **¿Qué tipo de comida le gusta?** |
| | *keh TEE-poh deh koh-MEE-dah leh GOOS-tah* |

*For a full list of food types, see Dining in Chapter 4.*

| | |
|---|---|
| Would you like to go ____ | **¿Le gustaría ir ____** |
| | *leh goos-tah-REE-ah eer* |
| to a concert? | **a un concierto?** |
| | *ah oon kohn-SYEHR-toh* |
| to the beach? | **a la playa?** |
| | *ah lah PLAH-yah* |
| dancing? | **a bailar?** |
| | *ah bah-ee-LAHR* |
| to a movie? | **al cine?** |
| | *ahl SEE neh* |
| to a museum? | **al museo?** |
| | *ahl moo-SEH-oh* |
| for a walk in the park? | **a caminar en el parque?** |
| | *ah kah-mee-NAHR ehn ehl PAHR-keh* |

| | |
|---|---|
| to the zoo? | **al zoológico?** |
| | *ahl soh-oh-LOH-hee-koh* |
| Would you like to | **¿Le gustaría ir ____** |
| get ____ | *leh goos-tah-REE-ah eer* |
| coffee? | **a tomar café?** |
| | *ah toh-MAHR kah-FEH* |
| dinner? | **a cenar?** |
| | *ah seh-NAHR* |
| lunch? | **a almorzar?** |
| | *ah ahl-mohr-SAHR* |
| What kind of books do | **¿Qué tipo de libros le gusta leer?** |
| you like to read? | *keh TEE-poh deh LEE-brohs leh* |
| | *GOOS-tah leh-EHR* |
| I like ____ | **Me gusta / gustan ____** |
| | *meh GOOS-tah / GOOS-tahn* |
| auto-biographies. | **las autobiografías.** |
| | *lahs ow-toh-bee-oh-grah-FEE-ahs* |
| biographies. | **las biografías.** |
| | *lahs bee-oh-grah-FEE-ahs* |
| dramas. | **los dramas.** |
| | *lohs DRAH-mahs* |
| history. | **la historia.** |
| | *lah ees-TOH-ryah* |
| mysteries. | **los misterios.** |
| | *lohs mees-TEHR-yohs* |
| novels. | **las novelas.** |
| | *lahs noh-VEH-lahs* |
| romance. | **los romances.** |
| | *lohs roh-MAHN-sehs* |
| Westerns. | **de vaqueros.** |
| | *deh vah-KEH-rohs* |

*For dating terms, see p214..*

## CONVERSATION STARTERS

**1. Soccer (*futbol*)**   Talking *futbol* is the perfect way to break an awkward silence with taxi drivers, acquaintances, or anyone else. The most docile individuals are likely to become animated as they discuss the progress of their favorite team. Substitute baseball in Venezuela.

**2. Ask for advice**   Go straight to the source and ask locals for the best place to visit or eat. People generally love to show off their country or town at its best.

**3. Food**   Nothing gets Uruguayans more excited than their favorite cut of meat and how to cook it. Ecuadorians will eagerly explain why they love eating guinea pig and rabbit, and Peruvians will argue that their national dish, *ceviche,* is more sushi than sushi.

**4. Drink**   Learn the ritual of drinking *mate* (an invitation to do so should not be declined), or argue about the best rum in Venezuela. Wine is another great conversation starter, especially in Argentina, Chile, and Brazil.

**5. Music**   With Latin America's wealth of musical styles, the subject of music is a great way to break the ice.

## NATIONAL PROFILES

It is said that Latin Americans are warmhearted and fun-loving, compounded with an anarchic attitude toward authority and a blissful rejection of logic. The truth is that this continent is so huge and populated by so many people and races, it's impossible to generalize with absolute accuracy. The beach-loving Brazilian of African descent is very different from the indigenous Andean of Incan descent. Add to this people of every European nationality, as well as Arabs, Indians, and Chinese, and you have a melting pot of appearances and persuasions.

Geography has had a tremendous influence on the people of Latin America. One of the reasons Colombia has remained so divided is that the high sierras isolate the various provinces. There is a fault line between people who live on the coast and those who live higher up, in the interior. The serious, hard-working citizens of cities like Quito (Ecuador) blame the laid-back *tropicalismo* along the coast for their country's woes. The people of the productive interior provinces of Argentina often look upon their counterparts in Buenos Aires as arrogant and undeserving of their wealth. It is said that the Uruguayan is enlightened and progressive, that the Ecuadorian is conservative in social matters, and that the Chilean is honest and law-abiding. But, of course, these stereotypes are only partially true.

**Values & Customs** If one thing unites Latin Americans, it's their love and respect for family. The family unit is the corner-stone of their society. Even in liberal-minded cities such as Buenos Aires, where divorce is commonplace, the extended family of stepsons and second wives is as compact as the traditional model.

The attitude toward law and order is more ambiguous. South America has an image of being vast and lawless, but the problem is often that there are too many laws. Excessive government regulations concerning the most mundane aspects of everyday life compel people to ignore the law or at least take a liberal, creative approach to its interpretation. Crime is every-body's concern—a subject that often borders on hysteria in the media. Despite the stereotype, the vast majority of South Americans abhor the illegal drugs trade for which their continent is infamous.

On a more personal level, Latin Americans possess a generosity that can be counterproductive. They hate to say no and will agree to anything with the full knowledge that it will never happen. Travelers often experience this firsthand when they ask for directions. Rather than admit that they don't know where the hotel or restaurant is, many South Americans will describe where they think it should be and may even decide to take you there.

South Americans generally love physical intimacy. They stand close together and touch as they speak. Often they will hold your elbow as you walk and talk, and the conversation is always primarily personal. Business, if there is any, takes second place.

The Latin attitude towards foreigners is overwhelmingly positive. Sure, anti-Americanism has been on the rise in recent years, but this rarely reaches down to an individual level. Locals are in general delighted that you've chosen to visit their country, and they're eager for you to enjoy your stay as much as possible. In poorer, more tropical countries, this respect can border on deference: Some people make the unnerving assumption that you are better then they are, at least when it comes to wealth and education. Of course, there are instances of "anti-gringoism," but these are isolated and easy to ignore.

## HANGING OUT ON THE BEACH

**Best Beaches for Families**    **Playa Caleta Abarca,** Vina del Mar, Chile, is only an hour from Santiago. But this sandy bay has all the amenities you'd expect for a day on the beach. At **Playa Tamarindo,** Costa Rica, families may opt to take boogie-boarding (or surfing) lessons (www.tamarindosurfschool.com) or just relax on the laid-back beaches of this lovely town. **Playa El Agua,** Isla Margarita, Venezuela, has 1³⁄₄ miles (3km) of white sand and palm trees, making it ideal for kids with excess energy. The beach is very busy in the summer months, especially on weekends when families come from far inland to picnic on the sand.

**Best Beaches for Couples**    At **Playa los Frailles,** in Parque Nacional Machalilla, Ecuador, a coastal cloud forest runs down to the pristine beaches on the Pacific Coast, making this little-known place a perfect hideaway for couples. **Playa de Amor** sits at the tip of the Baja Peninsula, near Los Cabos, Mexico. As its name suggests, Playa de Amor (it means the Beach of

Love) is romantic, beautiful, and serene. From the beach at **Francisqui,** Los Roques, Venezuela, you can charter a small boat to the romantic island of Los Roques and discover plenty of hidden coves to call your own paradise.

**Best Beaches for Singles**   The tiny island of **Playa Norte,** Isla Mujeres, Mexico, near Cancun, has only one beach, but everyone is super-friendly. Making new friends is second nature to both the locals and the laid-back visitors. **Bikini Beach,** la Barra, Punta del Este, Uruguay, is the St. Tropez of South America. "Punta" (as it is affectionately known), has something for everyone, including a very singles-friendly beach on a stretch of coast filled with hip clubs, happening cafes, and lots of beautiful people looking to meet each other. **Playa Cuyagua,** Ocumara de la Costa, Venezuela, is a breezy stretch of coast and a hip and happening destination for young and single beach-lovers.

## CLOSE ENCOUNTERS

**Servas** (an Esperanto word meaning "to serve") supports global goodwill and understanding by arranging free home stays of up to 2 nights. Travelers fill out an application, are interviewed for suitability, and pay an annual membership fee plus $25 for access to a list of hosts. Single-day visits, including a meal and sightseeing, can also be arranged. For details, visit www.servas.org. **Friendship Force International** also supports home stays around the world. Travelers pay a fee for a list of hosts for stays of up to a week. Contact them at ✆ **404/522-9490** or www.friendshipforce.org.

For less structured encounters, nothing beats Carnaval in Argentina and Uruguay, the week before the start of Lent; the Festival of the Virgen de la Candelaria, a 2-week explosion of music and dance in Peru; and New Year's Eve in Valparaíso, Chile.

## CHAPTER SIX

### MONEY & COMMUNICATIONS

This chapter covers money, the mail, phone, Internet service, and other tools you need to connect with the outside world.

### MONEY

Do you accept _____

**¿Aceptan _____**
*ah-SEHP-tahn*

Visa / MasterCard / Discover / American Express / Diners' Club? credit cards?

**Visa / MasterCard / Discover / American Express / Diners' Club?**
*Pronounced as in english*
**tarjetas de crédito?**
*tahr-HEH-tahs deh KREH-dee-toh*

bills?

**billetes?**
*bee-YEH-tehs*

coins?

**monedas?**
*moh-NEH-dahs*

checks?

**cheques?**
*CHEH-kehs*

travelers checks?

**cheques de viajero?**
*CHEH-kehs deh vyah-HEH-roh*

money transfer?

**transferencia de dinero?**
*trahns-feh-REHN-syah deh dee NEH-roh*

May I wire transfer funds here?

**¿Puedo hacer una transferencia de dinero aquí?**
*PWEH-doh ah-SEHR OO-nah trahns-feh-REHN-syah deh dee-NEH-roh ah-KEE*

Would you please tell me where to find _____

**Por favor, ¿puede decirme dónde puedo encontrar _____**
*pohr fah-VOHR PWEH-deh deh-SEER-meh DOHN-deh PWEH-doh ehn-kohn-TRAHR*

| | |
|---|---|
| a bank? | **un banco?**<br>*oon BAHN-koh* |
| a credit bureau? | **una agencia de crédito?**<br>*OO-nah ah-HEHN-syah deh*<br>*KREH-dee-toh* |
| an ATM? | **un cajero automático?**<br>*oon kah-HEH-roh ow-toh-MAH-*<br>*tee-koh* |
| a currency exchange? | **un lugar de cambio de moneda?**<br>*oon loo-HAHR deh KAHM-byoh*<br>*deh moh-NEH-dah* |
| A receipt, please. | **Un recibo, por favor.**<br>*oon reh-SEE-boh pohr fah-VOHR* |
| Would you tell me ____ | **Me puede decir ____**<br>*meh PWEH-deh deh-SEER* |
| today's interest rate? | **la tasa de interés de hoy?**<br>*lah TAH-sah deh een-teh-REHS*<br>*deh oy* |
| the exchange rate for<br>dollars to ____? | **la tasa de cambio de dólares**<br>**a ____?**<br>*lah TAH-sah deh KAHM-byoh*<br>*deh DOH-lah-rehs ah* |
| Is there a service<br>charge? | **¿Hay un cargo por servicio?**<br>*ay oon KAHR-goh pohr sehr-*<br>*VEES-yoh* |
| May I have a cash<br>advance on my credit<br>card? | **¿Puedo obtener un adelanto en**<br>**efectivo de mi tarjeta de crédito?**<br>*PWEH-doh ohb-teh-NEHR oon ah-*<br>*deh-LAHN-toh ehn eh-fehk-TEE-*<br>*voh deh mee tahr-HEH-tah deh*<br>*KREH-dee-toh* |
| Will you accept a<br>credit card? | **¿Aceptarían una tarjeta de**<br>**crédito?**<br>*ah-sehp-tah-REE-ahn OO-nah*<br>*tahr-HEH-tah deh KREH-dee-toh* |

## Listen Up: Bank Lingo

| | |
|---|---|
| **Por favor, firme aquí.**<br>*pohr fah-VOHR FEER-meh*<br>*ah-KEE* | Please sign here. |
| **Aquí está su recibo.**<br>*ah-KEE ehs-TAH soo reh-*<br>*SEE-boh* | Here is your receipt. |
| **Por favor, ¿puedo ver**<br>**su identificacion?**<br>*pohr fah-VOHR PWEH-doh*<br>*vehr soo ee-dehn-tee-fee-*<br>*kah-SYOHN* | May I see your ID, please? |
| **Aceptamos cheques**<br>**de viajero.**<br>*ah-sehp-TAH-mohs CHEH-*<br>*kehs deh vyah-HEH-roh* | We accept travelers checks. |
| **Solo en efectivo.**<br>*SOH-loh ehn eh-fehk-*<br>*TEE-voh* | Cash only. |

| | |
|---|---|
| May I have smaller bills, please. | **Me puede dar billetes más**<br>**pequeños, por favor.**<br>*meh PWEH-deh dahr bee-YEH-*<br>*tehs mahs peh-KEH-nyohs pohr*<br>*fah-VOHR* |
| Can you make change? | **¿Puede hacer cambio?**<br>*PWEH-deh ah-SEHR KAHM-byoh* |
| I only have bills. | **Sólo tengo billetes.**<br>*SOH-loh TEHNG-goh bee-YEH-tehs* |
| Some coins, please. | **Unas monedas por favor.**<br>*OO-nahs moh-NEH-dahs pohr*<br>*fah-VOHR* |

## ATM Machine

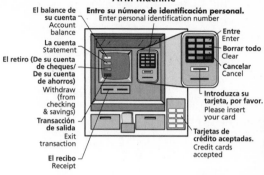

**Entre su número de identificación personal.**
Enter personal identification number

El balance de su cuenta
Account balance

La cuenta
Statement

El retiro (De su cuenta de cheques/ De su cuenta de ahorros)
Withdraw (from checking & savings)

Transacción de salida
Exit transaction

El recibo
Receipt

Entre
Enter

Borrar todo
Clear

Cancelar
Cancel

Introduzca su tarjeta, por favor.
Please insert your card

Tarjetas de crédito aceptadas.
Credit cards accepted

COMMUNICATIONS

## PHONE SERVICE

| | |
|---|---|
| Where can I buy or rent a cell phone? | **¿Dónde puedo comprar o alquilar un teléfono celular?** |
| | *DOHN-deh PWEH-doh kohm-PRAHR oh ahl-kee-LAHR oon teh-LEH-foh-noh seh-loo-LAHR* |
| What rate plans do you have? | **¿Qué planes de tarifas tienen?** |
| | *keh PLAH-nehs deh tah-REE-fahs TYEH-nehn* |
| Is this good throughout the country? | **¿Ésto es bueno en todo el país?** |
| | *EHS-teh ehs BWEH-noh ehn TOH-doh ehl pah-EES* |
| May I have a prepaid phone? | **¿Me puede dar un teléfono pre-pagado?** |
| | *meh PWEH-deh dahr oon teh-LEH-foh-noh preh-pah-GAH-doh* |

| | |
|---|---|
| Where can I buy a phone card? | **¿Dónde puedo comprar una tarjeta de llamadas?** *DOHN-deh PWEH-doh kohm-PRAHR OO-nah tahr-HEH-tah deh yah-MAH-dahs* |
| May I add more minutes to my phone card? | **¿Puedo añadirle más minutos a mi tarjeta de llamadas?** *PWEH-doh ah-nyah-DEER-leh mahs mee-NOO-tohs ah me tahr-HEH-tah deh yah-MAH-dahs* |

### MAKING A CALL

| | |
|---|---|
| May I dial direct? | **¿Puedo marcar directo?** *PWEH-doh MAHR-kahr dee-REHK-toh* |
| Operator please. | **Operadora, por favor.** *oh-peh-rah-DOH-rah pohr fah-VOHR* |
| I'd like to make an international call. | **Quisiera hacer una llamada internacional.** *kee-SYEH-rah ah-SEHR OO-nah yah-MAH-dah een-tehr-nah-syoh-NAHL* |

### Fuera de Servicio

Before you stick your coins or bills in a vending machine, watch out for the little sign that says *Fuera de Servicio* (Out of Service).

## Listen Up: Telephone Lingo

¿Diga? / ¿Bueno? /     Hello?
  ¿Hola?
*DEE-gah, BWEH-noh,*
*OH-lah*

¿A qué número?     What number?
*ah keh NOO-meh-roh*

Lo siento, la línea está     I'm sorry, the line is busy.
  ocupada.
*loh SYEHN-toh lah LEE-*
*neh-ah ehs-TAH oh-koo-*
*PAH-dah*

Por favor, cuelgue el     Please, hang up and redial.
  teléfono y marque el
  número de nuevo.
*pohr fah-VOHR KWEHL-*
*geh ehl teh-LEH-foh-noh*
*ee MAHR-keh ehl NOO-*
*meh-roh deh NWEH-voh*

Lo siento. Nadie     I'm sorry, nobody is answering.
  responde.
*loh SYEHN-toh NAH-*
*dyeh rehs-POHN-deh*

Su tarjeta tiene diez     Your card has ten minutes left.
  minutos.
*soo tahr-HEH-tah TYEH-*
*neh dyehs mee-NOO-tohs*

COMMUNICATIONS

| | |
|---|---|
| I'd like to make a collect call. | **Quisiera hacer una llamada a cobro revertido.**<br>*kee-SYEH-rah ah-SEHR OO-nah yah-MAH-dah ah KOH-broh reh-vehr-TEE-doh* |
| I'd like to use a calling card. | **Quisiera usar una tarjeta de llamadas.**<br>*kee-SYEH-rah oo-SAHR OO-nah tahr-HEH-tah deh yah-MAH-dahs* |
| Bill my credit card. | **Cargue a mi tarjeta de crédito.**<br>*KAHR-geh ah mee tahr-HEH-tah deh KREH-dee-toh* |
| May I bill the charges to my room? | **¿Puedo cargar los cargos a mi habitación?**<br>*PWEH-doh kahr-GAHR lohs KAHR-gohs ah mee ah-bee-tah-SYOHN* |
| May I bill the charges to my home phone? | **¿Puedo cargar los cargos a mi teléfono residencial?**<br>*PWEH-doh kahr-GAHR lohs KAHR-gohs ah mee teh-LEH-foh-noh reh-see-dehn-SYAHL* |
| Information, please. | **Información, por favor.**<br>*een-fohr-mah-SYOHN pohr fah-VOHR* |
| I'd like the number for ____. | **Quisiera el número para ____.**<br>*kee-SYEH-rah ehl NOO-meh-roh PAH-rah* |
| I just got disconnected. | **Me acaba de desconectar.**<br>*meh ah-KAH-bah dehs-koh-nehk-TAHR* |
| The line is busy. | **La línea está ocupada.**<br>*lah LEE-neh-ah ehs-TAH oh-koo-PAH-dah* |
| I lost the connection. | **Perdí la conexión.**<br>*pehr-DEE lah koh-nehk-SYOHN* |

## INTERNET ACCESS

Where is an Internet café?

**¿Dónde hay un café con acceso al Internet?**
*DOHN-deh aye oon kah-FEH kohn ahk-SEH-soh ahl een-tehr-NET*

Is there a wireless hub nearby?

**¿Hay un nodo de conexión inalámbrica cerca?**
*aye oon NOH-doh deh koh-nehk-SYOHN ee-nah-LAHM-bree-kah SEHR-kah*

How much do you charge per minute / hour?

**¿Cuánto cobra por minuto / hora?**
*KWAHN-toh KOH-brah pohr mee-NOO-toh / OH-rah*

Can I print here?

**¿Puedo imprimir aquí?**
*PWEH-doh eem-pree-MEER ah-KEE*

Can I burn a CD?

**¿Puedo quemar un CD?**
*PWEH-doh keh-MAHR oon seh-DEH*

Would you please help me change the language preference to English?

**¿Me puede ayudar a cambiar la opción de idioma al inglés?**
*meh PWEH-deh ah-yoo-DAHR ah kahm-BYAHR lah ohp-SYOHN deh ee-DYOH-mah ahl eeng-GLEHS*

| | |
|---|---|
| May I scan something? | **¿Puedo escanear algo?** *PWEH-doh ehs-kah-neh-AHR AHL-goh* |
| Can I upload photos? | **¿Puedo cargar mis fotos?** *PWEH-doh kahr-GAHR mees FOH-tohs* |
| Do you have a USB port so I can download music? | **¿Tiene un puerto de USB para poder descargar música?** *TYEH-neh oon PWEHR-toh deh oo-EH-seh-BEH PAH-rah poh-DEHR dehs-kahr-GAHR MOO-see-kah* |
| Do you have a machine compatible with iTunes? | **¿Tiene una máquina compatible con iTunes?** *TYEH-neh OO-nah MAH-kee-nah kohm-pah-TEE-bleh kohn ay-TOONS* |
| Do you have a Mac? | **¿Tiene una computadora Macintosh?** *TYEH-neh OO-nah kohm-poo-tah-DOH-rah ah mah-keen-TOHSH* |
| Do you have a PC? | **¿Tiene una computadora PC?** *TYEH-neh OO-nah kohm-poo-tah-DOH-rah peh-SEH* |
| Do you have a newer version of this software? | **¿Tiene la versión más nueva de este software?** *TYEH-neh lah vehr-SYOHN mahs NWEH-vah deh EHS-teh SOHFT-wehr* |
| Do you have broadband? | **¿Tiene conexión de Internet de alta velocidad?** *TYEH-neh koh-nehk-SYOHN deh een-tehr-NEHT deh AHL-tah veh-loh-see-DAHD* |
| How fast is your connection speed here? | **¿Cuán rápida es su conexión aquí?** *kwahn RAH-pee-dah ehs soo koh-nehk-SYOHN ah-KEE* |

## GETTING MAIL

| | |
|---|---|
| Where is the post office? | **¿Dónde está el correo?** *DOHN-deh ehs-TAH ehl koh-RREH-oh* |
| May I send an international package? | **¿Puedo enviar un paquete internacional?** *PWEH-doh ehn-vee-AHR oon pah-KEH-teh een-tehr-nah-syoh-NAHL* |
| Do I need a customs form? | **¿Necesito un formulario de aduanas?** *neh-seh-SEE-toh oon fohr-moo-LAHR-yoh deh ah-DWAH-nahs* |
| Do you sell insurance for packages? | **¿Vende seguros para paquetes?** *VEHN-deh seh-GOO-rohs PAH-rah pah-KEH-tehs* |
| Please, mark it fragile. | **Por favor, márquelo como frágil.** *pohr fah-VOHR MAHR-keh-loh koh-moh FRAH-heel* |
| Please, handle with care. | **Por favor, manéjelo con cuidado.** *pohr fah-VOHR mah-NEH-heh-loh kohn koo-ee-DAH-doh* |
| Do you have twine? | **¿Tiene cuerda?** *TYEH-neh KWEHR-dah* |
| Where is a DHL office? | **¿Dónde hay una oficina de DHL?** *DOHN-deh aye OO-nah oh-fee-SEE-nah deh deh AH-cheh EH-leh* |
| Do you sell stamps? | **¿Vende sellos?** *VEHN-deh SEH-yohs* |
| Do you sell postcards? | **¿Vende postales?** *VEHN-deh pohs-TAH-lehs* |
| May I send that first class? | **¿Puedo enviar esto por primera clase?** *PWEH-doh ehn-VEE-ahr EHS-toh pohr pree-MEH-rah KLAH-seh* |

COMMUNICATIONS

## Listen Up: Postal Lingo

| | |
|---|---|
| **¡Próximo!** | Next! |
| *PROHK-see-moh* | |
| **Por favor, póngalo aquí.** | Please, set it here. |
| *pohr fah-VOHR POHNG-* | |
| *gah-loh ah-KEE* | |
| **¿Qué clase?** | Which class? |
| *keh KLAH-seh* | |
| **¿Qué tipo de servicio** | What kind of service |
| **quiere?** | would you like? |
| *keh TEE-poh deh sehr-* | |
| *VEE-syoh KYEH-reh* | |
| **¿En qué puedo servirle?** | How can I help you? |
| *ehn keh PWEH-doh sehr-* | |
| *VEER-leh* | |
| **ventanilla de entregas** | dropoff window |
| *vehn-tah-NEE-yah deh ehn-* | |
| *TREH-gahs* | |
| **ventanilla de recogidos** | pickup window |
| *vehn-tah-NEE-yah deh reh-* | |
| *koh-HEE-dohs* | |

| | |
|---|---|
| How much to send that express / air mail? | **¿Cuánto cuesta enviar esto por correo urgente / correo aéreo?** |
| | *KWAHN-toh KWEHS-tah ehn-VEE-ahr EHS-toh pohr koh-RREH-oh oor-HEHN-teh / koh-RREH-oh ah-EH-reh-oh* |
| Do you offer overnight delivery? | **¿Ofrece entrega de un día para otro?** |
| | *oh-FREH-seh ehn-TREH-gah deh oon DEE-ah PAH-rah OH-troh* |

| | |
|---|---|
| How long will it take to reach the United States? | **¿Cuánto tardará en llegar a los Estados Unidos?** *KWAHN-toh tahr-dah-RAH ehn yeh-GAHR ah lohs ehs-TAH-dohs oo-NEE-dohs* |
| I'd like to buy an envelope. | **Quisiera comprar un sobre.** *kee-SYEH-rah kohm-PRAHR oon SOH-breh* |
| May I send it airmail? | **¿Puedo enviarlo por correo aéreo?** *PWEH-doh ehn-VYAHR-loh pohr koh-RREH-oh ah-EH-reh-oh* |
| I'd like to send it certified / registered mail. | **Quisiera enviarlo por correo certificado.** *kee-SYEH-rah ehn-VYAHR-loh pohr koh-RREH-oh sehr-tee-fee-KAH-doh* |

## MONEY MATTERS

**ATMs**  Automated teller machines in Latin America are linked to a network that most likely includes your bank at home. Using ATMs is a great way to obtain local currency without having to go to a bank or an exchange office. **Cirrus** (© **800/424-7787**; www.mastercard.com) and **PLUS** (© **800/843-7587**; www.visa.com) are the two most popular networks; check the back of your ATM card to see which network your bank belongs to, and use the toll-free numbers or check the websites to locate ATMs in your destination.

Be sure to check your daily withdrawal limit before you depart, and if you don't have a four-digit personal identification number (PIN), request one. Keep in mind that most banks impose a fee every time a card is used at an ATM other than its own, and that the bank from which you withdraw cash may charge a fee as well.

**Traveler's Checks**  In Latin America, most vendors prefer cash and credit cards over traveler's checks *(cheques de viajeros)*, although many hotels happily accept them. You can exchange traveler's checks at *casas de cambio* (money-exchange offices), usually for a significant fee. Many banks will not exchange traveler's checks, and those that do may have long lines.

You can buy traveler's checks at almost any bank. **American Express** sells them in denominations of $10, $20, $50, $100, $500, and $1,000 and charges a service fee of 1% to 4%. You can also get American Express traveler's checks by calling © **800/221-7282**. **Visa** (© **800/732-1322**) offers traveler's checks at Citibank locations nationwide for a service charge of 1.5% to 2%; checks come in denominations of $20, $100, $500, and $1,000. **AAA** members can obtain Visa checks without a fee at most AAA offices or by calling © **866/339-3378**. MasterCard also offers traveler's checks. Call © **800/223-9920** for a location near you. If you opt to carry traveler's checks, be sure to keep a record of their serial numbers, separate from the checks, to speed up your refund should they get lost or stolen.

**Credit Cards**   Credit cards are a safe way to carry money, and they provide a convenient record of all your expenses. You can withdraw cash advances from your credit cards at any bank, so long as you know your PIN. (Note that you'll start paying interest on the advance the moment you receive the cash, even if you pay your monthly bill on time.) Keep in mind that credit card companies try to protect themselves (and you) from theft by limiting the funds you can withdraw away from home, so call your credit card company before you leave and let them know where you're going and how much you plan to spend. Visa, MasterCard, American Express, and Diners Club are all commonly accepted in Latin America.

Your credit card company will likely charge a commission (up to 5%) on every foreign purchase you make.

## MAJOR LATIN AMERICAN CURRENCIES

**Argentina**   The *peso* is made up of 100 centavos. It was pegged to the U.S. dollar until the country's economic meltdown in late 2001, when it quickly devalued. Money is denominated in notes of 2, 5, 10, 20, 50, and 100 pesos; and in coins of 1, 2, and 5 pesos and 1, 5, 10, 25, and 50 centavos.

**Bolivia**   The unit of currency is the *boliviano* (Bs). You'll find coins with values of 1 and 2 bolivianos. Otherwise, all the currency is paper, in denominations of 2, 5, 10, 20, 50, and 100. It's very hard to make change, especially for a 100Bs note.

**Chile**   The Chilean *peso* comes in notes with denominations of 1,000; 2,000; 5,000; 10,000; and 20,000. There are currently six coins in circulation in denominations of 1, 5, 10, 50, 100, and 500. Chileans commonly call 1,000 pesos a *luca*.

**Costa Rica**   The unit of currency is the *colon*, which has been in a continual state of devaluation. The colon is divided into 100 centimos. Currently, two types of coins are in circulation. The older and larger nickel-alloy coins come in denominations of 1, 2, 5, 10, 25, and 50 centimos and 1, 2, 5, 10, and 20 colones. There are paper notes in denominations of 1,000; 2,000; 5,000; and 10,000 colones.

**Ecuador**    The official unit of currency in Ecuador is the **U.S. dollar**. You can use both American and Ecuadorian coins, divided into 100 cents. Otherwise, all the currency is in paper dollars, in denominations of $1, $5, $10, $20, $50, and $100.

**Mexico**    The currency is the *peso*. Bills come in denominations of 20, 50, 100, 200, and 500 pesos. Coins come in denominations of 1, 2, 5, 10, and 20 pesos, and 20 and 50 centavos (100 centavos = 1 peso).

**Peru**    The currency is the *nuevo sol*, abbreviated "S/" and usually referred to simply as the *sol* or *soles*. Bank notes are issued in 10, 20, 50, 100, and 200 soles. Visitors are advised to be very careful of counterfeit bank notes. A sol is divided into 100 centavos, with coins in denominations of 5, 10, 20, and 50. U.S. dollars are widely accepted across Peru for many commercial transactions.

**Uruguay**    The unit of currency is the *peso uruguayo* ($U), which comes in coin denominations of 1, 5, 10, 50, 100, 200, and 500 pesos; and bank notes of 50; 100; 200; 500; 1,000; 5,000; and 10,000.

**Venezuela**    The unit of currency, the *bolívar*, is popularly referred to as *bolos*, and abbreviated as "Bs." Paper bills come in denominations of 5; 10; 20; 50; 100; 500; 1,000; 2,000; 5,000; 10,000; 20,000; and 50,000 bolivares. There are coins of 5, 10, 20, 50, 100, and 500 bolivares.

## LOST OR STOLEN CREDIT CARDS

Make sure to pack your credit card company's emergency toll-free numbers so you can report the loss or theft of cards. "Identity theft" can be an even more serious problem especially if you've lost your driver's license. To be safe, you may want to place a fraud alert on your records with one of the three credit-reporting agencies, **Equifax** (© **800/766-0008,** www.equifax,com), **Experian** (© 888/397-3742, www.experian.com); and **TransUnion** (© 800/680-7289, www.transunion.com).

## STAYING CONNECTED

**Using A Cellphone**   The three letters that define much of the world's wireless capabilities are **GSM** (Global System for Mobiles). A big, seamless network, it makes for easy cross-border cellphone use, including an increasing number of Latin American countries. In the U.S., T-Mobile and Cingular use this system. All Europeans use it, too.

If your phone is on a multi-band GSM system, you can make and receive calls in the more populated areas of Latin America. Just call your wireless operator and ask for "international roaming." Unfortunately, per-minute charges can be high—usually $1 to $1.50 per minute—and you probably won't have service in remote areas. Another option is to rent a phone before you leave from **InTouchUSA** (© 800/872-7626; www.intouchusa.com) or **Cellular Abroad** (© 800/287-3020; www.cellularabroad.com). You can also buy an "unlocked" world phone before your trip. This allows you to install a cheap, prepaid SIM card memory phone chip (found at local retailers).

Renting a cellphone in Latin America is not much of an option unless you're in a large urban area, such as Mexico City, Guayaquil, or Santiago. Cellphone rentals are usually connected to a luxury or business hotel (the hotel itself owns the phones and rents them to guests); check before you book a room.

Across much of Latin America, there are telecommunications kiosks even in the remotest of areas. Sometimes these are located within a post office; other times they're in individual shops operated by the local telephone company. There are usually rows of cabins with phones; you dial your number and pay the cashier when you're done. Rates are relatively low and are usually posted when you enter; if not, ask the cashier.

COMMUNICATIONS

## CHAPTER SEVEN

### CULTURE

## CINEMA

| | |
|---|---|
| Is there a movie theater nearby? | **¿Hay un cine cerca?** |
| | *aye oon SEE-neh SEHR-kah* |
| What's playing tonight? | **¿Qué están dando esta noche?** |
| | *keh ehs-TAHN DAHN-doh ehs-TAH NOH-cheh* |
| Is that in English or Spanish? | **¿Es en inglés o español?** |
| | *ehs ehn eeng-GLEHS oh ehs-pah-NYOHL* |
| Are there English subtitles? | **¿Hay subtítulos en inglés?** |
| | *aye soob-TEE-too-lohs ehn eeng-GLEHS* |
| Is the theater air conditioned? | **¿El teatro tiene aire acondicionado?** |
| | *ehl teh-AH-troh TYEH-neh AYE-reh ah-kohn-dee-syoh-NAH-doh* |
| How much is a ticket? | **¿Cuánto cuesta un boleto?** |
| | *KWAHN-toh KWEH-stah oon boh-LEH-toh* |
| Do you have a _____ discount? | **¿Ofrecen un descuento para _____** |
| | *oh-FREH-sehn oon dehs-KWEHN-toh PAH-rah* |
| senior | **personas mayores de edad?** |
| | *pehr-SOH-nahs mah-YOH-rehs deh eh-DAHD?* |
| student | **estudiantes?** |
| | *ehs-too-DYAHN-tehs* |
| children's | **niños?** |
| | *NEE-nyohs* |

What time is the movie showing?

**¿A qué hora muestran la película?**
*ah keh OH-rah MWEHS-trahn lah peh-LEE-koo-lah*

How long is the movie?

**¿Cuán larga es la película?**
*kwahn LAHR-gah ehs lah peh-LEE-koo-lah*

May I buy tickets in advance?

**¿Puedo comprar los boletos por adelantado?**
*PWEH-doh kohm-PRAHR lohs boh-LEH-tohs pohr ah-deh-lahn-TAH-doh*

Is it sold out?

**¿Está todo vendido?**
*ehs-TAH TOH-doh vehn-DEE-doh*

When does it begin?

**¿A qué hora comienza?**
*ah keh OH-rah koh-MYEHN-sah*

# PERFORMANCES

Do you have ballroom dancing?

**¿Tienen un salón de bailes?**
*TYEH-nehn oon sah-LOHN deh bah-EE-lehs*

Are there any plays showing right now?

**¿Hay alguna obra en escena ahora mismo?**
*aye ahl-GOO-nah OH-brah ehn eh-SEH-nah ah-OH-rah MEES-moh*

Is there a dinner theater?

**¿Hay teatro de cena?**
*aye teh-AH-troh deh SEH-nah*

Where can I buy tickets?

**¿Dónde puedo comprar boletos?**
*DOHN-deh PWEH-doh kohm-PRAHR boh-LEH-tohs*

Are there student discounts?

**¿Ofrecen descuentos para estudiantes?**
*oh-FREH-sehn dehs-KWEHN-tohs PAH-rah ehs-too-DYAHN-tehs*

I need ____ seats.

**Quisiera ____ asientos.**
*kee-SYEH-rah ____ ah-SYEHN-tohs*

*For a full list of numbers, see p7.*

## Listen Up: Box Office Lingo

| | |
|---|---|
| **¿Qué le gustaría ver?** *keh leh goos-tah-REE-ah vehr* | What would you like to see? |
| **¿Cuántos?** *KWAHN-tohs* | How many? |
| **¿Para dos adultos?** *PAH-rah dohs ah-DOOL-tohs* | For two adults? |
| **¿Con mantequilla? ¿Sal?** *kohn mahn-teh-KEE-yah sahl* | With butter? Salt? |
| **¿Algo más?** *AHL-goh mahs* | Would you like anything else? |

An aisle seat.

**Un asiento de pasillo.**
*oon ah-SYEHN-toh deh pah-SEE-yoh*

Orchestra seat, please.

**Un asiento a nivel de orquesta, por favor.**
*oon ah-SYEHN-toh ah nee-VEHL deh ohr-KEHS-tah pohr fah-VOHR*

What time does the play start?

**¿A qué hora comienza la obra?**
*ah keh OH-rah koh-MYEHN-sah lah OH-brah*

Is there an intermission?

**¿Hay un interludio?**
*aye oon een-tehr-LOO-dyoh*

Do you have an opera house?

**¿Tienen un teatro de la ópera?**
*TYEH-nehn oon teh-AH-troh deh lah OH-peh-rah*

Is there a local symphony?

**¿Hay una sinfonía local?**
*aye OO-nah seen-foh-NEE-ah loh-KAHL*

| | |
|---|---|
| May I purchase tickets over the phone? | ¿Puedo comprar boletos por teléfono? |
| | *PWEH-doh kohm-PRAHR boh-LEH-tohs pohr teh-LEH-foh-noh* |
| What time is the box office open? | ¿A qué hora abre la boletería? |
| | *ah keh OH-rah AH-breh lah boh-leh-teh-REE-ah* |
| I need space for a wheelchair, please. | Necesito espacio para una silla de ruedas, por favor. |
| | *neh-seh-SEE-toh ehs-PAH-syoh PAH-rah OO-nah SEE-yah deh RWEH-dahs pohr fah-VOHR* |
| Do you have private boxes available? | ¿Tiene asientos de palco privados disponibles? |
| | *TYEH-neh ah-SYEHN-tohs deh PAHL-koh pree-VAH-dohs dees-poh-NEE-blehs* |
| Is there a church that gives concerts? | ¿Hay una iglesia que ofrece conciertos? |
| | *aye OO-nah ee-GLEH-syah keh oh-FREH-seh kohn-SYEHR-tohs* |
| A program, please. | Un programa, por favor. |
| | *oon proh-GRAH-mah pohr fah-VOHR* |
| Please show us to our seats. | Por favor llévenos a nuestros asientos. |
| | *pohr fah-VOHR YEH-veh-nohs ah NWEHS-trohs ah-SYEHN-tohs* |

CULTURE

## MUSEUMS, GALLERIES & SIGHTS

| | |
|---|---|
| Do you have a museum guide? | **¿Tiene un guía del museo?** *TYEH-neh oon GEE-ah dehl moo-SEH-oh* |
| Do you have guided tours? | **¿Ofrecen una excursión guiada?** *oh-FREH-sehn OO-nah ehs-koor-SYOHN gee-AH-dah* |
| What are the museum hours? | **¿Cuál es el horario del museo?** *kwahl ehs ehl oh-RAH-ryoh dehl moo-SEH-oh* |
| Do I need an appointment? | **¿Necesito una cita?** *neh-seh-SEE-toh OO-nah SEE-tah* |
| What is the admission fee? | **¿Cuánto es la tarifa de admisión?** *KWAHN-toh ehs lah tah-REE-fah deh ahd-mee-SYOHN* |
| Do you have ____ | **¿Ofrecen ____** *oh-FREH-sehn* |
| student discounts? | **descuentos para estudiantes?** *dehs-KWEHN-tohs PAH-rah ehs-too-DYAHN-tehs* |
| senior discounts? | **descuentos para personas mayores / ancianos?** *dehs-KWEHN-tohs PAH-rah pehr-SOH-nahs mah-YOH-rehs / ahn-SYAH-nohs* |
| Do you have services for the hearing impaired? | **¿Tienen servicios para las personas con impedimentos auditivos?** *TYEH-nehn sehr-VEE-syohs PAH-rah lahs pehr-SOH-nahs kohn eem-peh-dee-MEHN-tohs ow-dee-TEE-vohs* |
| Do you have audio tours in English? | **¿Ofrecen excursiones por audio en inglés?** *oh-FREH-sehn ehs-koor-SYOH-nehs pohr OW-dyoh ehn eeng-GLEHS* |

## FAVORITE MOMENTS IN LATIN AMERICA

**Visiting Iguazú (Iguaçu) Falls**   One of the world's most spectacular sights, Iguazú boasts more than 275 waterfalls fed by the Iguazú River, which can be visited from both the Argentine and the Brazilian sides. In addition to the falls, Iguazú encompasses a marvelous subtropical jungle with extensive flora and fauna.

**Walking in the Sun's Footsteps on The Isla del Sol, Bolivia**   The Incas trace their roots from Manco Capac and Mama Ocllo, the children of the Sun. Supposedly, the Sun stepped forth onto the Sun Island in Lake Titicaca to give birth to the first Incas. Nowadays, on the northwestern tip of the Sun Island, you can walk right up to rock formations that look like footsteps, which according to legend, were left here when the Sun came down to Earth to drop off Manco Capac and Mama Ocllo.

**Exploring the Copper Canyon in The Mexican Sierra** The canyons known collectively as the Copper Canyon are beautiful, remote, and unspoiled. The entire network is larger than the Grand Canyon, with high waterfalls, vertical canyon walls, and forests. This is the land of the Tarahumara Indians, who gained their legendary endurance from adapting to this wilderness.

**Sailing Past the Islands and Fiords of Southern Chile** Quietly sailing through the lush beauty of Chile's southern fiords is an unforgettable experience. There are two breathtaking trips: a 3-day ride between Puerto Natales and Puerto Montt, and a 1- to 6-day ride to the spectacular Laguna San Rafael Glacier. Backpackers on a shoestring (as well as those who need spiffier accommodations) all have options. These pristine, remote fiords are often said to be more dramatic than those in Norway. Farther south, a small cruise line takes passengers through Tierra del Fuego and past remote glaciers, peaks, and sea-lion colonies, stopping at the end of the world in Puerto Williams.

**Watching Blue-Footed Boobies Dance for Love in the Galápagos**    Birds are usually shy, especially during mating season. But in the Galápagos Islands (off the Ecuadorian coast), where wild animals have no fear of humans, you can watch male blue-footed boobies spread their wings, lift their beaks, and dance wildly in a performance known as "sky pointing," all in hope of attracting a mate. If the female likes what she sees, she'll do the same. It's a scene right out of a National Geographic documentary.

**Floating on Lake Titicaca**    The world's highest navigable body of water straddles the border between Peru and Bolivia. To locals, it is a mysterious and sacred place. A 1-hour boat ride from Puno takes you to the Uros floating islands, where communities dwell upon soft patches of reeds. Visitors have a rare opportunity to experience the ancient cultures of two inhabited natural islands, Amantani and Taquile, by staying with a local family. You won't find any cars or electricity here, but there are remarkable local festivals. The views of the ocean-like lake, at more than 12,000 ft. (3,600 m) above sea level, and the star-littered night sky alone are worth the trip.

**Gazing upon Machu Picchu, Peru**    However you get to it—whether you hike the fabled Inca Trail, hop aboard one of the prettiest train rides in South America, or zip in by helicopter—Machu Picchu more than lives up to its reputation as one of the most spectacular sites on earth. The ruins of the legendary "lost city of the Incas" sit majestically among the massive Andes, swathed in clouds. The ceremonial and agricultural center, never discovered or looted by the Spanish, dates from the mid-1400s but seems even more ancient. Exploring the site is a thrilling experience, especially at sunrise, when dramatic rays of light creep over the mountaintops.

**Visiting Punta del Este, Uruguay**    As *Porteños* (residents of Buenos Aires) will tell you, anyone who's anyone from Buenos Aires heads to Punta del Este for summer vacation. The glitzy Atlantic coast resort in Uruguay is packed, from

December through February, with South America's jet set, who come for the inviting beaches and outstanding nightlife.

**Watching a Scarlet Macaw in Flight over Carara National Park in Costa Rica** Home to Costa Rica's largest population of scarlet macaws, Carara Biological Reserve is a wonderful place to watch these noisy, colorful birds in flight. They arrive like clockwork every morning and then head for the coastal mangroves around dusk. Seeing them silhouetted against the fading sunlight is a magical moment not to be missed.

**Exploring the Madcap Streets of Valparaíso, Chile** The ramshackle, sinuous streets of Valparaíso offer a walking tour unlike any other. Valparaíso could be called the penniless older brother of San Francisco, California, and part of the fascination here is touring the faded remains of this once-thriving port town. Antique Victorian mansions and colorful tin houses line terraced walkways that wind around precipitous hills; to reach the top, there are a handful of 1900s funiculars. Sweeping views and atmospheric restaurants and cafes can be found at every turn. But Valparaíso's bars, which seem to have authored the word "bohemian," are what have brought this city notoriety.

**Riding El Teleférico in Mérida, Venezuela** The world's highest and longest cable car system will bring you to the summit of Pico Espejo at 15,629 ft. (4,765m). If you've ever wanted to ascend into thin air without the toil of actually climbing there, this is the way to go. Go early if you want the best views. But be careful: The effects of altitude can be felt, whether or not you actually climb.

**SIGHTSEEING**

## CHARMING TOWNS & VILLAGES

**San Martín de los Andes, Argentina** City planners in San Martín had the smart sense to do what Bariloche never thought of—limit building height to two stories and mandate continuity in the town's Alpine architecture. The result? Bariloche is crass whereas San Martín is class, and the town is a year-round playground to boot.

**The Isla del Sol, Bolivia**   There are actually several small villages on the Sun Island, but in total, only a few thousand people live here. There are no cars and barely any telephones. At rush hour, though, things get very chaotic: You may have to wait a few minutes while the locals herd their llamas from one end of the island to the other.

**San Cristobal de las Casas, Mexico**   San Cristobal is a beautiful colonial town of white stucco walls and red-tiled roofs, of cobblestone streets and narrow sidewalks, of graceful arcades and open plazas. It lies in a lush valley nearly 7,000 ft. (2,120m) high, surrounded by villages of Mayan-speaking Indians.

**Cafayate, Argentina**   Remote and rugged, Cafayate is surrounded by some of the highest vineyards in the world. Here, the vines are bursting with fruit and floral aromas due to the intense sunlight that hits them all summer. Cafayate is sleepy and laid-back and a great place to relax.

**San Pedro de Atacama, Chile**   Quaint, unhurried, and built of adobe brick, San Pedro de Atacama has drawn Santiaguinos and expatriates the world over to experience the mellow charm and New Age spirituality that waft through its dusty roads. San Pedro hasn't grown much over the past decade; it has simply reinvented itself. Its location in the driest desert in the world makes for starry skies and breathtaking views of the weird and wonderful land formations that are just a stone's throw away.

## CHAPTER EIGHT

## SHOPPING

This chapter covers the phrases you'll need to shop in a variety of settings, from the mall to the town square artisan market. We also threw in the terminology you'll need to visit the barber or hairdresser.

*For coverage of food and grocery shopping, see p112.*

## GENERAL SHOPPING TERMS

| | |
|---|---|
| Please tell me ____ | **¿Me puede decir ____**<br>*meh PWEH-deh deh-SEER* |
| how to get to a mall? | **cómo llego a un centro comercial?**<br>*KOH-moh YEH-goh ah oon SEHN-troh koh-mehr-SYAHL* |
| the best place for shopping? | **el mejor lugar para ir de compras?**<br>*ehl meh-HOHR loo-GAHR pah-rah EER deh KOHM-prahs* |
| how to get downtown? | **cómo llego al centro de la ciudad?**<br>*KOH-moh YEH-goh ahl SEHN-troh deh lah see-oo-DAHD* |

### Contrabandistas

Beware of unscrupulous vendors who attempt to sell you illegal, contraband, or fake goods. Most Latin American countries do not allow exportation of pre-Columbian artifacts. (In other words, the ones sold by street vendors aren't real.)

| Where can I find a \_\_\_\_ | ¿Dónde puedo encontrar una \_\_\_\_ |
| | DOHN-deh PWEH-doh ehn-kohn-TRAHR OO-nah |
| antique shop? | tienda de antigüedades? |
| | TYEHN-dah deh ahn-tee-gweh-DAH-dehs |
| bookstore? | librería? |
| | ee-breh-REE-ah |
| cigar shop? | tienda de cigarros? |
| | TYEHN-dah deh see-GAH-rrohs |
| designer fashion shop? | tienda de moda de diseñador? |
| | TYEHN-dah deh MOH-dah deh dee-seh-nyah-DOHR |
| jewelry store? | joyería? |
| | hoh-yeh-REE-yah |
| men's / women's / children's clothing store? | tienda de ropa para hombres / mujeres / niños? |
| | TYEHN-dah deh RROH-pah PAH-rah HOM-brehs / moo-HEH-rehs / NEE-nyohs |
| shoe store? | tienda de zapatos? |
| | TYEHN-dah deh sah-PAH-tohs |
| souvenir shop? | tienda de recuerdos? |
| | TYEHN-dah deh reh-KWEHR-dohs |

## Cuban Cigars

In Latin America, many shops purport to carry Cuban cigars, but it's just a line. Real Cuban cigars are sold only at stores certified by the Cuban government. Certification will be posted, with an anticounterfeiting hologram on the box. When in doubt: if it's cheap, it's fake. That said, most of the "Cubans" on the market, though they're actually from Honduras or the Dominican Republic, are excellent for the price.

| | |
|---|---|
| stationery store? | **tienda de útiles de escritura?** |
| | *TYEHN-dah deh OO-tee-lehs deh ehs-kree-TOO-rah* |
| toy store? | **juguetería?** |
| | *hoo-geh-teh-REE-ah* |
| vintage clothing store? | **tienda de ropa antigua?** |
| | *TYEHN-dah deh RROH-pah ahn-TEE-wah* |
| Where can I find a flea market? | **¿Dónde puedo encontrar un pulguero?** |
| | *DOHN-deh PWEH-doh ehn-kohn-TRAHR oon pool-GEH-roh* |

## CLOTHES SHOPPING

| | |
|---|---|
| I'd like to buy ____ | **Quisiera comprar ____** |
| | *kee-SYEH-rah kohm-PRAHR* |
| children's clothes. | **ropa para niños.** |
| | *RROH-pah PAH-rah NEE-nyohs* |
| men's shirts. | **camisas para hombres.** |
| | *kah-MEE-sahs PAH-rah OHM-brehs* |
| toys. | **juguetes.** |
| | *hoo-GEH-tehs* |
| women's shoes. | **zapatos para mujeres.** |
| | *sah-PAH-tohs PAH-rah moo-HEH-rehs* |

*For a full list of numbers, see p7.*

| | |
|---|---|
| I'm looking for a size ____ | **Busco una talla ____** |
| | *BOOS-koh OO-nah TAH-yah* |
| small. | **pequeño.** |
| | *peh-KEH-nyoh* |
| medium. | **mediano.** |
| | *meh-DYAH-noh* |
| large. | **grande.** |
| | *GRAHN-deh* |
| extra-large. | **extra grande.** |
| | *EHS-trah GRAHN-deh* |

los aretes
el collar

la camisa
la corbata
la chaqueta

el vestido
el reloj

el cinturón

los pantalones

los zapatos

| | |
|---|---|
| I'm looking for ___ | **Busco ___** |
| | *BOOS-koh* |
| cashmere. | **cachemir.** |
| | *kah-che-MEER* |
| a coat. | **un abrigo.** |
| | *oon ah-BREE-goh* |
| cotton pants. | **pantalones de algodón.** |
| | *pahn-tah-LOH-nehs deh ahl-goh-DOHN* |
| a hat. | **un sombrero.** |
| | *oon sohm-BREH-roh* |
| a silk blouse. | **una blusa de seda.** |
| | *OO-nah BLOO-sah deh SEH-dah* |
| socks. | **medias.** |
| | *MEH-dyahs* |
| sunglasses. | **gafas de sol.** |
| | *GAH-fahs deh sohl* |
| sweaters. | **suéteres.** |
| | *soo-EH-teh-rehs* |

las gafas

la camiseta

los jeans

los tennis

| | |
|---|---|
| a swimsuit. | **un traje de baño.**<br>*oon TRAH-heh deh BAH-nyoh* |
| underwear. | **ropa interior.**<br>*RROH-pah een-teh-RYOHR* |
| May I try it on? | **¿Puedo medírmelo?**<br>*PWEH-doh meh-DEER-meh-loh* |
| Do you have fitting rooms? | **¿Tiene probadores?**<br>*TYEH-neh proh-bah-DOH-rehs* |
| This is _____ | **Esto me queda _____**<br>*EHS-toh meh KEH-dah* |
| too tight. | **muy apretado.**<br>*MOO-ee ah-preh-TAH-doh* |
| too loose. | **muy suelto.**<br>*MOO-ee SWEHL-toh* |
| too long. | **muy largo.**<br>*MOO-ee LAHR-goh* |
| too short. | **muy corto.**<br>*MOO-ee KOHR-toh* |
| This fits great! | **¡Esto me queda bien!**<br>*EHS-toh meh KEH-dah byehn* |

| | |
|---|---|
| Thanks, I'll take it. | **Gracias, me lo llevo.**<br>*GRAH-syahs meh loh YEH-voh* |
| Do you have that in \_\_\_\_ | **¿Tiene eso en \_\_\_\_**<br>*TYEH-neh EH-soh ehn* |
| a smaller / larger size? | **una talla más pequeña / grande?**<br>*OO-nah TAH-yah mahs peh-KEH-nyah / GRAHN-deh* |
| a different color? | **un color diferente?**<br>*oon koh-LOHR dee-feh-REHN-teh* |
| How much is it? | **¿Cuánto es?**<br>*KWAHN-toh ehs* |

## ARTISAN MARKET SHOPPING

| | |
|---|---|
| Is there a craft / artisan market? | **¿Hay un mercado de artesanías?**<br>*aye oon mehr-KAH-doh deh ahr-teh-SAH-nee-ahs* |
| That's beautiful. May I look at it? | **¡Eso es hermoso! ¿Puedo verlo?**<br>*EH-soh ehs ehr-MOH-soh PWEH-doh VEHR-loh* |
| When is the farmers' market open? | **¿Cuándo está abierto el mercado de granjeros?**<br>*KWAHN-doh ehs-TAH ah-BYEHR-toh ehl mehr-KAH-doh deh grahn-HEH-rohs* |
| Is that open every day of the week? | **¿Eso está abierto todos los días de la semana?**<br>*EH-soh ehs-TAH ah-BYEHR-toh TOH-doh lohs DEE-ahs deh lah seh-MAH-nah* |
| How much does that cost? | **¿Cuánto cuesta eso?**<br>*KWAHN-toh KWEHS-tah EH-soh* |
| That's too expensive. | **Eso es muy caro.**<br>*EH-soh ehs MOO-ee KAH-roh* |
| How much for two? | **¿Cuánto por los / las dos?**<br>*KWAHN-doh pohr lohs / lahs dohs* |

### Listen Up: Market Lingo

| | |
|---|---|
| **Por favor pida que le asistan, antes de manejar la mercadería.** *pohr fah-VOHR PEE-dah keh leh ah-sees-TAHN ahn-TEHS deh mah-neh-HAHR lah mehr-kah-deh-REE-ah* | Please ask for help before handling goods. |
| **Aquí tengo su cambio.** *ah-KEE TEHNG-goh soo KAHM-byoh* | Here is your change. |
| **Dos por cuarenta, señor.** *dohs pohr kwah-REHN-tah sehn-YOHR* | Two for forty, sir. |

| | |
|---|---|
| Do I get a discount if I buy two or more? | **¿Me da un descuento si compro dos o más?** *meh dah oon dehs-KWEHN-toh see KOHM-proh dohs oh mahs* |
| Do I get a discount if I pay in cash? | **¿Me da un descuento si pago en efectivo?** *meh dah oon desh-KWEHN-toh see PAH-goh ehn eh-FEHK-tee-voh* |
| No thanks, maybe I'll come back. | **No gracias, quizás regreso más tarde.** *noh GRAH-syahs kee-SAHS reh-GREH-soh mahs TAHR-deh* |
| Would you take $____? | **¿Aceptaría $____?** *ah-SEHP-tah-REE-ah ____ DOH-lah-rehs* |

*For a full list of numbers, see p7.*

| | |
|---|---|
| That's a deal! | **¡Trato hecho!** |
| | *TRAH-toh EH-choh* |
| Do you have a less expensive one? | **¿Tiene uno -a menos caro -a?** |
| | *TYEH-neh oon / OO-nah MEH-nohs KAH-roh / KAH-rah* |
| Is there tax? | **¿Hay un impuesto?** |
| | *aye oon eem-PWEHS-toh* |
| May I have the VAT forms? (Europe only) | **¿Me puede dar los formularios IVA?** |
| | *meh PWEH-deh dahr lohs fohr-moo-LAHR-yohs ee-veh-AH* |

## BOOKSTORE / NEWSSTAND SHOPPING

| | |
|---|---|
| Is there a _____ nearby? | **¿Hay _____ cerca?** |
| | *aye _____ SEHR-kah* |
| a bookstore | **una librería** |
| | *OO-nah lee-breh-REE-ah* |
| a newsstand | **un puesto de periódicos** |
| | *oon PWEHS-toh deh pehr-YOH-dee-kohs* |
| Do you have _____ in English? | **¿Tiene _____ en inglés?** |
| | *TYEH-neh _____ ehn eeng-GLEHS* |
| books | **libros** |
| | *LEE-brohs* |
| books about local history | **libros acerca de la historia local** |
| | *LEE-brohs ah-SEHR-kah deh lah ees-TOHR-yah loh-KAHL* |
| magazines | **revistas** |
| | *reh-VEES-tahs* |
| newspapers | **periódicos** |
| | *pehr-YOH-dee-kohs* |
| picture books | **libros de fotos** |
| | *LEE-brohs deh FOH-tohs* |

# SHOPPING FOR ELECTRONICS

With some exceptions, shopping for electronic goods in Latin America or Spain is generally not recommended. Many DVDs, CDs, and other products contain different signal coding from that used in the United States or Canada, to help deter piracy. Radios, as well as older videos and cassette tapes, are probably the biggest exception though, and lots of U.S. market goods are available. Note: Electronic formats are the same for the United States and Canada.

| | |
|---|---|
| Can I play this in the United States? | **¿Puedo tocar esto en Estados Unidos?** *PWEH-doh toh-KAHR EHS-toh ehn ehs-TAH-dohs oo-NEE-dohs?* |
| Will this game work on my game console in the United States? | **¿Este juego funcionará en mi consola de juegos en los Estados Unidos?** *EHS-teh HWEH-goh foon-syoh-nah-RAH ehn mee kohn-SOH-lah deh HWEH-gohs ehn lohs ehs-TAH-dohs oo-NEE-dohs* |
| Do you have this in a U.S. market format? | **¿Tiene esto en un formato para el mercado de los Estados Unidos?** *TYEH-neh EHS-toh ehn oon fohr-MAH-toh PAH-rah ehl mehr-KAH-doh deh lohs ehs-TAH-dohs oo-NEE-dohs* |
| Can you convert this to a U.S. market format? | **¿Puede convertir esto a un formato para el mercado de los Estados Unidos?** *PWEH-deh kohn-vehr-TEER EHS-toh ah oon fohr-MAH-toh PAH-rah ehl mehr-KAH-doh deh lohs ehs-TAH-dohs oo-NEE-dohs* |

| | |
|---|---|
| Will this work with a 110 VAC adapter? | **¿Esto funcionará con un adaptador de 110 VAC?** *EHS-toh foon-syoh-nah-RAH kohn oon ah-dahp-tah-DOHR deh SYEHN-toh ee dyehs VOHL-tyohs deh koh-RRYEHN-teh ahl-TEHR-nah* |
| Do you have an adapter plug for 110 to 220? | **¿Tiene un enchufe adaptador de 110 a 220?** *TYEH-neh oon ehn-CHOO-feh ah-dahp-tah-DOHR deh SYEHN-toh ee dyehs ah doh-SYEHN-tohs ee VEH-een-teh* |
| Do you sell electronics adapters here? | **¿Vende adaptadores electrónicos aquí?** *VEHN-deh ah-dahp-tah-DOH-rehs eh-lehk-TROH-nee-kohs ah-KEE* |
| Is it safe to use my laptop with this adapter? | **¿Es seguro usar mi computadora portátil con este adaptador?** *ehs seh-GOO-roh oo-SAHR mee kohm-poo-tah-DOH-rah pohr-TAH-teel kohn EHS-teh ah-dahp-tah-DOHR* |
| If it doesn't work, may I return it? | **¿Si no funciona, puedo devolverlo?** *see noh foon-SYOH-nah PWEH-doh deh-vohl-VEHR-loh* |
| May I try it here in the store? | **¿Puedo probarlo aquí en la tienda?** *PWEH-doh proh-BAHR-loh ah-KEE ehn lah TYEHN-dah* |

## AT THE BARBER / HAIRDRESSER

| | |
|---|---|
| Do you have a style guide? | **¿Tiene una guía de estilo?** *TYEH-neh OO-nah GEE-ah deh eh-STEE-loh* |
| A trim, please. | **Un recorte, por favor.** *oon rreh-KOHR-teh pohr fah-VOHR* |

I'd like it bleached.

**Me gustaría el pelo descolorado.**
*meh goos-tah-REE-ah ehl PEH-loh
dehs-koh-loh-RAH-doh*

Would you change the
color ____

**¿Usted le cambiaría el color ____**
*oos-TEHD leh kahm-byah-REE-ah
ehl koh-LOHR*

　darker?

**más oscuro?**
*mahs oh-SKOO-roh*

　lighter?

**más claro?**
*mahs KLAH-roh*

Would you just touch it
up a little?

**¿Lo puede retocar un poco?**
*loh PWEH-deh reh-toh-KAHR oon
POH-koh*

I'd like it curled.

**Me gustaría rizado.**
*meh goos-tah-REE-ah ree-SAH-doh*

Do I need an
appointment?
Wash, dry, and set.

**¿Necesito una cita?**
*neh-seh-SEE-toh OO-nah SEE-tah*
**Lavado, secado y peinado.**
*lah-VAH-doh seh-KAH-doh ee
peh-ee-NAH-doh*

Do you do permanents?

**¿Hacen permanentes?**
*AH-sehn pehr-mah-NEHN-tehs*

May I make an
appointment?

**¿Puedo hacer una cita?**
*PWEH-doh ah-SEHR OO-nah
SEE-tah*

Please use low heat.

**Por favor use poco calor.**
*pohr fah-VOHR OO-seh POH-koh
kah-LOHR*

Please don't blow dry it.

**Por favor no lo seque con secadora.**
*pohr fah-VOHR noh loh SEH-keh
kohn seh-kah-DOH-rah*

Please dry it curly /
straight.

**Por favor séquelo rizado / lacio.**
*pohr fah-VOHR SEH-keh-loh kohn
ree-SAH-doh / LAH-syoh*

| | |
|---|---|
| Would you fix my braids? | **¿Puede arreglar mis trenzas?**<br>*PWEH-deh ah-rreh-GLAHR mees*<br>*TREHN-sahs* |
| Would you fix my highlights? | **¿Puede arreglar mis destellos?**<br>*PWEH-deh ah-rreh-GLAHR mees*<br>*dehs-TEH-yohs* |
| Do you wax? | **¿Hacen depilación con cera?**<br>*AH-sehn deh-pee-lah-SYOHN*<br>*kohn SEH-rah* |
| Please wax my ____ | **Por favor, depile mis ____**<br>*pohr fah-VOHR deh-PEE-leh mees* |
| legs. | **piernas.**<br>*PYEHR-nahs* |
| bikini line. | **área del bikini.**<br>*AH-reh-ah dehl bee-KEE-nee* |
| eyebrows. | **cejas.**<br>*SEH-hahs* |
| under my nose. | **debajo de mi nariz.**<br>*deh-BAH-hoh deh mee nah-REES* |
| Please trim my beard. | **Por favor recorte mi barba.**<br>*pohr fah-VOHR reh-KOHR-teh*<br>*mee BAHR-bah* |
| A shave, please. | **Una afeitada, por favor.**<br>*OO-nah ah-feh-ee-TAH-dah pohr*<br>*fah-VOHR* |
| Use a fresh blade please. | **Una navaja nueva por favor.**<br>*OO-nah nah-VAH-hah NWEH-vah*<br>*pohr fah-VOHR* |
| Sure, cut it all off. | **Seguro, córtelo todo.**<br>*seh-GOO-roh KOHR-teh-loh*<br>*TOH-doh* |

## UNDERSTANDING THE VAT

Known as *IVA* (pronounced eeba) in Latin America, VAT is a fact of life in most countries. The rate generally hovers around 12% but is as high as 21% in Argentina and a whopping 24% in Uruguay. In some countries, visitors can claim back this tax upon departure, so long as they purchase items at a store with tax-free shopping and spend more than $25 on each purchase. In most cases, you receive the money back (minus a commission) at the airport upon producing the form and the goods. Be sure to ask for forms and pack the goods separate from your check-in luggage.

## THE BEST BUYS & WHERE TO FIND THEM

### Antiques

Argentina is the best place for antiques, and nobody does it better than the **San Telmo Market**, Buenos Aires. A stroll around this weekend market will transport you back to the Belle Epoque. If you're not in Buenos Aires over a weekend, just head to Defensa Street (between Independencia and San Juan) where the streets are lined with palace-like antiques shops, open weekdays for the most discerning customer. Objects range from cathedral-size chandeliers to giant gramophones. Any item over 100 years old comes with a certificate of authenticity.

Recommended antiques stores in Buenos Aires include **El Churrinche**, Defensa 1031, for its elaborate lamps, and **Guevara Art Gallery**, Defensa 982, for a large array of Art Deco and Art Nouveau objects.

In Santiago, Chile, **Barrio Brasil** (near Parque de los Reyes) has a plethora of antiques stores and many bargains.

### Arts & Crafts

**Feria Artesanal de Angelmó** in Chile is an excellent hunting ground for gifts and souvenirs. The **Mercado Guajiro** in Caracas, Venezuela, has a large array of handmade souvenirs. **La Cancha**

in Cochabamba, Bolivia, is another market worth visiting. Northern Peru has excellent replicas of pre-Colombian relics. **Ayllu**, Corredor del Oeste, in Mendoza, Argentina, is a warehouse store containing arts and crafts from several countries in Latin America.

### Ceramics

**Hannsi Centro Artesanal**, El Hatillo, in Caracas, Venezuela, offers excellent ceramics and masks from Venezuelan tribes. The weekend fair at **Plaza Francia** in Buenos Aires, Argentina, will drive any potter potty. Looking for something handmade and intricate? Try **Vicunita Handicrafts**, Av. Rafael Pabón 777, Cochabamba, Bolivia.

### Exotic Goods

Some items for sale at the **Witchdoctors Market** in La Paz, Bolivia, defy classification, such as the dried llama fetuses. Other good luck charms include miniature houses (to hasten the prospect that you'll own the real thing some day). **Belen Market,** in the jungle town of Iquitos, Peru, is fascinating, though you probably won't buy much unless you're into magic potions, monkey heads, or 6-foot poison dart blowers.

### Hand-Woven Goods

If you're after ponchos and hammocks, Latin America is the right place to be, and you should have no trouble locating these items in whatever market you find yourself.

Ecuador offers the best quality and variety, especially in the town of **Otavalo**, north of Quito, Ecuador. This weekend market has become a 7-day affair with an emphasis on quality craftsmanship. You'll find an array of items, including hand-woven bags and alpaca scarves. You can also visit different studios in outlying regions, all within 2 hours: **Cotacahi** is known for leather work and **San Antonio de Ibarra** for its age-old woodcarving techniques.

In Peru, the cities of **Lima** and **Cuzco** are also good places to browse. Bolivia is hammock heaven, particularly in **La Paz**, around Calle Sagárnaga. A notable weekend market takes place in the town of **Tarabuco**, near Sucre. **Margarita Island** in Venezuela makes its own style of hammock known as *chinchorros*.

## Headware

The indigenous tribes of Ecuador, Peru, and Bolivia each wear their own style of hat. Stroll through any highland city and you'll find shops specializing in them. Cuenca, Ecuador, is the home of the Panama hat, while Venezuela and Argentina are strictly for cowboys. For something woolly and head hugging, the shops in **Copacabana**, Bolivia, can't be beat.

## Jewelry

The Caribbean city of **Cartagena**, in Colombia, is the place for emeralds. Specialist shops line the cobbled streets, and unbelievable bargains are available for cut and uncut stones. (Some dealers are unscrupulous, so know what you're looking for.)

**Santa Cruz,** in Bolivia, is a retail center for unique jewelry. **Joyeria Andrea**, Junin 177, specializes in a stone called the Bolivian, a mix of amethyst and citrine (a yellow stone resembling topaz). Bolivia is also a good place to find quality silver jewelry. Check out **Kuka Pradel**, Av. 6 de Agosto 2190, La Paz. The silver mining town of **Potosi**, Bolivia, is also a hunting ground for silver. **Cordoba** in central Argentina is notable for stores selling precious stones.

## Leather Goods

Contrary to popular belief, it was not the Spanish or Portuguese that conquered South America, so much as the cow. Abandoned herds proliferated on the pampas and savannahs of Argentina and Brazil, and meat and leather became the foundation of both economies. The tradition of excellent leather-making continues to this day. Argentina is the most popular and affordable place to buy leather goods. You'll find quality-made bags, belts, and wallets on most city center streets and shopping malls. Buenos Aires is the epicenter of the trade.

**Murillo Street** in Villa Crespo, Buenos Aires, is where the leather wholesalers gather; a cab ride away from the more heavily touristed areas of the city, you'll find a half-dozen streets lined with high-quality leather retailers. **Calle Florida** in Buenos Aires is Leather Central, though the overzealous salesmen may put you off, and the prices are much higher than what you'll find on Murillo Street. **Peter Kent**, Avenida Alvear 1820, Buenos Aires, is a luxury leather store popular with wealthy *Porteños*. Look out for *capyvara*, a soft, dimpled leather taken from the largest rodent in the world. **Artencueros**, Galeria Rue des Artisans, Arenales 1239, Buenos Aires, specializes in women's jackets and skirts. **Blaque**, Galerias Pacifico, Florida 737, Buenos Aires, is the luggage expert, and **Sybil Lane**, Galeria Pacifico in Buenos Aires, is well known for its well-designed bags and boots. For something more down to earth but of lesser quality try **Mataderos Market**, a gaucho fair in the southwestern suburb of Mataderos, Buenos Aires. In the wine country, another notable leather shop is **Alain de France**, Palero 20, Mendoza City.

## Wine & Spirits

The huge **El Mundo de Vin** at Av. Isidora Goyenechea 2931 in Santiago, Chile, has a wonderful array of wines—mostly Chilean, from hard-to-find boutique wineries.

The wine-growing region of Mendoza, Argentina, offers great bargains for quality wines that are half the price you'd pay back home; the variety can be overwhelming. **Marcelino Wineshop**, Benegas and Zapata, Mendoza City, Argentina, offers an excellent variety of boutique wines, with shipping included in the price. **Ligier**, Avenida Santa Fe 800, Buenos Aires, also delivers.

### STAYING FIT

Is there a gym nearby?

**¿Hay un gimnasio cerca?**
*aye oon heem-NAH-syoh SEHR-kah*

Do you have free weights?

**¿Tienen pesas de mano?**
*TYEH-nehn PEH-sahs deh MAH-noh*

I'd like to go for a swim.

**Me gustaría nadar.**
*meh goos-tah-REE-ah nah-DAHR*

Do I have to be a member?

**¿Tengo que ser miembro?**
*TEHNG-goh keh sehr MYEHM-broh*

May I come here for one day?

**¿Puedo venir por un día, nada más?**
*PWEH-doh veh-NEER pohr oon DEE-ah NAH-dah mahs*

How much does a membership cost?

**¿Cuánto cuesta la membresía?**
*KWAHN-toh KWEHS-tah lah mehm-breh-SEE-ah*

I need to get a locker please.

**Necesito un casillero.**
*neh-seh-SEE-toh oon kah-see-YEH-roh*

| | |
|---|---|
| Do you have a lock? | **¿Tiene un candado?** <br> *TYEH-neh oon kahn-DAH-doh* |
| Do you have a treadmill? | **¿Tiene una caminadora?** <br> *TYEH-neh OO-nah kah-mee-nah-DOH-rah* |
| Do you have a stationary bike? | **¿Tiene una bicicleta estacionaria?** <br> *TYEH-neh OO-nah bee-see-KLEH-tah ehs-tah-syoh-NAH-ryah* |
| Do you have handball / squash courts? | **¿Tiene canchas de balonmano / squash?** <br> *TYEH-neh KAHN-chahs deh bah-lohn-MAH-noh / skwahsh?* |
| Are they indoors? | **¿Son bajo techo?** <br> *sohn BAH-hoh TEH-cho* |
| I'd like to play tennis. | **Me gustaría jugar tenis.** <br> *meh goos-tah-REE-ah hoo-GAHR TEH-nees* |
| Would you like to play? | **¿Le gustaría jugar?** <br> *leh goos-tah-REE-ah hoo-GAHR* |
| I'd like to rent a racquet. | **Quisiera alquilar una raqueta.** <br> *kee-SYEH-roh ahl-kee-LAHR OO-nah rrah-KEH-tah* |
| I need to buy some ____ | **Necesito comprar ____** <br> *neh-seh-SEE-toh kohm-PRAHR* |
| new balls. | **bolas nuevas.** <br> *BOH-lahs NWEH-vahs* |
| safety glasses. | **gafas de protección.** <br> *GAH-fahs deh proh-tehk-SYOHN* |
| May I rent a court for tomorrow? | **¿Puedo alquilar una cancha para mañana?** <br> *PWEH-doh ahl-kee-LAHR OO-nah KAHN-chah PAH-rah mah-NYAH-nah* |
| May I have clean towels? | **¿Me puede dar toallas limpias?** <br> *meh PWEH-deh dahr toh-AH-yahs LEEM-pyahs* |

| | |
|---|---|
| Where are the showers / locker-rooms? | **¿Dónde están las duchas / los vestuarios?** *DOHN-deh ehs-TAHN lahs DOO-chas / lohs vehs-TWAHR-yohs* |
| Do you have a workout room for women only? | **¿Tienen un cuarto de entrenamiento para mujeres solamente?** *TYEH-nehn oon KWAHR-toh deh ehn-treh-nah-MYEHN-toh PAH-rah moo-HEH-rehs soh-lah-MEHN-teh* |
| Do you have aerobics classes? | **¿Tienen clases de aeróbicos?** *TYEH-nehn KLAH-sehs deh ah-eh-ROH-bee-kohs* |
| Do you have a women's pool? | **¿Tienen una piscina para mujeres?** *TYEH-nehn OO-nah pee-SEE-nah PAH-rah moo-HEH-rehs* |
| Let's go for a jog. | **Vamos a trotar.** *VAH-mohs ah troh-TAHR* |
| That was a great workout. | **Fue un tremendo entrenamiento.** *fweh oon treh-MEHN-doh ehn-treh-nah-MYEHN-toh* |

## CATCHING A GAME

| | |
|---|---|
| Where is the stadium? | **¿Dónde está el estadio?** *DOHN-deh ehs-TAH ehl ehs-TAH-dyoh* |

| | |
|---|---|
| Where can I see a cockfight? | ¿Dónde puedo ver una pelea de gallos?<br>*DOHN-deh PWEH-doh vehr OO-nah peh-LEH-ah deh GAH-yohs* |
| Do you have a bullfight? | ¿Tienen una corrida de toros?<br>*TYEH-nehn OO-nah koh-RREE-dah deh TOH-rohs* |
| Who is your favorite toreador / matador? | ¿Quién es su toreador / matador favorito?<br>*kyehn ehs soo toh-reh-ah-DOHR / mah-tah-DOHR fah-voh-REE-toh* |
| Who is the best goalie? | ¿Quién es el mejor portero?<br>*kyehn ehs ehl meh-HOHR pohr-TEH-roh* |
| Are there any women's teams? | ¿Hay equipos de mujeres?<br>*aye eh-KEE-pohs deh moo-HEH-rehs* |
| Do you have any amateur / professional teams? | ¿Tienen algún equipo aficionado / profesional?<br>*TYEH-nehn ahl-GOON eh-KEE-poh ah-fee-syoh-NAH-doh / proh-feh-syoh-NAHL* |
| Is there a game I could play in? | ¿Hay algún juego en el que yo puedo jugar?<br>*aye ahl-GOON HWEH-goh ehn ehl keh yoh PWEH-doh hoo-GAHR* |
| Which is the best team? | ¿Cuál es el mejor equipo?<br>*kwahl ehs ehl meh-HOHR eh-KEE-poh* |
| Will the game be on television? | ¿El juego será televisado?<br>*ehl HWEH-goh seh-RAH teh-leh-vee-SAH-dah* |
| Where can I buy tickets? | ¿Dónde puedo comprar boletos?<br>*DOHN-deh PWEH-doh kohm-PRAHR boh-LEH-tohs* |

| | |
|---|---|
| The best seats, please. | **Los mejores asientos, por favor.** |
| | *lohs meh-HOH-rehs ah-SYEHN-tohs pohr fah-VOHR* |
| The cheapest seats, please. | **Los asientos más baratos, por favor.** |
| | *lohs ah-SYEHN-tohs mahs bah-RAH-tohs pohr fah-VOHR* |
| How close are these seats? | **¿Cuán cerca están estos asientos?** |
| | *kwahn SEHR-kah ehs-TAHN EHS-tohs ah-SYEHN-tohs* |
| May I have box seats? | **¿Me puede dar asientos de palco?** |
| | *meh PWEH-deh dahr ah-SYEHN-tohs deh PAHL-koh* |
| Wow! What a game! | **¡Caray! ¡Que juego!** |
| | *kah-RAH-ee keh HWEH-goh* |
| Go Go Go! | **¡Dale, dale, dale!** |
| | *DAH-leh, DAH-leh, DAH-leh* |
| Oh No! | **¡O no!** |
| | *oh NOH* |
| Give it to them! | **¡Dale!** |
| | *DAH-leh* |
| Go for it! | **¡Ve por él!** |
| | *Veh pohr ehl* |
| Score! | **¡Anota!** |
| | *ah-NOH-tah* |
| What's the score? | **¿Cuál es la puntuación?** |
| | *kwahl ehs lah poon-twah-SYOHN* |
| Who's winning? | **¿Quién está ganando?** |
| | *kyehn ehs-TAH gah-NAHN-doh* |

## HIKING

| | |
|---|---|
| Where can I find a guide to hiking trails? | **¿Dónde puedo encontrar un guía para los senderos de excursionismo?** |
| | *DOHN-deh PWEH-doh ehn-kohn-TRAHR oon GEE-ah PAH-rah lohs sehn-DEH-rohs deh ehs-koor-syoh-NEES-moh* |

Do we need to hire a guide?

**¿Necesitamos contratar a un guía?**
*neh-seh-see-TAH-mohs kohn-trah-TAHR ah oon GEE-ah*

Where can I rent equipment?

**¿Dónde puedo alquilar equipo?**
*DOHN-deh PWEH-doh ahl-kee-LAHR eh-KEE-poh*

Do they have rock climbing there?

**¿Tienen escalada de rocas ahí?**
*TYEH-nehn ehs-kah-LAH-dah deh RROH-kahs ah-EE*

We need more ropes and carabiners.

**Necesitamos más cuerda y carabineros.**
*neh-seh-see-TAH-mohs mahs KWEHR-dah ee kah-rah-bee-NEH-rohs*

Where can we go mountain climbing?

**¿Dónde podemos ir de alpinismo?**
*DOHN-deh poh-DEH-mohs eer deh ahl-pee-NEES-moh*

Are the routes _____

**¿Todas las rutas están _____**
*TOH-dahs lahs ROO-tahs ehs-TAHN*

well marked?

**bien marcadas?**
*byehn mahr-KAH-dahs*

in good condition?

**en buenas condiciones?**
*ehn BWEH-nahs kohn-dees-YOH-nehs*

What is the altitude there?
¿Cuál es la altitud allí?
*kwahl ehs lah ahl-tee-TOOD ah-YEE*

How long will it take?
¿Cuánto tomará?
*KWAHN-toh toh-mah-RAH*

Is it very difficult?
¿Es muy difícil?
*ehs MOO-ee dee-FEE-seel*

I'd like a challenging climb but I don't want to take oxygen.
Me gustaría un ascenso desafiante, pero no quiero tener que llevar oxígeno.
*meh goos-tah-REE-ah oon ah-SEHN-soh deh-sah-fee-AHN-teh peh-roh noh KYEH-roh teh-NEHR keh yeh-VAHR ohk-SEE-heh-noh*

I want to hire someone to carry my excess gear.
Quisiera contratar a alguien para cargar mi exceso de equipo.
*kee-SYEH-rah kohn-trah-TAHR ah AHLG-yehn PAH-rah kahr-GAHR mee ehk-SEH-soh deh eh-KEE-poh*

We don't have time for a long route.
No tenemos tiempo para una ruta larga.
*noh teh-NEH-mohs TYEHM-poh PAH-rah OO-nah RROO-tah LAHR-gah*

I don't think it's safe to proceed.
No creo que sea seguro continuar.
*noh KREH-oh keh SEH-ah seh-GOO-roh kohn-tee-NWAHR*

Do we have a backup plan?
¿Tenemos un plan de respaldo?
*teh-NEH-mohs oon plahn deh rrehs-PAHL-dah*

If we're not back by tomorrow, send a search party.
Si no hemos regresado para mañana, envía un grupo de rescate.
*see noh EH-mohs rreh-greh-SAH-doh PAH-rah mah-NYAH-nah ehn-VEE-ah oon GROO-poh deh rrehs-KAH-teh*

| Are the campsites marked? | ¿Los campamentos están marcados? |
| | *lohs kahm-pah-MEHN-tohs ehs-TAHN mahr-KAH-dohs* |
| Can we camp off the trail? | ¿Podemos acampar a lejos del sendero? |
| | *poh-DEH-mohs ah-kahm-PAHR ah LEH-hohs dehl sehn-DEH-roh* |
| Is it okay to build fires here? | ¿Está bien construir fogatas aquí? |
| | *ehs-TAH byehn kohn-stroo-EER foh-GAH-tahs ah-KEE* |
| Do we need permits? | ¿Necesitamos permisos? |
| | *neh-seh-see-TAH-mohs pehr-MEE-sohs* |

*For more camping terms, see p87.*

## BOATING OR FISHING

| When do we sail? | ¿Cuándo partimos / salimos? |
| | *KWAHN-doh pahr-TEE-mohs / sah-LEE-mohs* |
| Where are the life preservers? | ¿Dónde están los salvavidas? |
| | *DOHN-deh ehs-TAHN lohs sahl-vah-VEE-dahs* |
| Can I purchase bait? | ¿Puedo comprar carnada? |
| | *PWEH-doh kohm-PRAHR kahr-NAH-dah* |
| Can I rent a pole? | ¿Puedo alquilar una caña de pescar? |
| | *PWEH-doh ahl-kee-LAHR OO-nah KAH-nyah deh pehs-KAHR* |

| How long is the voyage? | ¿Cuán largo es el viaje? |
| --- | --- |
| | kwahn LAHR-goh ehs ehl VYAH-heh |
| Are we going up river or down? | ¿Vamos río arriba o río abajo? |
| | VAH-mohs REE-oh ah-RREE-bah oh REE-oh ah-BAH-hoh |
| How far are we going? | ¿Por cuanta distancia vamos? |
| | pohr KWAHN-tah dee-STAHN-seeah VAH-mohs |
| How fast are we going? | ¿Qué tan rápido vamos? |
| | keh tahn RRAH-pee-doh VAH-mohs |
| How deep is the water here? | ¿Cuán profunda es el agua aquí? |
| | kwahn proh-FOON-dah ehs ehl AH-wah ah-KEE |
| I got one! | ¡Pesqué uno! |
| | pehs-KEH OO-noh |
| I can't swim. | No sé nadar. |
| | noh seh nah-DAHR |
| Can we go ashore? | ¿Podemos ir a la orilla? |
| | poh-DEH-mohs eer ah lah oh-REE-yah |

*For more boating terms, see p66.*

## DIVING

| I'd like to go snorkeling. | **Quisiera bucear con tubo respiratorio.** |
| --- | --- |
| | kee-SYEH-rah boo-seh-AHR kohn TOO-boh rehs-pee-rah-TOH-ryoh |
| I'd like to go scuba diving. | **Quisiera ir de buceo con tanques de oxígeno.** |
| | kee-SYEH-rah eer deh boo-SEH-oh kohn TAHN-kehs deh ohk-SEE-heh-noh |

| I have a NAUI / PADI certification. | **Tengo certificación NAUI / PADI.** *TEHNG-goh sehr-tee-fee-kah-SYOHN EH-neh ah oo ee / peh ah deh ee* |
| I need to rent gear. | **Necesito alquilar equipo.** *neh-seh-SEE-toh ahl-kee-LAHR eh-KEE-poh* |
| We'd like to see some shipwrecks if we can. | **Quisiéramos ver algunos naufragios si podemos.** *kee-SYEH-rah-mohs vehr ahl-GOO-nohs now-FRAH-hyohs see poh-DEH-mohs* |
| Are there any good reef dives? | **¿Hay buenos lugares para buceo de arrecifes?** *aye BWEH-nohs loo-GAH-rehs PAH-rah boo-SEH-oh deh ah-rreh-SEE-fehs* |
| I'd like to see a lot of sea-life. | **Quisiera ver mucha vida marina.** *kee-SYEH-rah vehr MOO-chah VEE-dah mah-REE-nah* |
| Are the currents strong? | **¿Las corrientes son fuertes?** *lahs koh-RRYEHN-tehs sohn FWEHR-tehs* |
| How clear is the water? | **¿Qué tan clara es el agua?** *keh tahn KLAH-rah ehs ehl AH-wah* |
| I want / don't want to go with a group | **Quiero / No quiero ir con un grupo.** *KYEH-roh / NOH kyeh-roh eer kohn oon GROO-poh* |
| Can we charter our own boat? | **¿Podemos fletar nuestro propio bote?** *poh-DEH-mohs fleh-TAHR NWEHS-troh PROH-pyoh BOH-teh* |

## SURFING

I'd like to go surfing.

**Quisiera ir de surfing.**
*kee-SYEH-rah eer deh soor-FEENG*

Are there any good beaches?

**¿Hay buenas playas?**
*aye BWEH-nahs PLAH-yahs*

Can I rent a board?

**¿Puedo alquilar una tabla?**
*PWEH-doh ahl-kee-LAHR OO-nah TAH-blah*

How are the currents?

**¿Cómo son las corrientes?**
*KOH-moh sohn lahs koh-RRYEHN-tehs*

How high are the waves?

**¿Cuán altas son las olas?**
*kwahn AHL-tahs sohn lahs OH-lahs*

Is it usually crowded?

**¿Generalmente está llena de personas?**
*heh-neh-rahl-MEHN-teh ehs-TAH YEH-nah deh pehr-SOH-nahs*

Are there facilities on that beach?

**¿Hay facilidades en esa playa?**
*aye fah-see-lee-DAH-dehs ehn EH-sah PLAH-yah*

Is there wind surfing there also?

**¿Hay windsurfing allí también?**
*aye weend-soor-FEENG ah-YEE tahm-BYEHN*

## GOLFING

I'd like to reserve a tee-time, please.

**Quisiera reservar tiempo para jugar golf, por favor.**
*kee-SYEH-rah rreh-sehr-VAHR TYEHM-poh PAH-rah hoo-GAHR gohlf, pohr fah-VOHR*

Do we need to be members to play?

**¿Tenemos que ser miembros para jugar?**
*teh-NEH-mohs keh sehr MYEHM-brohs PAH-rah hoo-GAHR*

How many holes is your course?

**¿De cuántos hoyos es su campo?**
*deh KWAHN-tohs OH-yohs ehs soo KAHM-poh*

What is par for the course?

**¿Qué es par para el campo?**
*keh ehs PAHR PAH-rah ehl KAHM-poh*

I need to rent clubs.

**Necesito alquilar los palos.**
*neh-seh-SEE-toh ahl-kee-LAHR lohs PAH-lohs*

I need to purchase a sleeve of balls.

**Necesito alquilar una funda de bolas.**
*neh-seh-SEE-toh ahl-kee-LAHR OO-nah FOON-dah deh BOH-lahs*

I need a glove.

**Necesito un guante.**
*neh-seh-SEE-toh oon GWAHN-teh*

I need a new hat.

**Necesito un sombrero nuevo.**
*neh-seh-SEE-toh oon sohm-BREH-roh NWEH-voh*

| | |
|---|---|
| Do you require soft spikes? | **¿Ustedes requieren zapatos con púas blandas?** |
| | *oos-TEH-dehs rreh-KYEH-rehn sah-PAH-tohs kohn POO-ahs BLAHN-dahs* |
| Do you have carts? | **¿Tienen carritos?** |
| | *TYEH-nehn kah-RREE-tohs* |
| I'd like to hire a caddy. | **Quisiera contratar a alguien que cargue mis palos.** |
| | *kee-SYEH-rah kohn-trah-TAHR ah AHLG-yehn keh KAHR-geh mees PAH-lohs* |
| Do you have a driving range? | **¿Tienen un campo de práctica?** |
| | *TYEH-nehn oon KAHM-poh deh PRAHK-tee-kah* |
| How much are the greens fees? | **¿Cuánto es la cuota por jugar?** |
| | *KWAHN-toh ehs lah KWOH-tah PAH-rah hoo-GAHR* |
| Can I book a lesson with the pro? | **¿Puedo reservar una lección con el profesional?** |
| | *PWEH-doh rreh-sehr-VAHR OO-nah lehk-SYOHN kohn ehl proh-feh-syoh-NAHL* |
| I need to have a club repaired. | **Necesito reparar un palo de golf.** |
| | *neh-seh-SEE-toh rreh-pah-RAHR oon PAH-loh deh gohlf* |
| Is the course dry? | **¿El campo está seco?** |
| | *ehl KAHM-poh ehs-TAH SEH-koh* |
| Are there any wildlife hazards? | **¿Hay peligros de vida silvestre?** |
| | *aye peh-LEEG-rohs deh VEE-dah seel-VEHS-treh* |
| How many meters is the course? | **¿De cuántos metros es el campo?** |
| | *deh KWAHN-tohs MEH-trohs ehs ehl KAHM-poh* |
| Is it very hilly? | **¿Está lleno de colinas pequeñas?** |
| | *ehs-TAH YEH-noh deh koh-LEE-nahs peh-KEH-nyahs* |

## ACTIVE SPORTS

### Climbing

Many a mountaineer has traveled to Latin America to scale some of the highest summits in the world. The snowy peaks of **Patagonia** offer some of the most challenging climbs on the continent. But you don't have to head all the way down south. In Ecuador, you can climb the glacier-covered **Cotopaxi**, which at 19,037 ft. (5,804m) is the highest active volcano on earth.

### Diving

The Galápagos Islands, off the coast of **Ecuador**, offer some of the most exciting dives on the planet. You'll have the opportunity to see schools of hammerhead sharks, as well as exotic underwater life. Serious divers should consider booking a special diving cruise around the islands. The Caribbean coast of **Venezuela** is also a popular dive spot.

### Mountain Biking

The 5,000 mile-long (8,050km) Andes mountain range offers some excellent mountain-biking opportunities. From Ecuador down to Patagonia, you'll find mountain-biking outfitters galore. But be careful: The roads are often poorly maintained. Some routes are narrow and open onto steep precipices. It's important to rent a high-quality bike that can handle the conditions. The South American Explorers Club advises bikers to use Kona, Trek, or Cannondale brand bikes; cheaper bikes may not be able to survive the rough terrain.

### River Rafting

The **Amazon** is the world's second-longest river, and running it or one of its many tributaries is one of the great thrills in South America. The wildest parts run through Ecuador, Peru, and Brazil. And in **central Chile**, as the water rages down from the Andes to the Pacific, you'll find some of the wildest white-water rafting anywhere.

## Skiing

The ski areas in Chile and southern Argentina are considered the Alps of South America, and July and August are peak season. In Argentina, the glitterati head to **Bariloche**, while Chileans consider the ski resorts **Valle Nevado** (east of Santiago) and **Portillo** to be sacred ground.

## Snorkeling

The Pacific Coast isn't as enticing, but visitors to the **Galápagos** will find that the snorkeling there is out of this world. The lively fishing village of **Taganga, Santa Matha, Columbia**, is a great jumping off point from which to explore the coast of Tayrona Park. At **La Cienaga, Ocumara de la Costa, Venezuela**, you'll find a beautiful lagoon with crystal clear water, accessible only by boat, brilliant for a day under water.

## Surfing

It has been said that some of the longest breaks in the world occur off the coast of **Peru.** But small beach towns that cater to the surfing set dot the whole Pacific coast of South America. The **Galápagos** Islands have also begun to attract serious surfers to their windy shores. Not surprisingly, the Pacific can get quite cold; be sure to bring a wet suit. For warmer waters, surfers should head to the Caribbean coast of **Venezuela,** where **Henry Pitter National Park** has become a hot spot.

## Swimming & Other Watersports

The Atlantic coast of South America offers wonderful watersports opportunities. **Punta del Este** in Uruguay is one of the premier South American beach resorts. From December through March, the Argentine elite come here to sail, swim, water-ski, or just get close to the sea. The warm Caribbean waters off Venezuela are also great for snorkeling, water-skiing, and windsurfing.

The best windsurfing can be found at **Miramar, Mar de Plata, Argentina**, on the South Atlantic coast. **Montañita, Ecuador**, is one of the hippest hang-out beaches for windsurfing gringos. It's a haven for budget travelers, too. At

**Mancora, Northern Peru**, the wind and waves aren't the only attractions. Mancora has endless white beaches and excellent seafood restaurants.

## FUTBOL

Soccer is the most popular sport in Latin America. This beautiful game dominates headlines and TV schedules and draws huge, raucous crowds to giant stadiums. If you want to get inside the life and culture of a Latin American country, you owe it to yourself to experience at least one match. When you book your room, ask your hotel concierge to reserve tickets for you, and offer a tip when you check in.

## THE BEST OUTFITTERS

### Climbing

**Climb Ecuador** (© 212/362-4721; www.climbecuador.com), is an excellent company that offers well-organized climbing trips to Ecuador, Peru, and Bolivia. In Quito, the **Ecuadorian Alpine Institute**, (© 5932/256-5465; www.volcanoclimbing.com), runs tailor-made expeditions along the Andes Mountain range in Ecuador and Peru. California-based **H2O Patagonia** (© 866/525-2395; www.h2opatagonia.com), offers climbing expeditions all over Chilean Patagonia for the advanced climber.

### Diving

**Caribbean Divers** (© 575/422-0878; www.caribbeandiver-scol.com), offers diving trips to the spectacular coast of Tayrona National Park, Colombia. **Scuba Iguana** (© 593/5-526-497; www.scubaiguana.com), uses English-speaking guides to lead multi-day diving expeditions in the Galapagos Islands. **Coconut Tree Divers** (© 445-4016; www.coconuttreedivers.com), is a highly recommended company based in Roatan, Honduras. They organize dives all over the Honduras coast.

## Mountain Biking

**Backroads** (© 510/527-1555; www.backroads.com), is a well-known company, in Berkeley, CA, that organizes biking trips from Ecuador to Argentina. **MTB Tours** (© 011/4776-3727; www.mtbtours.com), in Argentina, organizes tailor-made biking trips to Brazil, Chile, Uruguay, and Patagonia.

## River Rafting

**Argentina Rafting** (© 0261/429-6325; www.argentinarafting.com), in Mendoza City, is the biggest and best operator on the Mendoza river in Argentina. **Earthquest Adventure** (© 206/334-3404; www.earthquestadventure.com), is an excellent Seattle-based outfitter that organizes adventure trips throughout South America, including kayaking trips down waterfalls in Venezuela, and kayak tours around Chiloe Island, Chile.

## Skiing

**Adventures on Skis** (www.adventuresonskis.com), is a Massachusetts-based company that specializes in ski trips to many areas of the world, including Argentina and Chile. **Chilean Andean Snow Adventure**, in Maryland (© 1-888/449-2272; www.casatours.com), organizes ski trips to the best slopes of Chile and Argentina.

## Surfing

**Surf Express** (© 1-888/566-4147 or 321/779-2124; www.surfex.com), in Florida, offers tailor-made surfing adventures in Peru and Ecuador. **Surfing Adventures** (© 800/796-9110; www.surfingadventures.com), is another small Florida-based outfitter that organizes surfing trips to the most up-and-coming surf destinations in Latin America, including Tamarindo in Costa Rica and Sunzal and La Libertad in El Salvador.

## CHAPTER TEN

### NIGHTLIFE

*For coverage of movies and cultural events, see p168, Chapter Seven, "Culture."*

## CLUB HOPPING

| | |
|---|---|
| Where can I find ____ | **¿Dónde puedo encontrar ____** *DOHN-deh PWEH-doh ehn-kohn-TRAHR* |
| a good nightclub? | **un buen club nocturno?** *oon bwehn kloob nohk-TOOR-noh* |
| a club with a live band? | **un club con banda en vivo?** *oon kloob kohn BAHN-dah ehn VEE-voh* |
| a reggae club? | **un club de reggae?** *oon kloob deh RREH-geh* |
| a hip hop club? | **un club de música hip-hop?** *oon kloob deh MOO-see-kah EEP-ohp / HEEP-hohp* |
| a techno club? | **un club de música techno?** *oon kloob deh MOO-see-kah TEHK-noh* |
| a jazz club? | **un club de jazz?** *oon kloob deh jahs* |
| a country-western club? | **un club de música country?** *oon kloob deh MOO-see-kah KOHN-tree* |
| a gay / lesbian club? | **un club de gays?** *oon kloob deh gehs* |
| a club where I can dance? | **un club dónde pueda bailar?** *oon kloob DOHN-deh PWEH-dah bah-ee-LAHR* |

| | |
|---|---|
| a club with Spanish / Mexican music? | **un club con música latina / mexicana?**<br>*oon kloob kohn MOO-see-kah lah-TEE-nah / meh-hee-KAH-nah* |
| the most popular club in town? | **el club más popular en el pueblo?**<br>*ehl kloob mahs poh-poo-LAHR ehn ehl PWEH-bloh* |
| a singles bar? | **una cantina para solteros?**<br>*OO-nah kahn-TEE-nah PAH-rah sohl-TEH-rohs* |
| a piano bar? | **una cantina con piano?**<br>*OO-nah kahn-TEE-nah kohn PYAH-noh* |
| the most upscale club? | **el club de más clase?**<br>*ehl kloob deh mahs KLAH-seh* |
| What's the hottest bar these days? | **¿Cuál es la cantina más popular de estos días?**<br>*kwahl ehs lah kahn-TEE-nah mahs poh-poo-LAHR deh EHS-tohs DEE-ahs* |
| What's the cover charge? | **¿Cuánto es el cargo de entrada?**<br>*KWAHN-toh ehs ehl KAHR-goh deh ehn-TRAH-dah* |
| Do they have a dress code? | **¿Tienen un código de vestimenta?**<br>*TYEH-nehn oon KOH-dee-goh deh vehs-tee-MEHN-tah* |

NIGHTLIFE

## Cover Your Culo

Be careful with the verb culear. *Culear* is "to shake one's bottom" or "dance," but in Colombia it means "to have sex." Because *el culo* is a vulgar term for derriere, *culear* may mean "to have anal sex" in many Latin American countries.

| | |
|---|---|
| Is it expensive? | **¿Es caro?** |
| | *ehs KAH-roh* |
| What's the best time to go? | **¿A qué hora es lo mejor para ir?** |
| | *ah keh OH-rah ehs loh meh-HOHR PAH-rah eer* |
| What kind of music do they play there? | **¿Qué tipo de música tocan ahí?** |
| | *keh TEE-poh deh MOO-see-kah TOH-kahn ah-EE* |
| Is it smoking? | **¿Permiten fumar?** |
| | *pehr-MEE-tehn foo-MAHR* |
| Is it nonsmoking? | **¿Se prohíbe fumar?** |
| | *seh proh-EE-beh foo-MAHR* |
| I'm looking for ____ | **Estoy buscando ____** |
| | *ehs-TOY boos-KAHN-doh* |
| a good cigar shop. | **una buena tienda de cigarros.** |
| | *OO-nah BWEH-nah TYEHN-dah deh see-GAH-rrohs* |
| a pack of cigarettes. | **un paquete de cigarrillos.** |
| | *oon pah-KEH-teh deh see-gah-REE-yohs* |

## Do You Mind If I Smoke?

| | |
|---|---|
| **¿Tiene un cigarrillo?** | Do you have a cigarette? |
| *TYEH-neh oon see-gah-RREE-yoh* | |
| **¿Tiene lumbre?** | Do you have a light? |
| *TYEH-neh LOOM-breh* | |
| **¿Le puedo ofrecer lumbre / encender su cigarrillo?** | May I offer you a light? |
| *leh PWEH-doh oh-freh-SEHR LOOM-breh / ehn-sehn-DEHR so see-gah-RREE-yoh* | |
| **Prohibido fumar.** | Smoking not permitted. |
| *proh-ee-BEE-doh foo-MAHR* | |

I'd like \_\_\_\_ | **Quisiera \_\_\_\_**
*kee-SYEH-rah*

 a drink please. | **una bebida por favor.**
*OO-nah beh-BEE-dah pohr fah-VOHR*

 a bottle of beer please. | **una botella de cerveza.**
*OO-nah boh-TEH-yah deh sehr-VEH-sah*

 a beer on tap please. | **una cerveza de barril por favor.**
*OO-nah sehr-VEH-sah deh bah-RREEL pohr fah-VOHR*

 a shot of \_\_\_\_ please. | **un trago de \_\_\_\_ por favor.**
*oon TRAH-goh deh \_\_\_\_ pohr fah-VOHR*

*For a full list of drinks, see p100.*

Make it a double please! | **¡Hazlo doble por favor!**
*AHS-loh DOH-bleh pohr fah-VOHR*

With ice, please. | **Con hielo, por favor.**
*kohn YEH-loh pohr fah-VOHR*

And one for the lady / the gentleman! | **¡Y uno para la dama / el caballero!**
*ee OO-noh PAH-rah lah DAH-mah / ehl kah-bah-YEH-roh*

How much for a bottle / glass of beer? | **¿Cuánto por una botella / un copa de cerveza?**
*KWAHN-toh pohr OO-nah boh-TEH-yah / oon KOH-pah deh sehr-VEH-sah*

I'd like to buy a drink for that girl / guy over there. | **Quisiera comprarle una bebida a aquella chica / aquel chico allá.**
*kee-SYEH-rah kohm-PRAHR-leh OO-nah beh-BEE-dah ah ah-KEH-yah CHEE-kah / ah-KEHL CHEE-koh ah-YAH*

A pack of cigarettes, please. | **Un paquete de cigarrillos, por favor.**
*oon pah-KEH-teh deh see-gah-RREE-yohs pohr fah-VOHR*

**NIGHTLIFE**

| Do you have a lighter or matches? | **¿Tiene un encendedor o fósforos?** |
| | *TYEH-neh oon ehn-sehn-dah-DOHR oh FOHS-foh-rohs* |
| Do you smoke? | **¿Usted fuma?** |
| | *oos-TEHD FOO-mah* |
| Would you like a cigarette? | **¿Le gustaría un cigarrillo?** |
| | *leh goos-tah-REE-yah oon see-gah-RREE-yoh* |
| May I run a tab? | **¿Puedo crear una cuenta?** |
| | *PWEH-doh kreh-AHR OO-nah KWEHN-tah* |
| What's the cover? | **¿Cuánto es el cargo de entrada?** |
| | *KWAHN-toh ehs ehl KAHR-goh deh ehn-TRAH-dah* |

## ACROSS A CROWDED ROOM

| Excuse me; may I buy you a drink? | **¿Con permiso, ¿puedo comprarle una bebida?** |
| | *kohn pehr-MEE-soh PWEH-doh kohm-PRAHR-leh OO-nah beh-BEE-dah* |
| You look amazing. | **Se ve maravilloso -a.** |
| | *seh veh mah-rah-vee-YOH-soh -sah* |

| | |
|---|---|
| You look like the most interesting person in the room. | **Usted se ve como la persona más interesante aquí.**<br>*oos-TEHD seh veh koh-moh lah pehr-SOH-nah mahs een-teh-reh-SAHN-teh ah-KEE* |
| Would you like to dance? | **¿Le gustaría bailar?**<br>*leh goos-tah-REE-ah bah-ee-LAHR* |
| Do you like to dance fast or slow? | **¿Le gusta bailar rápido o lento?**<br>*leh GOOS-tah bah-ee-LAHR RRAH-pee-doh oh LEHN-toh* |
| Give me your hand. | **Déme su mano.**<br>*DEH-meh soo MAH-noh* |
| What would you like to drink? | **¿Qué le gustaría tomar?**<br>*keh leh goos-tah-REE-ah toh-MAHR* |
| You're a great dancer. | **Usted es un gran bailador / una gran bailadora.**<br>*oos-TEHD ehs oon grahn bah-ee-lah-DOHR / OO-nah grahn bah-ee-lah-DOH-rah* |
| I don't know that dance! | **¡Yo no se ese baile!**<br>*yoh noh seh EH-seh BAYE-leh* |
| Do you like this song? | **¿Le gusta esta canción?**<br>*leh GOOS-tah EHS-tah kahn-SYOHN* |
| You have nice eyes! | **¡Usted tiene / Tú tienes ojos lindos!**<br>*oo-STEHD TYEH-neh / too TYEH-nehs OH-hohs LEEN-dohs* |

*For a full list of features, see p133.*

| | |
|---|---|
| May I have your phone number? | **¿Me puede dar su número de teléfono?**<br>*meh PWEH-deh dahr soo NOO-meh-roh deh teh-LEH-foh-noh* |

## GETTING CLOSER

You're very attractive.

**Tú eres muy atractivo -a.**
*too EH-rehs MOO-ee ah-trahk-TEE-voh -vah*

I like being with you.

**Me gusta estar contigo.**
*meh GOOS-tah ehs-TAHR kohn-TEE-goh*

I like you.

**Me gustas.**
*meh GOOS-tahs*

I want to hold you.

**Quiero abrazarte.**
*KYEH-roh ah-brah-SAHR-teh*

Kiss me.

**Bésame.**
*BEH-sah-meh*

May I give you _____

**¿Te puedo dar _____**
*teh PWEH-doh dahr*

a hug?

**un abrazo?**
*oon ah-BRAH-soh*

a kiss?

**un beso?**
*oon BEH-soh*

Would you like _____

**¿Te gustaría _____**
*teh goos-tah-REE-ah*

a back rub?

**un masaje en la espalda?**
*oon mah-SAH-heh ehn lah ehs-PAHL-dah*

a massage?

**un masaje?**
*oon mah-SAH-heh*

## SEX

| | |
|---|---|
| Would you like to come inside? | **¿Te gustaría entrar?** <br> *teh goos-tah-REE-ah ehn-TRAHR* |
| May I come inside? | **¿Puedo entrar?** <br> *PWEH-doh ehn-TRAHR* |
| Let me help you out of that. | **Déjame ayudarte a quitarte eso.** <br> *DEH-hah-meh ah-yoo-DAHR-teh ah kee-TAHR-teh EH-soh* |
| Would you help me out of this? | **¿Me puedes ayudar a quitarme esto?** <br> *meh PWEH-dehs ah-yoo-DAHR ah kee-TAHR-meh EHS-toh* |
| You smell so good. | **Hueles tan bueno.** <br> *WEH-lehs tahn BWEH-noh* |
| You're beautiful / handsome. | **Eres bella / guapo.** <br> *EH-rehs BEH-yah / GWAH-poh* |
| May I? | **¿Puedo?** <br> *PWEH-doh* |
| OK? | **¿Está bien?** <br> *ehs-TAH byehn* |
| Like this? | **¿Así?** <br> *ah-SEE* |
| How? | **¿Cómo?** <br> *KOH-moh* |

## HOLD ON A SECOND

| | |
|---|---|
| Please don't do that. | **Por favor no hagas eso.** <br> *pohr fah-VOHR noh AH-gahs EH-soh* |
| Stop, please. | **Para, por favor.** <br> *PAH-rah pohr fah-VOHR* |
| Do you want me to stop? | **¿Quieres que pare?** <br> *KYEH-rehs keh PAH-reh* |
| Let's just be friends. | **Seamos sólo amigos.** <br> *seh-AH-mohs SOH-loh ah-MEE-gohs* |

## Don't Mix the Message

| | |
|---|---|
| **Te deseo.**<br>*teh deh-SEH-oh* | I desire you. This is pretty much a physical expression. |
| **Te quiero.**<br>*teh KYEH-roh* | While this literally means "I want you," in Spanish, it implies "I love you" in the romantic and erotic sense. |
| **Te amo.**<br>*teh AH-moh* | This is used very seriously. If you're not the person's parent or grandparent, you'd better not be saying this without a ring in your pocket. |

| | |
|---|---|
| Do you have a condom? | **¿Tienes un condón?**<br>*TYEH-nehs oon kohn-DOHN* |
| Are you on birth control? | **¿Estás usando anticonceptivos?**<br>*ehs-TAHS oo-SAHN-doh ahn-tee-kohn-sehp-TEE-vohs* |
| I have a condom. | **Tengo un condón.**<br>*TEHNG-goh oon kohn-DOHN* |
| Do you have anything you should tell me first? | **¿Tienes que decirme algo primero?**<br>*TYEH-nehs keh deh-SEER-meh AHL-goh pree-MEH-roh* |

## BACK TO IT

| | |
|---|---|
| That's it. | **Eso es.**<br>*EH-soh ehs* |
| That's not it. | **Eso no es.**<br>*EH-soh noh ehs* |
| Here. | **Ahí.**<br>*ah-EE* |
| There. | **Allá.**<br>*ah-YAH* |

*For a full list of features, see p133.*
*For a full list of body parts, see p230.*

| More. | **Más.** |
| | *mahs* |
| Harder | **Más duro.** |
| | *mahs DOO-roh* |
| Faster | **Más rápido.** |
| | *mahs RRAH-pee-doh* |
| Deeper | **Más profundo.** |
| | *mahs proh-FOON-doh* |
| Slower. | **Más lento.** |
| | *mahs LEHN-toh* |
| Easier. | **Más suave.** |
| | *mahs SWAH-veh* |

## COOLDOWN

| You're great. | **Eres tremendo -a.** |
| | *EH-rehs treh-MEHN-doh -dah* |
| That was great. | **Eso estuvo fabuloso.** |
| | *EH-soh ehs-TOO-voh fah-boo-LOH-soh* |
| Would you like ____ | **¿Te gustaría ____** |
| | *teh goos-tah-REE-ah* |
| a drink? | **un trago?** |
| | *oon TRAH-goh* |
| a snack? | **un bocadillo?** |
| | *oon boh-kah-DEE-yoh* |
| a shower? | **una ducha?** |
| | *OO-nah DOO-cha* |
| May I stay here? | **¿Puedo quedarme aquí?** |
| | *PWEH-doh keh-DAHR-meh ah-KEE* |
| Would you like to stay here? | **¿Te gustaría quedarte aquí?** |
| | *teh goos-tah-REE-ah keh-DAHR-teh ah-KEE* |
| I'm sorry. I have to go now. | **Lo siento. Me tengo que ir ahora.** |
| | *loh SYEHN-toh meh TEHN-goh keh eer ah-OH-rah* |
| Where are you going? | **¿Adónde vas?** |
| | *ah-DOHN-deh vahs* |

| | |
|---|---|
| I have to work early. | **Tengo que trabajar temprano.** <br> *TEHN-goh keh trah-bah-HAHR tehm-PRAH-noh* |
| I'm flying home in the morning. | **Regreso a casa en la mañana.** <br> *rreh-GREH-soh ah KAH-sah ehn lah mah-NYAH-nah* |
| I have an early flight. | **Tengo un vuelo temprano.** <br> *TEHNG-goh oon VWEH-loh tehm-PRAH-noh* |
| I think this was a mistake. | **Creo que esto fue un error.** <br> *KREH-oh keh EHS-toh fweh oon eh-RROHR* |
| Will you make me breakfast too? | **¿Puedes hacerme desayuno también?** <br> *PWEH-dehs ah-SEHR-meh deh-sah-YOH-noh tahm-BYEHN* |
| Stay. I'll make you breakfast. | **Quédate. Te haré desayuno.** <br> *KEH-dah-teh teh ah-REH deh-sah-YOO-noh* |

## IN THE CASINO

| | |
|---|---|
| How much is this table? | **¿Cuánto cuesta esta mesa?** <br> *KWAHN-toh KWEHS-tah EHS-tah MEH-sah* |
| Deal me in. | **Repártame las cartas.** <br> *reh-PAHR-tah-meh lahs KAHR-tahs* |
| Put it on red! | **¡Ponlo en rojo!** <br> *POHN-loh ehn ROH-hoh* |
| Put it on black! | **¡Ponlo en negro!** <br> *POHN-loh ehn NEH-groh* |
| Let it ride! | **¡Déjalo ir!** <br> *DEH-hah-loh eer* |
| 21! | **¡21!** <br> *veh-een-TYOO-noh* |
| Snake-eyes! | **¡Ojos de serpiente!** <br> *OH-hohs deh sehr-PYEHN-teh* |

| | |
|---|---|
| Seven. | **Siete.** |
| | *SYEH-teh* |

*For a full list of numbers, see p7.*

| | |
|---|---|
| Damn, eleven. | **Maldición, once.** |
| | *mahl-dees-YOHN OHN-seh* |
| I'll pass. | **Paso.** |
| | *PAH-soh* |
| Hit me! | **¡Dame!** |
| | *DAH-meh* |
| Split. | **Rompa.** |
| | *RROHM-pah* |
| Are the drinks complimentary? | **¿Las bebidas son complementarias?** |
| | *lahs beh-BEE-dahs sohn kohm-pleh-mehn-TAH-ryahs* |
| May I bill it to my room? | **¿Puedo facturarlo a mi habitación?** |
| | *PWEH-doh fahk-too-RAHR-loh ah mee ah-bee-tah-SYOHN* |
| I'd like to cash out. | **Quisiera llevarme el dinero.** |
| | *kee-SYEH-rah yeh-VAHR-meh ehl dee-NEH-roh* |
| I'll hold. | **Me quedo.** |
| | *meh KEH-doh* |
| I'll see your bet. | **Veo tu apuesta.** |
| | *VEH-oh too ah-PWEHS-tah* |
| I call. | **Igualo tu apuesta.** |
| | *ee-GWAH-loh too ah-PWEHS-tah* |
| Full house! | **¡Full house!** |
| | *fool OWS* |
| Royal flush. | **Escalera real.** |
| | *ehs-kah-LEH-rah reh-AHL* |
| Straight. | **Escalera.** |
| | *ehs-kah-LEH-rah* |

NIGHTLIFE

# LATIN AMERICAN MUSIC

Here's the best of what the region has to offer:

## Changa

Europe has techno. Venezuela has changa, a Caribbean mix of electronic beats and risqué, repetitive lyrics.

## Classical & Opera

Buenos Aires is undoubtedly the classical music center of South America. The season of the world-renowned Teatro Colon runs from early March until early November. Other venues worthy of mention are Teatro Avenida and Teatro Margarita Xirgu. Homegrown talent of international standing includes pianists Daniel Barenboim and Martha Argerich, and tenors José Cura and Marcelo Alvarez.

## Cumbia

There are two types of *cumbia*. One is a catchy Latin beat from the coast of Colombia, where enthusiasts dance like long grass in the breeze. The other is a tropical gangster rap of tinny beats and obscene lyrics, hugely popular in the poorer suburbs of Buenos Aires.

## Folklorico

*Folklorico* is many things to many people, depending on where you are. In Ecuador it means the magic of the panpipes, while in Argentina it means roaring gauchos and handkerchief-waving maidens. In Chile it means pot-banging melodies, while in Paraguay, it's petticoat-wearing, locals doing the can-can.

## Joropo

What must be one of South America's most bizarre types of music, *joropo* comes from the badlands of southern Venezuela and involves wailing cowboys with giant harps and a dance that resembles a galloping horse. The best place to hear it is at one of the many town festivals that occur throughout the year in the region of Los Llanos, Venezuela.

### Ranchera

Mexico's very own type of country and western. Sequined mariachis with trumpets, guitars, and accordions blaze their way through songs about love, liberty, and where my horse has gone. The San Marcos National Fair (Mexico) is the annual hoedown, taking place every April.

### Reggaeton

Born in Panama and Puerto Rico but now sweeping the continent, reggaeton is an energetic mix of hip-hop, pop, and reggae. It's a dance music distinguished by its frenetic drum machine beat and Jamaican-style dance-hall gyrations.

### Salsa

Salsa is the soundtrack to South America. It's a high energy hybrid that pounds your ears on hair-tingling bus journeys and throbs in your head as you sit in taxis on hot and humid city streets. Cuba is its spiritual home but other places worthy of note are Margarita Island, Venezuela, and Cali, Colombia.

### Samba

The pounding heartbeat of Brazil is an energetic mix of percussion and melody. Samba is now a huge musical movement with many sub-genres, all of which come together at the biggest party in the world—the Rio Carnival.

### Tango

Buenos Aires is the home of tango—it's often referred to as the *Tangolopolis*, so plentiful are the opportunities to stretch and swoon. Events vary from high-end tourist shows in baroque theaters to crowded dance halls where audience participation is everything. Never a museum piece, tango is very much alive and ever changing, as in the case of laid-back *tango electronica* (electronic tango—a softer version), just one of many new innovations on this traditional music form. The World Tango Championship takes place every August in various venues around Buenos Aires.

NIGHTLIFE

## RECOMMENDED FILMS

***The Mission* (1986)**    A sweeping, cinematic account of the Jesuit exit from South America. Directed by Rodrigo Mendoza.

***Amores Perros* (2000)**    A visceral tale of love, murder, and dog fighting in Mexico City. Directed by Alejandro Gonzalez Iñarritu.

***Y Tu Mama También* (2001)**    A Mexican road movie about friendship, sex, and older women. Directed by Alfonso Cuarón.

***The Dancer Upstairs* (2002)**    A compelling account of the Shining Path insurrection in Peru and the capture of the movement's leader. Directed by John Malkovich.

***Historias Minimas* (2002)**    A lonely old man goes on an Argentine road trip in search of his estranged dog. Directed by Carlos Sorin.

***Nueva Reinas* (2002)**    Two Argentine con-men team up for the ultimate scam. Directed by Fabiam Bielinsky.

***City of God* (2003)**    A beautiful but savage portrait of life in a Rio de Janeiro slum. Directed by Fernando Meirelles and Katia Lund.

***Man on Fire* (2004)**    A taut, violent thriller that affords insight into police corruption in Mexico City. Directed by Tony Scott.

***The Motorcycle Diaries* (2004)**    Based on the true story of a young Che Guevara touring South America. Directed by Walter Salles.

## RECOMMENDED BOOKS

***At Play in the Field of the Lord,*** by Peter Matthiessen Zealous missionaries and world-weary mercenaries come to a boil in the Peruvian jungle.

***Aunt Julia and the Scriptwriter,*** by Mario Vargas Llosa The surreal account, by Peru's best known writer, of a soap opera writer and a misplaced love affair.

*Collected Fictions,* by Jorge Luis Borges   Argentina's greatest writer draws you into his labyrinth.

*House of the Spirits,* by Isabel Allende   A meticulously detailed family saga spanning four generations of life in Chile.

*In Patagonia,* by Bruce Chatwin   More than just a travelogue, Chatwin uses history, fiction, and repetition to give a searing account of Patagonia.

*One Hundred Years of Solitude,* by Gabriel Garcia Marquez   A jungle town epic by Colombia's magical realist master.

*The Fruit Palace,* by Charles Nicholl   One man's hilarious account of his brave but inept attempt to penetrate the Colombian cocaine trade.

## MODERN MUSIC STARS & GROUPS

**Cafe Tacuba**   A talented Mexican group that plays alternative rock/pop.

**Charlie Garcia**   Argentina's answer to Mick Jagger and Frank Zappa.

**Inti Illimani**   A well-established Chilean ensemble of musicians who play traditional Andean music.

**Juanes**   Another talented Colombian who sings catchy, earnest pop.

**Mana**   Aging Mexican rockers who play a mix of ballads and stadium anthems.

**Molotov**   As the name implies, an explosive punk outfit from Mexico who make biting social commentary.

**Shakira**   The bum-jiggling Colombian rock goddess sings in both Spanish and English.

**Susana Baca**   A Peruvian singer of *lando*, rhythmic Afro-Peruvian coastal music.

## CHAPTER ELEVEN

## HEALTH & SAFETY

This chapter covers the terms you'll need to maintain your health and safety—including the most useful phrases for the pharmacy, the doctor's office, and the police station.

## AT THE PHARMACY

| | |
|---|---|
| Please fill this prescription. | **Por favor, despache esta receta.** *pohr fah-VOHR dehs-PAH-cheh EHS-tah rreh-SEH-tah* |
| Do you have something for ___ | **¿Tiene algo para ___** *TYEH-neh AHL-goh PAH-rah* |
| a cold? | **un resfriado?** *oon rrehs-FRYAH-doh* |
| a cough? | **la tos?** *lah TOHS* |
| I need something ___ | **Necesito algo para ___** *neh-seh-SEE-toh AHL-goh PAH-rah* |
| to help me sleep. | **ayudarme a dormir.** *ah-yoo-DAHR-meh ah dohr-MEER* |
| to help me relax. | **ayudarme a relajarme.** *ah-yoo-DAHR-meh ah rreh-lah-HAHR-meh* |
| I want to buy ___ | **Quiero comprar ___** *KYEH-roh kohm-PRAHR* |
| aspirin. | **aspirina.** *ahs-pee-REE-nah* |
| condoms. | **condones.** *kohn-DOH-nehs* |
| antibiotic cream. | **una crema antibiótica.** *OO-nah KREH-mah ahn-tee-BYOH-tee-koh* |

| | |
|---|---|
| an antihistamine. | **un antihistamínico.** |
| | *oon ahn-tee-ees-tah-MEE-nee-koh* |
| insect repellant. | **repelente contra insectos.** |
| | *rreh-peh-LEHN-teh KOHN-trah een-SEHK-tohs* |
| medicine with codeine. | **medicina con codeína.** |
| | *meh-dee-SEE-nah kohn koh-deh-EE-nah* |
| non-aspirin pain reliever. | **un analgésico sin aspirina.** |
| | *oon ah-nahl-HEH-see-koh seen ahs-pee-REE-nah* |
| I need something for ____ | **Necesito algo para ____.** |
| | *neh-seh-SEE-toh AHL-goh PAH-rah* |
| acne. | **el acné.** |
| | *ehl ahk-NEH* |
| congestion. | **la congestión.** |
| | *lah kohn-hehs-TYOHN* |
| corns. | **los callos.** |
| | *lohs KAH-yohs* |
| constipation. | **el estreñimiento.** |
| | *ehl ehs-treh-nyee-MYEHN-toh* |
| diarrhea. | **la diarrea.** |
| | *lah dyah-RREH-ah* |
| indigestion. | **la indigestión.** |
| | *lah een-dee-hehs-TYOHN* |
| motion sickness. | **el enfermedad de movimiento.** |
| | *ehl ehn-fehr-mee-DAHD deh moh-vee-MYEHN-toh* |
| nausea. | **la náusea.** |
| | *lah NOW-seh-ah* |
| seasickness. | **el mareos.** |
| | *ehl mah-REH-ohs* |
| warts. | **las verrugas.** |
| | *lahs veh-RROO-gahs* |

HEALTH & SAFETY

## AT THE DOCTOR'S OFFICE

| | |
|---|---|
| I would like to see ____ | **Quisiera ver a ____.** |
| | *kee-SYEH-rah vehr ah* |
| a doctor. | **un doctor.** |
| | *oon dohk-TOHR* |
| a chiropractor. | **un quiropráctico.** |
| | *oon kee-roh-PRAHK-tee-koh* |
| a gynecologist. | **un ginecólogo.** |
| | *oon hee-neh-KOH-loh-goh* |
| an eye / ears / nose / throat specialist. | **un especialista en ojos / oídos / nariz / garganta.** |
| | *oon ehs-peh-syah-LEES-tah ehn OH-hohs / oh-EE-dohs / nah-REES / gahr-GAHN-tah* |
| a dentist. | **un dentista.** |
| | *oon dehn-TEES-tah* |
| an optometrist. | **un optómetra.** |
| | *oon ohp-TOH-meh-trah* |
| Do I need an appointment? | **¿Necesito una cita?** |
| | *neh-seh-SEE-toh OO-nah SEE-tah* |
| I have an emergency. | **Tengo una emergencia.** |
| | *TEHNG-goh OO-nah eh-mehr-HEHN-syah* |
| I need an emergency prescription refill. | **Necesito un reabastecimiento de emergencia de mi receta.** |
| | *neh-seh-SEE-toh oon rreh-ah-bahs-teh-see-MYEHN-toh deh eh-mehr-HEHN-syah deh mee rreh-SEH-tah* |
| Please call a doctor. | **Por favor llame a un doctor.** |
| | *pohr fah-VOHR YAH-meh ah oon dohk-TOHR* |
| I need an ambulance. | **Necesito una ambulancia.** |
| | *neh-seh-SEE-toh OO-nah ahm-boo-LAHN-syah* |

## SYMPTOMS

*For a full list of body parts, see p230.*

| | |
|---|---|
| My ____ hurts. | **Me duele mi ____.** |
| | *meh DWEH-leh mee* |
| My ____ is stiff. | **Mi ____ está tenso.** |
| | *mee ____ ehs-TAH TEHN-soh* |
| I think I'm having a heart attack. | **Creo que estoy teniendo un ataque cardiaco.** |
| | *KREH-oh keh ehs-TOY teh-NYEHN-doh oon ah-TAH-keh kahr-DYAH-koh* |
| I can't move. | **No me puedo mover.** |
| | *noh meh PWEH-doh moh-VEHR* |
| I fell. | **Me caí.** |
| | *meh kah-EE* |
| I fainted. | **Me desmayé.** |
| | *meh dehs-mah-YEH* |
| I have a cut on my ____. | **Tengo un corte en mi ____.** |
| | *TEHNG-goh oon KOHR-teh ehn mee* |
| I have a headache. | **Tengo dolor de cabeza.** |
| | *TEHNG-goh doh-LOHR deh kah-BEH-sah* |
| My vision is blurry | **Mi visión está borrosa.** |
| | *mee vee-SYOHN ehs-TAH boh-RROH-sah* |
| I feel dizzy. | **Me siento mareado.** |
| | *meh-SYEHN-toh mah-reh-AH-doh* |
| I think I'm pregnant. | **Creo que estoy embarazada.** |
| | *KREH-oh keh ehs-TOY ehm-bah-rah-SAH-dah* |
| I don't think I'm pregnant. | **No creo estar embarazada.** |
| | *noh KREH-oh ehs-TAHR ehm-bah-rah-SAH-dah* |
| I'm having trouble walking. | **Tengo dificultad al caminar.** |
| | *TEHNG-goh dee-fee-kool-TAHD ahl kah-mee-NAHR* |

HEALTH & SAFETY

el cuello
los senos
el ombligo
las caderas
las muñecas
el trasero
la vagina
los muslos
las piernas
los tobillos

los hombros
las manos
los dedos
los brazos
el pecho
el torso
el estómago
la cintura
el pene
las pantorrillas
los pies
los dedos del pie

| | |
|---|---|
| I can't get up. | **No me puedo levantar.**<br>*noh meh PWEH-doh leh-vahn-TAHR* |
| I was mugged. | **Me asaltaron.**<br>*meh ah-sahl-TAH-rohn* |
| I was raped. | **Me violaron.**<br>*meh vee-oh-LAH-rohn* |
| A dog attacked me. | **Me atacó un perro.**<br>*meh ah-tah-KOH oon PEH-rroh* |
| A snake bit me. | **Me mordió una serpiente.**<br>*meh mohr-dee-OH OO-nah sehr-PYEHN-teh* |
| I can't move my ____ without pain. | **No puedo mover mi ____ sin sentir dolor.**<br>*noh PWEH-doh moh-VEHR mee ____ seen sehn-TEER doh-LOHR* |
| I think I sprained my ankle. | **Creo que me torcí el tobillo.**<br>*KREH-oh keh meh tohr-SEE ehl toh-BEE-yoh* |

## MEDICATIONS

I need morning-after pills.

**Necesito píldoras para la mañana siguiente.**
*neh-seh-SEE-toh PEEL-doh-rahs PAH-rah lah mah-NYAH-nah see-GYEHN-teh*

I need birth control pills.

**Necesito píldoras anticonceptivas.**
*neh-seh-SEE-toh PEEL-doh-rahs ahn-tee-kohn-sehp-TEE-vahs*

I lost my eyeglasses and need new ones.

**Perdí mis gafas y necesito unos nuevos.**
*pehr-DEE mees GAH-fahs ee neh-seh-SEE-toh OO-nohs NWEH-vohs*

I need new contact lenses.

**Necesito lentes de contacto nuevos.**
*neh-seh-SEE-toh LEHN-tehs deh kohn-TAHK-toh NWEH-vohs*

I need erectile dysfunction pills.

**Necesito píldoras para la disfunción eréctil.**
*neh-seh-SEE-toh PEEL-doh-rahs PAH-rah lah dees-foon-SYOHN eh-REHK-teel*

It's cold in here!

**¡Hace frío aquí!**
*AH-seh FREE-oh ah-KEE*

I am allergic to ____

**Soy alérgico a ____**
*soy ah-LEHR-hee-koh ah*

  penicillin.

  **la penicilina.**
  *lah peh-nee-see-LEE-nah*

  antibiotics.

  **los antibióticos.**
  *lohs ahn-tee-BYOH-tee-kohs*

  sulfa drugs.

  **los sulfonamides.**
  *lohs sool-foh-nah-MEE-dehs*

  steroids.

  **los esteroides.**
  *lohs ehs-teh-ROH-EE-dehs*

I have asthma.

**Tengo asma.**
*TEHNG-goh AHS-mah*

HEALTH & SAFETY

## DENTAL PROBLEMS

| | |
|---|---|
| I have a toothache. | **Tengo dolor de dientes.** *TEHNG-goh doh-LOHR deh DYEHN-tehs* |
| I chipped a tooth. | **Se me partió un diente.** *seh meh pahr-tee-OH oon DYEHN-teh* |
| My bridge came loose. | **Mi puente se soltó.** *mee PWEHN-teh seh sohl-TOH* |
| I lost a crown. | **Perdí una corona.** *pehr-DEE OO-nah koh-ROH-nah* |
| I lost a denture plate. | **Perdí mi dentadura postiza.** *pehr-DEE mee dehn-tah-DOO-rah pohs-TEE-sah* |

## AT THE POLICE STATION

| | |
|---|---|
| I'm sorry, did I do something wrong? | **Lo siento, ¿hice algo mal?** *loh SYEHN-toh EE-seh AHL-goh mahl* |
| I am _____ | **Soy _____** *soy* |
| American. | **americano.** *ah-meh-ree-KAH-noh* |
| British. | **británico.** *bree-TAH-nee-koh* |
| Canadian. | **canadiense.** *kah-nah-DYEHN-seh* |
| Irish. | **irlandés.** *eer-lahn-DEHS* |
| Australian. | **australiano.** *ows-trah-LYAH-noh* |
| New Zealander. | **de Nueva Zelanda.** *deh NWEH-vah seh-LAHN-dah* |
| The car is a rental. | **El auto es alquilado.** *ehl OW-toh ehs ahl-kee-LAH-doh* |

## Listen Up: Police Lingo

**Su licencia, registro y seguro por favor.**
*soo lee-SEHN-syah rreh-HEES-troh ee seh-GOO-roh pohr fah-VOHR*

Your license, registration and insurance, please.

**La multa es diez dólares y me la puede pagar directo.**
*lah MOOL-tah ehs dyehs DOH-lah-rehs ee meh lah PWEH-deh pah-GAHR dee-REHK-toh*

The fine is $10. You can pay me directly.

**Su pasaporte, por favor.**
*soo pah-sah-POHR-teh pohr fah-VOHR*

Your passport please?

**¿A dónde va?**
*ah DOHN-deh vah*

Where are you going?

**¿Por qué tiene tanta prisa?**
*pohr keh TYEH-neh TAHN-tah PREE-sah*

Why are you in such a hurry?

---

Do I pay the fine to you?

**¿Le pago la multa a usted?**
*leh PAH-goh lah MOOL-tah ah oos-TEHD*

Do I have to go to court?

**¿Tengo que ir a corte?**
*TEHNG-goh keh eer ah KOHR-teh*

When?

**¿Cuándo?**
*KWAHN-doh*

I'm sorry, my Spanish isn't very good.

**Lo siento, mi español no es muy bueno.**
*loh SYEHN-toh mee ehs-pah-NYOHL noh ehs MOO-ee BWEH-noh*

HEALTH & SAFETY

| | |
|---|---|
| I need an interpreter. | **Necesito un intérprete.** |
| | *neh-seh-SEE-toh oon een-TEHR-preh-teh* |
| I'm sorry, I don't understand the ticket. | **Lo siento, no entiendo la multa.** |
| | *loh SYEHN-toh noh ehn-TYEHN-doh lah MOOL-tah* |
| May I call my embassy? | **¿Puedo llamar a mi embajada?** |
| | *PWEH-doh yah-MAHR ah mee ehm-bah-HA-dah* |
| I was robbed. | **Me robaron.** |
| | *meh rroh-BAH-rohn* |
| I was mugged. | **Me asaltaron.** |
| | *meh ah-sahl-TAH-rohn* |
| I was raped | **Me violaron.** |
| | *meh vee-oh-LAH-rohn* |
| Do I need to make a report? | **¿Tengo que hacer un informe?** |
| | *TEHNG-goh keh ah-SEHR oon een-FOHR-meh* |
| Somebody broke into my room. | **Alguien entró en mi habitación.** |
| | *AHLG-yehn ehn-TROH ehn mee ah-bee-tahs-YOHN* |
| Someone stole my purse / wallet. | **Alguien robó mi bolso / cartera.** |
| | *AHLG-yehn rroh-BOH mee BOHL-soh / kahr-TEH-rah* |

# HEALTH & SAFETY

**Tropical Illnesses**  In the rural, tropical areas of Ecuador, Venezuela, Bolivia, Peru, and Colombia, there is a small risk of **malaria.** Mosquitoes carrying malaria usually can't survive in altitudes over 5,000 ft. (1,500 m.), so if you're traveling in the Andes, you shouldn't have to worry. To protect yourself, apply mosquito repellent with DEET, wear long-sleeved shirts and trousers, and use mosquito nets. You can also take anti-malaria drugs before you go; some have nasty side effects, so consult with your doctor first. **Dengue fever,** transmitted by an aggressive daytime mosquito, is also a risk in tropical areas. As with malaria, the best prevention is to avoid mosquito bites; there is no vaccine available to protect you from infection. Impure water is another source of disease; when in doubt, drink bottled water. And remember: Ice can carry bacteria, too.

**Bugs & Bites**  Snakes, scorpions, and spiders rarely bite without provocation. Keep your eyes open and never walk barefoot. If you're in the jungle or rainforest, be sure to shake your clothes and check your shoes before putting them on.

**High-Altitude Hazards**  The most common ailment affecting people who travel to high elevations such as Quito, Cusco, or La Paz is **altitude sickness.** Common symptoms include headaches, nausea, sleeplessness, and a tendency to tire easily. The most common remedy is to take it easy for your first day or two, avoiding strenuous exercise. It also helps to abstain from alcohol and drink lots of bottled water. You can also take the drug acetazolamide; consult your doctor first.

The **sun** can also be very dangerous at high altitudes. Be sure to bring plenty of high-powered sunblock and perhaps a wide-brimmed hat. Don't let the cold weather fool you—even when it's cold, the sun can inflict serious damage to your skin.

**Toiletries**  Most toiletries are available in larger cities. The exception is **tampons**; be sure to bring enough from home. For some reason, the **toothpaste** in Latin America can be of poor quality, so bring your own. Except in the most rural areas, **film** and **batteries** are easy to find. It can be difficult, however, to find common medicines. We recommend packing a **medicine kit**, just in case. Because food and water poisoning are common, bring medicine to treat diarrhea. Pain relievers and cold medication are also recommended. Consider bringing multivitamins and bromelain, which is said to aid in the digestion of parasites. If you're traveling to jungle or coastal areas, mosquito repellent with DEET is imperative.

Be sure to bring extra contact lenses or prescription glasses, and pack them with your medicines, in your carry-on luggage. Bring the generic names of medications; local chemists may not be familiar with every brand. Check with a specialist in tropical medicines about shots to take in remote areas of the continent.

**Travel Alerts**   Before you depart, check for travel advisories from the **U.S. State Department** (www.travel.state.gov) or the **Canadian Department of Foreign Affairs** (www.voyage. gc.ca).

**Clothing**   If you're traveling in the Andes (parts of Venezuela, Ecuador, Peru, Bolivia, Chile, and western Argentina), be prepared for cold weather. **Layering** is the name of the game here. It can get hot during the day and very cold at night. We recommend a lightweight sweater or sweatshirt, a T-shirt, a fleece jacket, and a windbreaker. Some hotels don't have heat, so bring flannel or heavy pajamas. At night, you may even need a hat and gloves.

Contrary to popular belief, it gets cold in Buenos Aires (Argentina), Santiago (Chile), and Montevideo (Uruguay), especially from June through September, so bring a **jacket** to these countries. If you're heading to the Galápagos, waterproof sandals will be your best friends. During these cooler months you should also consider bringing a **wet suit**. The snorkeling is great this time of year, but the water can be frigid.

**Crime**   Theft at airports and bus stations is not unheard of, so put a lock on your luggage. Put something colorful on your luggage—a sticker, a piece of string—to distinguish it from hundreds of similar bags coming off the conveyer belt. Don't wear expensive jewelry. Keep your wallet in your front pocket. Stash your money in at least two places. Get cash as you go along; with the proliferation of ATMs, there's no reason to bring all your cash with you. Keep your credit card numbers, and the numbers you need to call if you lose your cards, in a separate place. Consider bringing two credit cards in case you lose one, or in case one doesn't work. If you're driving, lock your belongings in the trunk (don't rent a wagon or SUV without an enclosed trunk; they're invitations to thieves).

## INSURANCE MATTERS

Check your existing insurance policies and credit card coverage before you buy travel insurance. You may already be covered. **Trip-Cancellation Insurance** If you have to back out of a trip, if you have to go home early, or if your travel supplier goes bankrupt, trip-cancellation insurance helps you get your money back. Permissible reasons for cancellation can range from sickness to natural disasters to the State Department declaring your destination unsafe for travel.

In this unstable world, trip-cancellation insurance is a good buy, particularly if you're getting tickets well in advance—who knows what state the world will be in 6 months or a year from now? Policy details vary, so read the fine print—and make sure your airline is on the list of carriers covered in case of bankruptcy. A good resource is **Travel Guard Alerts**, a list of companies considered high-risk by Travel Guard International (see website below). Protect yourself further by paying for the insurance with a credit card—by law, consumers can get their money back on goods and services not received if they report the loss within 60 days after the charge is listed on their credit card statement. For information, contact one of the following insurers: **Access America** (② 1-800/729-6021 or 866/807-3982; www.accessamerica.com); **Travel Guard International** (② 800/826-4919; www.travelguard.com); **Travel**

**Insured International** (© 800/243-3174; www.travelin-sured.com); and **Travelex Insurance Services** (© 888/457-4602; www.travelex-insurance.com).

**Medical Insurance**    For travel overseas, most health plans (including Medicare and Medicaid) do not provide complete coverage, and the ones that do often require you to pay for services upfront and reimburse you only after you return home. As a safety net, you may want to buy travel medical insurance, particularly if you're traveling to a remote or high-risk area where emergency evacuation is a possible scenario. If you require additional medical insurance, try **MEDEX Assistance** (© 410/453-6300; www.medexassist.com) or **Travel Assistance International** (© 800/821-2828; www.travelassistance.com; for general information on services, call the company's Worldwide Assistance Services, Inc., at © 800/777-8710).

## SOUTH OF THE BORDER

For years, Mexico was known as the place where bribes—called *mordidas* (bites)—were routinely expected. That's no longer true. Offering a bribe today, especially to a police officer, is frequently considered an insult, and can land you in deeper trouble.

# CHAPTER TWELVE

## CULTURE GUIDE

### LANGUAGE

You'll find that the differences in Spanish spoken throughout Latin América are quite pronounced (no pun intended). Spanish is not widely spoken among Brazilians, but it helps if you speak at least some Spanish, which shares a number of similarities with Portuguese, especially with regard to vocabulary.

#### Idiosyncrasies of Latin American Spanish

**Argentine Spanish** has a rich, almost Italian sound, with the double "ll" and "y" pronounced with a "j" sound. So *llave* (key) sounds like "*zha*-ve" and *desayuno* (breakfast) sounds like "de-sa-*zhu*-no." *Usted* (the formal "you") is used extensively, and *vos* is a form of "you" that's even more familiar than *tú* (informal "you"). Among the peculiarly Argentine terms you may come across are: *bárbaro* (very cool); *Porteño* (a resident of Buenos Aires); *pasos* (steps in a tango); *bandoneón* (a cousin of the accordion, used in tango music); and *subte* (the Buenos Aires subway).

**Uruguayan Spanish** closely resembles the Spanish spoken in Buenos Aires.

**Bolivian Spanish** (like Peruvian Spanish, below) is influenced by its high altitude and large indigenous culture. Common terms include *soroche* (altitude sickness), *trufis* (minivans), and *flotas* (long-distance buses). Instead of *de nada* (you're welcome), it's common for Bolivians to say *no hay de que*. *Chola* refers to women who live in the cities but still wear traditional dress. Be careful when using this term; it can be considered derogatory. People who can trace their ancestors back to both Spain and pre-Columbian Bolivia are known as *mestizos*. To understand the local culture, it's

239

important to be aware of *Pachamama* (Mother Earth), whom Bolivians hold in the highest regard.

**Chilean Spanish** has a singsong feel; sentences often end on a high-pitched note. Chileans habitually drop the "s" off the end of words such as *gracias* (thank you) and *más* (more), which end up sounding more like "*gra*-cia" and "*ma*." Words that end in -*ido* or -*ado* frequently drop the "d"; for example, *pesado* (heavy) is pronounced "peh-*sao*." When using the familiar *tú* verb conjugation, Chileans—especially younger Chileans—exchange the standard -*as* or -*es* ending for -*ai* or -*i*, so ¿*Cómo estás?* (How are you?) becomes ¿*Cómo estái?* Chileans add emphasis to *sí* or *no* by tacking on the suffix -*pues*, which is then shortened to -*po*, as in ¡*Sí, po!* *Ya* is commonly used for "yes" or "okay," and ¡*Ya, po!* means "Enough!" *Cachai* (You know?) is peppered through conversations. Two very Chilean sayings are *al tiro* (right away) and *harto* (a lot or many).

**Costa Rican Spanish** is neither the easiest nor the most difficult dialect to understand. Ticos speak at a relatively relaxed speed and enunciate clearly, without dropping too many final consonants. The y and ll sounds are subtly, almost inaudibly, pronounced. Perhaps the most defining idiosyncrasy of Costa Rican Spanish is the way Ticos overemphasize—are said to almost chew—their r's.

**Ecuadorian Spanish** won't hold many surprises if you've studied Spanish in high school. When greeting strangers, be sure to always use the formal *usted*; you can switch to the informal *tú* when you get to know the person a bit better. One common phrase that is unique to Ecuador is *a la orden* (you're welcome), instead of *de nada*. It's also typical to add *no más* to commands and directions. In stores and at markets, vendors will often say *Siga no más*, which essentially means "Feel free to look around."

**Peruvian Spanish** is also straightforward and fairly free of the quirks and national slang that force visitors to page through their dictionaries in desperation. But you will hear people saying *chibolo* for *muchacho* (boy); *churro* and *papasito* for *guapo* (good-looking); *jato* instead of *casa* (house); *chapar* (literally to grab or get), slangier than *besar* (to kiss); *¡Que paja está!* or *¡Está buenísimo!* (It's great); and *mi pata* to connote a dude or chick from your posse. As in Bolivia, *Pachamama* (Mother Earth) tends to make it into conversation remarkably frequently.

Of course, Spanish is but one of the official languages of Peru. **Quechua** (the language of the Inca Empire) was recently given official status and is still widely spoken, especially in the highlands, and there's a movement afoot to include Aymara as a national language. A couple dozen other native tongues are still spoken. A predominantly oral language (the Incas had no written texts), Quechua is full of glottal and magical, curious sounds. As it is written today, it is mystifyingly vowel-heavy and apostrophe-laden, full of q's, k's, and y's; try to wrap your tongue around *Munayniykimanta* (Excuse me) or *Hayk' atan kubrawanki llamaykikunanmanta?* (How much is it to hire a llama?). Colorful phrases mix and match Spanish and Amerindian languages: *hacer la tutumeme* is the same as *ir a dormir*, or to go to sleep.

**Venezuelan Spanish** is similar to that spoken throughout the islands and coastal regions, given Venezuela's extensive coastline and historic ties to the Caribbean basin. As in Cuba, the Dominican Republic, Puerto Rico, and **Panama**, the accent is thick, the speech is fast, and final consonants are often dropped. Venezuelans rarely use the familiar second person singular *tú* or *vos*, preferring to employ the more formal *usted* in most instances, even among friends and acquaintances. Some typically Venezuelan words and slang you may come across include *bolo* (short for Bolívar, the unit of currency); *caraqueño -a* (person from Caracas); and *tepui* or *tepuy* (distinct flat-topped mesas representative of the southern region).

# FESTIVALS & CULTURAL CELEBRATIONS

## January

**Dia de los Reyes (Three Kings Day), Mexico**   This nationwide holiday commemorates the biblical story of the Three Kings bringing gifts to the Christ Child. On this day, children receive gifts, as they do on Christmas elsewhere. Friends and families gather to share the Rosca de Reyes, a special cake with a Baby Jesus doll inside. *Jan 6.*

**Fiesta of Palmares, Palmares, Costa Rica**   The largest and best organized of the traditional Costa Rican fiestas includes bullfights, a horseback parade *(tope)*, a wide range of concerts, carnival rides, and food booths. *First two weeks of Jan.*

## February

**Dia de la Candelaria (Candlemas), Mexico**   Across the country there are dances, processions, food, music, and other festivities that mix pre-Hispanic and European traditions marking the end of winter.

**Carnaval, Argentina, Mexico, Uruguay**   At the start of Lent, the liveliest Carnaval festivities are held in Argentina, Mexico and Uruguay. In Salta, Argentina, citizens throw a large parade, which includes caricatures of public officials and "water bomb" fights. In Uruguay, Montevideo is the center for the main events, including parades, dance parties, and general debauchery. In Mexico, people from all over the country go to Mazatlán for parades, outdoor mariachi concerts, and all-night parties.

**Festival of the Virgen de la Candelaria, Bolivia and Peru**   Lively festivities are held in honor of one of the most beloved religious symbols in Bolivia and Peru. In Copacabana, Bolivia, the home of the Virgin, the celebration includes parades and dancing in the street. In Puno, Peru, it's one of the largest and most colorful folk religious festivals in the Americas, with abundant music and dance troupes, many in fantastic costumes and masks. *Feb 2.*

**Festival de la Canción (Festival of Song), Viña del Mar, Chile**  This gala showcases Latin American and international performers during a 5-day festival of concerts held in the city's outdoor amphitheater. The spectacle draws thousands of visitors to an already packed Viña del Mar, so plan your hotel reservations accordingly. *Late Feb.*

**Fiesta of the Diablitos, Rey Curre village, Costa Rica**  Boruca Indians wearing wooden devil and bull masks perform dances representative of the Spanish conquest of Central America; there are fireworks displays and an Indian handicrafts market. *Late Feb.*

## March

**Annual Witches Conference, Lake Catemaco, Veracruz, Mexico**  Shamans, white witches, black witches, and practitioners of macumba, Caribbean, Afro, and Antillean rituals gather on the shores of the lake. *Last Friday night in Mar.*

## April

**Festival Internacional de Teatro (Caracas International Theater Festival), Venezuela**  This festival brings together scores of troupes and companies from around the world and across Venezuela for a 2-week celebration of the theater arts. Performances are held in various theaters (and languages) around Caracas, as well as in the streets and plazas. Begun some 3 decades ago, this is the premier theater festival in Latin America. For more information, contact the *Ateneo de Caracas* (© 0212/573-4400). *Early-mid Apr.*

**Semana Santa (Holy Week), Mexico**  The entire country celebrates the last week in the life of Christ, from Palm Sunday to Easter Sunday, with somber religious processions almost nightly, spoofs of Judas, and reenactments of biblical events, plus food and craft fairs. The week following is a traditional vacation period. This is the busiest season for travel in Mexico, so book months in advance if you're heading to the country at this time. *Early Apr.*

**Semana Santa, Uruguay**    During Holy Week, Uruguay shuts down. In Montevideo and the smaller cities, you'll find gaucho-style barbecues everywhere. There are also parades with local folk music. *Wed-Fri before Easter.*

## June

**Gaucho Parade, Salta, Argentina**    The parade features music by folk artists and gauchos dressed in traditional red ponchos with black stripes, leather chaps, black boots, belts, and knives. *June 16.*

**Corpus Christi, Cuenca, Ecuador**    During this weeklong event, Cuenca is at its most festive. The streets around the main plaza are closed and a carnival atmosphere prevails with games, special food stalls, and nightly fireworks. Thousands of balloons are sent into the sky over the city on closing night. The exact date varies, but it's usually *mid-June.*

**Corpus Christi, Mexico**    This day, celebrated all over Mexico, honors the Body of Christ (the Eucharist) with processions, Masses, and food. Festivities include performances of *voladores* (flying pole dancers) beside the church and at the ruins of El Tajín, Veracruz. In Mexico City, children dressed as Indians and carrying decorated baskets of fruit gather with their parents in front of the cathedral. Painted *mulitas* (mules), handmade from dried cornhusks, are traditionally sold outside churches. *Dates vary.*

**Inti Raymi (Festival of the Sun), Argentina, Ecuador, Peru**    This Inca Festival of the Sun—the mother of all pre-Hispanic festivals—celebrates the winter solstice and honors the sun god with traditional pageantry, parades, and dances. In Argentina, celebrations take place in towns throughout the northwest on the night before the summer solstice (around June 20). In Peru, thousands of visitors fill Cuzco's hotels; the principal event takes place on June 24 at the Sacsayhuamán ruins and includes the sacrifice of a pair of llamas. General celebrations continue for several days. In Ecuador, Inti Raymi merges with the fiestas of San Pablo and San Juan to create one big holiday in the Otavalo area. *June 24-29.*

July
**Fiesta of the Virgin of the Sea, Puntarenas, Costa Rica**   A regatta of colorfully decorated boats carrying a statue of Puntarenas's patron saint marks this festival. *Saturday closest to July 16.*

August
**Independence Day, Bolivia**   To celebrate this holiday, Bolivians flock to Sucre, where the leaders of the Bolivian independence movement signed the declaration of independence in 1825. For several days before and afterward, there are colorful parades, fireworks, and all sorts of celebrations. If you can't make it to Sucre, you'll find people partying throughout the country, especially in Copacabana. *Aug 6.*

September
**Virgen del Valle, Isla de Margarita, Venezuela**   The patron saint of sailors, fishermen, and all other seafarers is honored with street fairs and a colorful blessing of the fleet. *Sept 8-15.*

**Independence Day, Mexico**   This national holiday celebrates Mexico's independence from Spain with parades, picnics, and family reunions. At 11pm on September 15, the president gives the famous independence *grito* (shout) from the National Palace in Mexico City. At least half a million people crowd into the *zocalo* (main plaza), and the rest of the country watches on TV or participates in local celebrations. Tall buildings in downtown Mexico City are draped in the national colors (red, green, and white), and the *zocalo* is ablaze with lights. The people of Queretaro and San Miguel de Allende, where Independence leaders lived and met, also celebrate elaborately; the schedule of events is essentially the same in every village, town, and city across Mexico. *Sept 15-16.*

**Independence Day and Armed Forces Day, Chile**   Chile's rich cultural heritage comes to life with plenty of drinking, dancing, rodeos, and military parades. This holiday can stretch into a 3- or 4-day weekend. The best place to witness the celebrations is in the Central Valley south of Santiago. *Sept 18-19.*

## October

**Fiesta del Maiz, Upala, Costa Rica**    At this lively and colorful celebration of the corn harvest, local beauty queens wear outfits made from corn plants. *Oct 12.*

**El Señor de los Milagros (Lord of the Miracles), Lima, Peru**    Lasting nearly 24 hours and involving tens of thousands of participants, many of whom are dressed in purple, this procession celebrates a Christ image painted by an Angolan slave that survived the 1746 earthquake and has since become the most venerated image in the capital. *Oct 18.*

**Fiestas de Octubre (October Festivals), Guadalajara, Mexico**    This most Mexican of cities celebrates for a month with its trademark mariachi music. It's a bountiful display of popular culture and fine arts, and a spectacular spread of traditional food, Mexican beer, and wine.

## November

**Day of the Dead, Mexico**    This national holiday lasts for 2 days. All Saints' Day—honoring saints and deceased children—and All Souls' Day, honoring deceased adults. Relatives gather at cemeteries countrywide, carrying candles and food, and often spend the night beside graves of loved ones. Weeks before, bakers begin producing bread in the shape of mummies. Sugar skulls emblazoned with glittery names are sold everywhere. Many days before, homes and churches erect altars laden with bread, fruit, flowers, candles, favorite foods, and photographs of saints and of the deceased. *Nov 1-2.*

**All Souls' Day and Independence Day, Cuenca, Ecuador**    The city celebrates both the Day of the Dead and its independence day with parties, art shows, parades, dances in the streets, and food festivals. *Nov 2-3.*

## December

**Feast of the Virgin of Guadalupe, Mexico**    One of Latin America's most moving and beautiful displays of traditional culture takes place at the Basilica of Guadalupe, north of Mexico City, where the Virgin is said to have appeared.

Religious processions, street fairs, dancing, fireworks, and Masses honoring the patroness of Mexico take place nationwide. It's customary for children to dress up as Juan Diego, wearing mustaches and red bandanas. Almost every village celebrates this day, often with processions of children carrying banners, and with *charreadas* (rodeos), bicycle races, dancing, and fireworks. *Dec 12.*

**Santuranticuy Festival, Cuzco, Peru**   Hundreds of artisans sell traditional carved Nativity figures and saints' images at one of the largest handicrafts fairs in Peru, in Cuzco's Plaza de Armas. *Dec 24.*

## NATIONAL PROFILES

The population of Latin America is extremely diverse, and it would be difficult to generalize about its cultural makeup. But it's safe to say that of all the different people who live here, a large majority can trace their roots back to Spain, Portugal, Africa, or the Americas. Because of the Spanish and Portuguese influence, *mestizos* (people of both Amerindian and either Spanish or Portuguese ancestry) are also in the majority. From the late 19th century through 1930, the look of Latin America began to gradually change. Millions of Italians emigrated mainly to Brazil, Argentina, and Uruguay. Significant numbers of Germans went to Mexico. Syrians and Lebanese went to Ecuador, and a large number of Japanese began to settle in parts of southern Brazil.

### Argentina

To understand how Argentina's European heritage impacts its South American identity, you must identify its cultures and how they overlap. *Tango*, the sensual dance originated in the suspect corners of Buenos Aires's San Telmo neighborhood, was legitimized in the ballrooms of France, and was then exported to Argentina to become the nation's great art form. Beyond the borders of Argentina's capital and largest city, you will find a land of vibrant extremes—from the Northwest's desert plateau to the flat grasslands of the pampas, from the rainforest jungle of Iguazú to the towering blue-white glaciers of Patagonia. The land's geographic diversity is reflected in its people: Witness the contrast between the capital's largely immigrant population and the indigenous people of the Northwest. Greater Buenos Aires, in which a third of Argentines live, is separated from the rest of Argentina both culturally and economically. Considerable suspicion exists between *Porteños*, as the people of Buenos Aires are called, and the rest of the Argentines. Residents of the fast-paced metropolis who consider themselves more European than South American share little in common with the indigenous people of the Northwest, who trace their roots to the Incas and take pride in a slower, more rural life.

### Bolivia

Bolivia has the highest percentage of indigenous people in all of South America. The country is twice as big as France, but its population is only 8.8 million (about the same as New York City's). And because of the country's rugged vastness, its indigenous groups have remained isolated and have been able to hold on to their traditions. In the rural highlands, lifestyles still revolve around agriculture and traditional weaving. It is also common to see people all over the country chewing coca leaves, a thousands-year-old tradition that is believed to give people energy. The customs of the indigenous people are in full flower not only in rural areas but in cities such as La Paz. In addition, Bolivians all over, particularly in rural highland areas, are known for their love of traditional music.

It is a testament to the tenacity of Bolivian traditions that millions of Bolivians still speak *Aymara*, a language that predates not only the Spanish conquest of Bolivia but also the Inca conquest. Millions more speak *Quechua*, the language of the Incas. In fact, only half the population speaks Spanish as their first language. Of course, in the cities there are many *mestizos*, and most people speak Spanish.

Almost all Bolivians today are Roman Catholic, though traditional indigenous rituals are still practiced, even by devout Catholics. In the 18th and 19th centuries, a distinct "Mestizo Baroque" movement developed, where mestizo artists used indigenous techniques to create religious art. Even today, the mixture of the two influences is evident throughout Bolivian society. In Copacabana, where the Virgin of the Candelaria is one of the most revered Catholic symbols in all of South America, you can climb Calvario, the hill that looms over the cathedral, and receive blessings or have your coca leaves read by traditional Andean priests.

## Chile

About 95% of Chile's population is *mestizo*, a mix of indigenous and European blood that includes Spanish, German (in the Lake District), and Croatian (in southern Patagonia). Other nationalities, such as Italian, Russian, and English, have had a more modest influence. Indigenous groups, such as the Aymara in the northern desert and the Mapuche in the Lake District, still exist in large numbers, although nothing compared to their size before the Spanish conquest. It is estimated that there are more than a half million Mapuches, many of whom live on poverty-stricken *reducciones* (communities), where they continue to use their language and carry on their customs. In southern Chile and Tierra del Fuego, indigenous groups such as Alacalufe and Yagan have been diminished to only a few remaining representatives, and some, such as the Patagonian Ona, have been completely extinguished. One-third of Chile's 15 million residents live in the Santiago metropolis alone.

Until the late 1800s, the Roman Catholic Church exerted a heavy influence over all political, educational, and social spheres of society. Today, although more than 85% of the population claims faith in the Catholic religion, only a fraction attends Mass regularly. The church has lost much of its sway over government, but it still is the dominant influence when the government deals with issues such as abortion and divorce. It is estimated that less than 10% of Chileans are Protestants, mostly Anglican and Lutheran descendants of British and German immigrants, and fewer are Pentecostal. The remaining few belong to tiny communities of Jewish, Mormon, and Muslim faiths.

Chile is a country whose rich cultural tapestry reflects its wide-ranging topography. From this range of cultures and landscapes have arisen some of Latin America's most prominent poets and writers, notably Nobel Prize winners Pablo Neruda and Gabriela Mistral, as well as contemporary writers Isabel Allende and José Donoso. Despite an artistically sterile period during the Pinochet regime, when any form of art deemed suspicious or offensive was censored (meaning nothing was permitted beyond safe, traditional entertainment), modern art has begun to bloom. Even folkloric art and music are finding a fresh voice. Chile is also known for theater, and visitors to Santiago will find dozens of excellent productions to choose from. The national Chilean dance is the *cueca*, a courtship dance between couples that is said to imitate the mating ritual between chickens! The *cueca* is danced by couples who perform a one-two stomp while flitting and twirling a handkerchief.

### Costa Rica

With only about 4 million people, Costa Rica is a small country. More than half the population lives in the Central Valley and is classified as urban. Nearly 96% of the population is of Spanish or otherwise European descent, and it is not at all unusual to see fair-skinned and blond Costa Ricans. This is largely because, when the Spaniards first arrived, the indigenous population was small and thereafter quickly reduced to even more of a minority by wars and disease. In general, Costa Ricans (who call themselves Ticos, a practice that stems from their tendency to add a diminutive, either *"tico"* or *"ito,"* to the ends of words to connote familiarity or affection) are a friendly, outgoing people. In conversation and interaction with visitors, Ticos are very open and helpful.

In a region plagued by internal strife and civil wars, Costa Ricans are proud of their peaceful history, political stability, and relatively high level of development. However, this can also translate into arrogance and prejudice toward immigrants from neighboring countries, particularly Nicaraguans, who make up a large percentage of the workforce on the banana and coffee plantations.

Modern Costa Rica is a nation of contrasts. On one hand, it's the most technologically advanced and politically stable nation in Central America, and it has the largest middle class. Even the smallest towns have electricity, the water is (mostly) safe to drink, and the phone system is relatively good. On the other hand, Costa Rica finds itself in the midst of a huge economic transition. In real terms, the gap between rich and poor has been widening for many years. Government, banking, and social institutions are regularly embroiled in scandal.

Tourism has become the nation's principal source of income, surpassing both cattle and ranching and exports of coffee, pineapples, and bananas. More than a million tourists visit Costa Rica each year. Increasingly, Ticos whose fathers and grandfathers were farmers find themselves hotel owners, tour guides, and waiters. Costa Rican cuisine is not especially memorable, mostly because there's so much international food available around the country to cater to the huge influx of visitors. "The Switzerland of Central America" is also not particularly known for its cultural offerings. However, the country's natural environment makes up for it. It is home to 5% of the planet's biodiversity; more than 10,000 identified species of plants, 850 species of birds, 800 species of butterflies, and 500 species of mammals, reptiles, and amphibians are found here.

## Ecuador

About 25% of the Ecuadorian population is indigenous, and more than 55% of the population is *mestizo*. An additional 10% of Ecuadorians are Afro-Ecuadorian, descendants of African slaves who were forced to work in the coastal areas. Caucasian, Asian, and Middle Eastern immigrants account for the remaining 10%. During the cocoa boom of the late 19th century, many Ecuadorians moved from the heavily populated highland areas to work on the fertile coast. In the past 100 years, there has also been a significant migration of people from the rural highlands to the major cities. El Oriente (the eastern, Amazon basin region of Ecuador) remains the least populated area in the whole country; only 3% of the population lives here.

In the highland areas, the local people have managed to hold on to their traditional culture. It's very common to see people still celebrating ancient holidays such as the Inti Raymi—a festival welcoming the summer solstice. In Otavalo, in the northern highlands, the people still wear traditional clothing, and they have also kept their artisan traditions alive. The finest handicrafts in the country can be found here.

Because of the Amazon basin's isolated location, the locals here were able to escape domination by the Spanish, and managed to maintain thousand-year-old rituals and customs. Some groups never had contact with "the outside world" until the 1960s and 1970s. Visitors to the Ecuadorian jungle who are taken to Amazonian villages will find that the people here live very much as their ancestors did thousands of years ago.

When it comes to art in Ecuador, it has been hard for artists to break from the old colonial mode. Oswaldo Guayasamín is one of Ecuador's most important modern artists. Some of his most famous pieces are expressions of outrage at the military governments in South America in the 1970s.

Music in Ecuador is still strongly influenced by the large traditional Andean population in the country. If you head to any local festival in the Andes, you can be assured that you will find groups of colorfully dressed men playing drums and reed instruments.

## Mexico

With more than 110 million inhabitants, Mexico is one of the most populated countries in Latin America. Five million Mexicans still speak a native language, close to almost 5 centuries following the Conquest, and 800,000 of those do not speak Spanish at all. The states with the highest population of Indians are Oaxaca, Chiapas, Yucatan, Michoacan, and Puebla. Twenty-two million people live in Mexico City, the capital, but the rate of population growth is starting to decrease (from 3.2% per year in the 1970s, to 1.6% at present).

By most measurements, the disparity between rich and poor has increased in the last 30 to 40 years. Cycles of boom and bust weigh heavier on the poor than on the rich. But in the face of all this, Mexican society shows great resilience, due in part to the values Mexicans live by. For them, family and friends, social gatherings, and living in the present remain eminently important. In Mexico, there is always time to meet relatives or friends for a drink, a cup of coffee, or a special occasion.

Frida Kahlo may very well be the best known Mexican artist, and the museum dedicated to her in Mexico City is a must-see for art lovers. But the capital is also one of the world's foremost cultural destinations, with hundreds of performing arts venues taking place on any given night of the year. Opera, theater, ballet, and dance, along with concerts of symphonic, rock, and popular music abound. The mariachis (who play the music of Mexico) are also popular. They play songs ranging from traditional boleros to Mozart and the Beatles, but their style of presentation is unique to Mexico. Known for their distinctive dress, strolling presentation, and mix of brass and guitars, they epitomize the romance and tradition of the country. Mexico is rich with culture, and its cuisine is popular the world over. Every state has its specialty, the most famous being the chocolate mole from Oaxaca.

## Peru

Peru's 27 million people are predominantly mestizo and Andean Indian, but there are also significant minority groups of Afro-Peruvians (descendants of African slaves, confined mainly to a coastal area south of Lima), immigrant Japanese and Chinese populations that are among the largest on the continent, and smaller groups of European immigrants, including Italians and Germans. Their religion is mainly Roman Catholic, though many people still practice pre-Columbian religious rituals inherited from the Incas.

Peru has, after Bolivia and Guatemala, the largest percentage of Amerindians in Latin America. Perhaps half the country lives in the sierra, or highlands, and most of these people, commonly called *campesinos* (peasants), live in either small villages or rural areas. Descendants of Peru's many Andean indigenous groups who live in remote rural areas continue to speak the native languages Quechua (made an official language in 1975) and Aymara or other Amerindian tongues. For the most part, they adhere to traditional regional dress. However, massive peasant migration to cities from rural highland villages has contributed to a dramatic weakening of indigenous traditions and culture across Peru.

Indigenous Amazonian tribes in Peru's jungle are dwindling in number, and today the population is less than two million. Though visitors are unlikely to come into contact with groups of non-Spanish-speaking native peoples, many traditions and languages have yet to be extinguished, especially in the jungle.

Amerindian (Altiplano and Andina) music, is played on wind instruments such as bamboo panpipes and quena flutes, as well as *charangos* (small, bright-sounding, guitarlike instruments), among others. For many, this *música folklórica* is the very sound of Peru, but there are also significant strands of *música criolla* (based on a mix of European and African forms, played with guitar) and *cajón,* (a wooden box used as a percussion instrument), bouncy-sounding *huayno* rhythms played by *orquestas típicas*, and Afro-Peruvian music, adapted from music brought by African slaves.

Peru has one of the richest handicrafts traditions in the Americas. Many ancient traditions, such as the drop spindle (weaving done with a stick and spinning wooden wheel) are still employed in many regions. Wonderful alpaca wool sweaters, ponchos, and shawls; tightly woven and brilliantly colored blankets and tapestries; and many other items of great quality are on display throughout Peru.

## Uruguay

There are 3.3 million Uruguayans, 93% of whom are of European descent. About 5% of the population is of African descent, and 1% is mestizo. The majority of Uruguayans are Roman Catholic. Most live in the capital or one of only 20 other significant towns. Uruguay enjoys high literacy, long life expectancy, and a relatively high standard of living. Despite Uruguay's recent economic troubles, this middle-income nation remains largely sheltered from the pervasive poverty and extreme socioeconomic differences characterizing much of Latin America.

Uruguay has a rich artistic and literary heritage. Among the country's notable artists are the sculptor José Belloni and the painter Joaquín Torres-García, founder of Uruguay's Constructivist movement. Top writers include José Enrique Rodó, a famed essayist; Mauricio Rosencof, a politically active playwright; and journalist Eduardo Galeano.

## Venezuela

Venezuela has a population of approximately 24 million people, some 80% of whom live in a narrow urban belt running along the Caribbean coast and slightly inland. Venezuela is a young country, with an estimated half the population under 20 and around 70% under 35. Almost 70% of the population is mestizo, or a mix of Spanish, European, indigenous, and African ancestry. Another 19% are considered white, and 10%

are black. While indigenous peoples make up only about 1% of the population, their influence and presence are noticeable. Venezuela has more than 20 different indigenous tribes totaling some 200,000 people. The principal tribes are the Guajiro, found north of Maracaibo; the Pémon, Piaroa, Yekuana, and Yanomami, who live in the Amazon and Gran Sabana regions; and the Warao of the Orinoco Delta.

More than 90% of the population claims to be Roman Catholic, although church attendance is relatively low and Venezuelans are not considered the most devout of followers on the continent. There is a growing influx of U.S.-style Protestant denominational churches, as well as small Jewish and Muslim populations. The country's indigenous peoples were an early target of Catholic missionary fervor, although their traditional beliefs and faith do survive. One of the most interesting religious phenomena in the country is the cult of María Lionza, a unique syncretic sect that combines elements of Roman Catholicism, African voodoo, and indigenous rites.

Although Venezuela has its fair share of European-influenced colonial and religious art, its most important art, literature, and music are almost all modern. Jesús Soto is perhaps the country's most famous artist. A pioneer and leading figure of the kinetic art movement, Soto has major and prominent works in public spaces around Caracas. Novelist, essayist, and one-time president of Venezuela, Rómulo Gallegos is the defining literary figure in Venezuela. One important literary figure from the revolutionary era is Andrés Bello, a poet, journalist, historian, and close friend of Simón Bolívar.

Venezuelans love to dance, and no one has been getting them up and moving longer and more consistently than Oscar D'León. Alternately known as El Rey (The King), El León (The Lion), and El Diablo (The Devil) of salsa, D'León has been recording and performing live for more than 30 years, and he shows no sign of slowing down.

# CENTRAL AMERICA

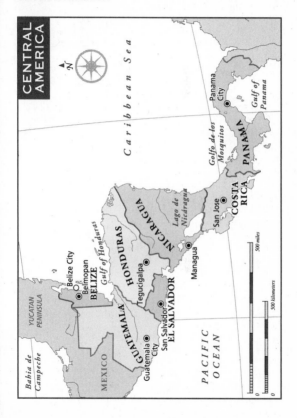

## SOUTH AMERICA

## DICTIONARY KEY

| | | | |
|---|---|---|---|
| n | noun | m | masculine |
| v | verb | f | feminine |
| adj | adjective | s | singular |
| prep | preposition | pl | plural |
| adv | adverb | | |

All verbs are listed in infinitive (to + verb) form, cross-referenced to the appropriate conjugations page. Adjectives are listed first in masculine singular form, followed by the feminine ending.
*For food terms, see the Menu Reader (p103) and Grocery section (p112) in Chapter 4, Dining.*

ENGLISH—SPANISH

**A**

**able, to be able to (can)** v poder **p31**

**above** adj sobre

**accept, to accept** v aceptar **p22**

> **Do you accept credit cards?** *¿Acepta tarjetas de crédito?*

**accident** n el accidente m

> **I've had an accident.** *He tenido un accidente.*

**account** n la cuenta f

> **I'd like to transfer to / from my checking / savings account.** *Quisiera transferir a / de mi cuenta de cheques / ahorros.*

**acne** n el acné m

**across** prep a través de, al otro lado de

> **across the street** al otro lado de la calle

**actual** adj actual

**adapter plug** n el enchufe adaptador m

**address** n la dirección f

> **What's the address?** *¿Cuál es la dirección?*

**admission fee** n el precio de entrada m

**in advance** por adelantado

**African-American** adj afroamericano -a

**afternoon** n la tarde f

> **in the afternoon** en la tarde

**age** n la edad f

> **What's your age?** *¿Cuántos años tiene?*

**agency** n la agencia f

> **car rental agency** la agencia de alquiler de autos

**agnostic** adj agnóstico -a

**air conditioning** n el aire acondicionado m

> **Would you lower / raise the air conditioning?** *¿Puede bajar / subir el aire acondicionado?*

**airport** n el aeropuerto m

**I need a ride to the airport.** *Necesito llegar al aeropuerto.*

**How far is it from the airport?** *¿Cuán lejos está del aeropuerto?*

**airsickness bag** *n* la bolsa para mareos *f*

**aisle (in store)** *n* el pasillo *m*

**Which aisle is it in?** *¿En qué pasillo está?*

**alarm clock** *n* el reloj despertador *m*

**alcohol** *n* el alcohol *m*

**Do you serve alcohol?** *¿Sirven alcohol?*

**I'd like nonalcoholic beer.** *Quisiera una cerveza sin alcohol.*

**all** *n* el todo *m*

**all** *adj* todo -a

**all of the time** todo el tiempo

**That's all, thank you.** *Eso es todo, gracias.*

**allergic** *adj* alérgico -a

**I'm allergic to ___.** *Soy alérgico -a a ___.* See and for common allergens.

**altitude** *n* la altitud *f*

**aluminum** *n* el aluminio *m*

**ambulance** *n* la ambulancia *f*

**American** *adj* americano -a

**amount** *n* la cantidad *f*

**angry** *adj* enojado -a

**animal** *n* el animal *m*

**another** *adj* otro -a ,

**answer** *n* la contestación *f*

**answer, to answer (phone call, question)** *v* contestar p22

**Answer me, please.** *Contéstame por favor.*

**antibiotic** *n* el antibiótico *m*

**I need an antibiotic.** *Necesito un antibiótico.*

**antihistamine** *n* el antihistamínico *m*

**anxious** *adj* ansioso -a

**any** *adj* cualquier, cualquiera

**anything** *n* cualquier cosa

**anywhere** *adv* dondequiera, cualquier lugar

**April** *n* abril

**appointment** *n* la cita *f*

**Do I need an appointment?** *¿Necesito una cita?*

**are** *v* See be, to be. p27, 28

**Argentinian** *adj* argentino -a

**arm** *n* el brazo *m*

**arrive, to arrive** *v* llegar p22

**arrival(s)** *n* las llegadas *f*

**art** *n* el arte *m*

**exhibit of art** exhibición de arte

**art** *adj* de arte

**art museum** museo de arte

**artist** *n* el artista *m*, la artista *f*

**Asian** *adj* asiático -a

**ask for (request)** *v* pedir p32

**ask a question** *v* preguntar p22

**aspirin** *n* la aspirina *f*

**assist** *v* ayudar p22

**assistance** n la asistencia f
**asthma** n el asma f
 **I have asthma.** Tengo asma.
**atheist** adj ateo -a
**ATM** n el cajero automático m
 **I'm looking for an ATM.**
 Estoy buscando un cajero
 automático.
**attend** v asistir p23
**audio** adj audio, auditivo
**August** n agosto
**aunt** n la tía f
**Australia** n Australia
**Australian** adj australiano -a
**autumn** n el otoño m
**available** adj disponible

**B**
**baby** n el / la bebé m / f
**baby** adj de bebés, para
 bebés
 **Do you sell baby food?**
 ¿Venden comida para
 bebés?
**babysitter** n la niñera f
 **Do you have babysitters
 who speak English?** ¿Tiene
 niñeras que hablen inglés?
**back** n la espalda f
 **My back hurts.** Me duele la
 espalda.
**back rub** n el masaje de
 espalda m
**backed up (toilet)** adj tapado -a
 **The toilet is backed up.** El
 inodoro está tapado.
**bag** n la bolsa f, el bolso m

**airsickness bag** bolsa para
 mareos
 **My bag was stolen.** Mi
 bolsa fue robada.
 **I lost my bag.** Perdí mi
 bolsa.
**bag** v empacar p22
**baggage** n el equipaje m
**baggage** adj de equipaje
 **baggage claim** reclamo de
 equipaje
**bait** n la carnada f, el cebo m
**balance (on bank account)** n
 el balance m
**balance** v balancear p22
**balcony** n el balcón m
**ball (sport)** n la bola f
**ballroom dancing** n el baile
 de salón m
**band (musical)** n la banda f
**band-aid** n vendaje m,
 venda f
**bank** n el banco m
 **Can you help me find a
 bank?** ¿Puede ayudarme a
 encontrar un banco?
**bar** n la cantina f, la taberna f
**barber** n el barbero m
**bass (instrument)** n el contrabajo m
**bath** n el baño m
**bathroom (restroom)** n el
 baño m
 **Where is the nearest public
 bathroom?** ¿Dónde está el
 baño público más cercano?

**bathtub** n la bañera f, la tina de baño f

**bathe, to bathe oneself** v bañarse **p22, 35**

**battery (for flashlight)** n la pila f

**battery (for car)** n la batería f, el acumulador m, la acumuladora f

**bee** n la abeja f

  **I was stung by a bee.** Me picó una abeja.

**be, to be (temporary state, condition, mood)** v estar **p27**

**be, to be (permanent quality)** v ser **p28**

**beach** n la playa

**beard** n barba f

**beautiful** adj bello -a

**bed** n la cama f

**beer** n la cerveza f

  **beer on tap** cerveza de barril

**begin** v comenzar **p31**

**behave** v comportar **p22**

**behind** adv detrás

**below** adv debajo

**belt** n el cinturón m

  **conveyor belt** correa transportadora

**berth** n el camarote m

**best** mejor

**bet, to bet** v apostar **p35** (like jugar)

**better** mejor

**big** adj grande

**bilingual** adj bilingüe

**bill (currency)** n el billete m

**bill** v facturar **p22**

**biography** n la biografía f

**biracial** adj biracial

**bird** n el pájaro m

**birth control** n los anticonceptivos m ,

**birth control** adj anticonceptivo -a ,

  **I'm out of birth control pills.** Se me acabaron las pastillas anticonceptivas.

  **I need more birth control pills.** Necesito más pastillas anticonceptivas.

**bit (small amount)** n un poco m

**black** adj negro -a

**blanket** n la cobija f, la frazada f

**bleach** n el blanqueador m

**blind** adj ciego -a

**block** v bloquear **p22**

**blond(e)** adj rubio -a

**blouse** n la blusa f

**blue** adj azul

**blurry** adj borroso -a

**board** n bordo

  **on board** a bordo

**board** v abordar **p22**

**boarding pass** n la boleta de abordaje f

**boat** n el barco m

**Bolivian** adj boliviano -a

**bomb** n la bomba f

**book** n el libro m

**bookstore** n la librería f

**boss** n el jefe m, la jefa f

**bottle** *n* la botella *f*

> **May I heat this (baby) bottle someplace?** ¿Puedo calentar esta botella en algún lugar?

**box (seat)** *n* el palco *m*

**box office** *n* la boletería *f*

**boy** *n* el niño *m*

**boyfriend** *n* el novio *m*

**braid** *n* la trenza *f*

**braille, American** *n* el braille americano *m*

**brake** *n* el freno *m*

> **emergency brake** el freno de emergencia

**brake** *v* frenar p22

**brandy** *n* el brandy *m*

**bread** *n* el pan *m*

**break** *v* romper p22

**breakfast** *n* el desayuno *m*

> **What time is breakfast?** ¿A qué hora es el desayuno?

**bridge (across a river, dental)** *n* el puente *m*

**briefcase** *n* el maletín *m*

**bright** *adj* brillante

**broadband** *n* la banda ancha *f*

**bronze** *adj* bronce

**brother** *n* el hermano *m*

**brown** *adj* café, castaño -a, moreno -a, pardo -a

**brunette** *n* el moreno *m*, la morena *f*

**Buddhist** *n* el budista *m*, la budista *f*

**budget** *n* el presupuesto *m*

**buffet** *n* el bufé *m*

**bug** *n* el insecto *m*, el bicho *m*

**bull** *n* el toro *m*

**bullfight** *n* la corrida de toros *f*

**bullfighter** *n* el torero *m*, el matador *m*

**burn** *v* quemar p22

> **Can I burn a CD here?** ¿Puedo quemar un CD aquí?

**bus** *n* el autobús *m*

> **Where is the bus stop?** ¿Dónde es la parada de autobuses?
>
> **Which bus goes to ____?** ¿Cuál autobús va hacia ____?

**business** *n* el negocio *m*

**business** *adj* de negocios

> **business center** centro de negocios

**busy** *adj* concurrido -a (restaurant), ocupado -a (phone)

**butter** *n* la mantequilla *f*

**buy, to buy** *v* comprar p22

## C

**café** *n* el café *m*

> **Internet café** cibercafé

**call, to call** *v* llamar (shout) telefonear (phone) p22

**camp, to camp** *v* acampar p22

**camper** *n* el campista *m*

**camping** *adj* para acampar

> **Do we need a camping permit?** ¿Necesitamos un permiso para acampar?

**campsite** n el campamento m

**can** n la lata f

**can (able to)** v poder **p31**

**Canada** n Canadá

**Canadian** adj canadiense

**cancel, to** v cancelar **p22**

My flight was canceled. *Mi vuelo fue cancelado.*

**canvas** n el lienzo m (for painting), la lona f (material)

**cappuccino** n el cappuccino m

**car** n el auto m

car rental agency *agencia de alquiler de autos*

I need a rental car. *Necesito un auto alquilado.*

**card** n la tarjeta f

Do you accept credit cards? *¿Aceptan tarjetas de crédito?*

May I have your business card? *¿Me puede dar su tarjeta de presentación?*

**car seat (child's safety seat)** n el asiento para niños m

Do you rent car seats for children? *¿Ustedes alquilan asientos para niños para el auto?*

**carsickness** n el mareo de auto m

**cash** n el efectivo m

cash only *efectivo solamente*

**cash, to cash** v hacer efectivo **p30**

to cash out (gambling) *hacer efectivo*

**cashmere** n el cachemir m

**casino** n el casino m

**cat** n el gato m, la gata f

**Catholic** adj católico -a

**cavity (tooth cavity)** n la carie f

I think I have a cavity. *Creo que tengo una carie.*

**CD** n el CD m, el disco compacto m

**CD player** n el lector de discos compactos m

**celebrate, to celebrate** v celebrar **p22**

**cell phone** n el teléfono celular m

**centimeter** n el centímetro m

**chamber music** n la música de cámara f

**change (money)** n el cambio m

I'd like change, please. *Quisiera obtener cambio, por favor.*

This isn't the correct change. *Esto no es el cambio correcto.*

**change (to change money, clothes)** v cambiar **p22**

**changing room** n el cuarto de cambio m

**charge, to charge (money)** v cobrar **p22**

**charge, to charge (a battery)** v recargar **p22**

**charmed** adj encantado -a

**charred (meat)** adj achicharrado -a

**charter, to charter** v fletar p22

**cheap** adj barato -a

**check** n el cheque m

Do you accept travelers' checks? ¿Aceptan cheques de viajero?

**check, to check** v verificar p22

**checked (pattern)** adj a cuadros

**check-in** n registro

What time is check-in? ¿A qué hora es el registro?

**check-out** n la salida f

check-out time la hora de salida

What time is check-out? ¿A que hora es la salida?

**check out, to check out** v despedirse p32, 35 (like pedir)

**cheese** n el queso m

**chicken** n el pollo m

**child** n el niño m, la niña f

**children** n los niños m

Are children allowed? ¿Se permiten niños?

Do you have children's programs? ¿Tienen programas para niños?

Do you have a children's menu? ¿Tienen un menú para niños?

**Chinese** adj chino -a

**chiropractor** n el quiropráctico m

**church** n la iglesia f

**cigar** n el cigarro m

**cigarette** n el cigarrillo m

a pack of cigarettes un paquete de cigarrillos

**cinema** n el cine m, el cinema m

**city** n la ciudad f

**claim** n el reclamo m

I'd like to file a claim. Quisiera presentar un reclamo.

**clarinet** n el clarinete m

**class** n la clase f

business class clase de negocios

economy class clase económica

first class primera clase

**classical (music)** adj clásico -a

**clean** adj limpiado -a

**clean, to clean** v limpiar p22

Please clean the room today. Por favor limpia la habitación hoy.

**clear** v aclarar p22

**clear** adj claro -a

**climbing** n la escalada f

**climb, to climb** v escalar, subir p22, 23

to climb a mountain escalar una montaña

to climb stairs subir las escaleras

**close, to close** v cerrar pp31 (like comenzar)

**close (near)** cerca, cercano

**closed** adj cerrado -a

**cloudy** *adj* nublado -a

**clover** *n* el trébol *m*

**go clubbing, to go clubbing** *v* ir a los clubes nocturnos p25

**coat** *n* el abrigo *m*

**cockfight** *n* la pelea de gallos *f*

**coffee** *n* el café *m*

   **iced coffee** *café helado*

**cognac** *n* el coñac *m*

**coin** *n* la moneda *f*

**cold** *n* el resfriado *m*

   **I have a cold.** *Tengo un resfriado.*

**cold** *adj* frío -a

   **I'm cold.** *Tengo frío.*

   **It's cold out.** *Hace frío.*

**coliseum** *n* el coliseo *m*

**collect** *adj* a cobro revertido

   **I'd like to place a collect call.** *Quisiera hacer una llamada a cobro revertido.*

**collect, to collect** *v* recolectar p22

**college** *n* la universidad *f*

**Colombian** *adj* colombiano -a

**color** *n* el color *m*

**color** *v* colorear p22

**computer** *n* la computadora *f*

**concert** *n* el concierto *m*

**condition** *n* la condición *f*

   **in good / bad condition** *en buena / mala condición*

**condom** *n* el condón *m*

   **Do you have a condom?** *¿Tienes un condón?*

   **not without a condom** *no sin un condón*

**confirm, to confirm** *v* confirmar p22

   **I'd like to confirm my reservation.** *Quisiera confirmar mi reservación.*

**confused** *adj* confundido -a

**congested** *adj* congestionado -a

**connection speed** *n* la velocidad de conexión *f*

**constipated** *adj* estreñido -a

   **I'm constipated.** *Estoy estreñido -a.*

**contact lens** *n* el lente de contacto *m*

   **I lost my contact lens.** *Perdí mi lente de contacto.*

**continue, to continue** *v* continuar p22

**convertible** *n* el convertible *m*

**cook, to cook** *v* cocinar p22

   **I'd like a room where I can cook.** *Quisiera una habitación donde pueda cocinar.*

**cookie** *n* la galleta *f*

**copper** *adj* cobre

**corner** *n* la esquina *f*

   **on the corner** *en la esquina*

**correct** *v* corregir p23

**correct** *adj* correcto -a

   **Am I on the correct train?** *¿Estoy en el tren correcto?*

**cost, to cost** *v* costar p35 (like *jugar*)

   **How much does it cost?** *¿Cuánto cuesta?*

**Costa Rican** *adj* costarricense

**costume** n el disfraz m
**cotton** n el algodón m
**cough** n la tos f
**cough** v toser **p23**
**counter (in bar)** n el mostrador m
**country-and-western** n la música country f
**court (legal)** n la corte f
**court (sport)** n la cancha f
**courteous** adj cortés
**cousin** n el primo m, la prima f
**cover charge (in bar)** n el cargo de entrada m
**cow** n la vaca f
**crack (in glass object)** n la grieta f
**craftsperson** n el artesano m, la artesana f
**cream** n la crema f
**credit card** n la tarjeta de crédito f

**Do you accept credit cards?** ¿Aceptan tarjetas de crédito?

**crib** n la cuna f
**crown (dental)** n la corona f
**curb** n el borde de la acera m
**curl** n el rizo m
**curly** adj rizado -a
**currency exchange** n el cambio de moneda m ,

**Where is the nearest currency exchange?** ¿Dónde está el cambio de moneda más cercano?

**current (water)** n la corriente f

**customs** n aduana f
**cut (wound)** n el corte m, la cortadura f

**I have a bad cut.** Tengo una cortadura seria.

**cut, to cut** v cortar **p22**
**cybercafé** n el cibercafé m

**Where can I find a cybercafé?** ¿Dónde puedo encontrar un cibercafé?

## D

**damaged** adj dañado -a
**Damn!** expletive ¡Maldición!
**dance** v bailar **p22**
**danger** n el peligro m
**dark** n la oscuridad f
**dark** adj oscuro -a
**daughter** n la hija f
**day** n el día m

**the day before yesterday** el día antes de ayer / anteayer

**these last few days** estos últimos días

**dawn** n la madrugada m
**at dawn** al amanecer
**deaf** adj sordo -a
**deal (bargain)** n la ganga f

**What a great deal!** ¡Que ganga increíble!

**deal (cards)** v repartir **p23**
**Deal me in.** Repárteme.
**December** n diciembre
**declined** adj rechazado -a

**Was my credit card declined?** ¿Mi tarjeta de crédito fue rechazada?

**declare** v declarar p22

I have nothing to declare.
*No tengo nada que declarar.*

**deep** adj profundo -a

**delay** n el retraso m

How long is the delay?
*¿Cuán largo es el retraso?*

**delighted** adj deleitado -a

**democracy** n la democracia f

**dent** v abollar p22

He / She dented the car. *Él / Ella abolló el auto.*

**dentist** n el dentista m

**denture** n la dentadura f

denture plate *dentadura*

**departure** n la salida f

**designer** n el diseñador m, la diseñadora f

**dessert** n el postre m

dessert menu *el menú de postres*

**destination** n el destino m

**diabetic** adj diabético -a

**dial (a phone)** v marcar p22

dial direct *marcar directo*

**diaper** n el pañal m

Where can I change a diaper? *¿Dónde puedo cambiar un pañal?*

**diarrhea** n la diarrea f

**dictionary** n el diccionario m

**different (other)** adj diferente

**difficult** adj difícil

**dinner** n la cena f

**directory assistance (phone)** n la asistencia telefónica f

**disability** n la incapacidad f

**disappear** v desaparecer p33 (like *conocer*)

**disco** n el disco m

**disconnected** adj desconectado -a

Operator, I was disconnected. *Operadora, fui desconectado -a.*

**discount** n el descuento m

Do I qualify for a discount? *¿Cualifico para un descuento?*

**dish** n el plato m

**dive** v bucear p22

scuba dive *buceo con tanques de oxígeno*

**divorced** adj divorciado -a

**dizzy** adj mareado -a

**do, to do** v hacer p30

**doctor** n el doctor m, la doctora f,

**doctor's office** n la oficina del doctor m

**dog** n el perro m

service dog *perro de servicio*

**dollar** n el dólar m

**door** n la puerta f

**double** adj doble

double bed *cama doble*
double vision *visión doble*

**down** adj abajo

**download** v descargar p22

**downtown** n el centro de la ciudad m

**dozen** n la docena f

**drain** n el drenaje m

**drama** n el drama m

**drawing (work of art)** *n el dibujo m*

**dress (garment)** *n el vestido m*

**dress (general attire)** *n la vestimenta f*

What's the dress code? *¿Cuál es el código de vestimenta?*

**dress** *v vestirse* **p32** (like *pedir*)

Should I dress up for that affair. *Debería vestirme para ese evento.*

**dressing (salad)** *n el aderezo m*

**dried** *adj secado -a*

**drink** *n la bebida f*

I'd like a drink. *Quisiera una bebida.*

**drink, to drink** *v beber* **p23**

**drip** *v gotear* **p22**

**drive** *v guiar, manejar* **p22**

**driver** *n el chofer m*

**driving range** *n el campo para golpear pelotas m*

**drum** *n el tambor m*

**dry** *adj seco -a*

This towel isn't dry. *Esta toalla no está seca.*

**dry, to dry** *v secar* **p22**

I need to dry my clothes. *Necesito secar mi ropa.*

**dry cleaner** *n la tintorería f*

**dry cleaning** *n la limpieza en seco f*

**duck** *n el pato m*

**duty-free** *adj libre de impuestos*

**duty-free shop** *n la tienda libre de impuestos f*

**DVD** *n el DVD m*

Do the rooms have DVD players? *¿Las habitaciones tienen lectores de DVD?*

Where can I rent DVDs or videos? *¿Dónde puedo alquilar DVD o videos?*

**E**

**early** *adj temprano -a*

It's early. *Es temprano.*

**eat** *v comer* **p23**

to eat out *comer afuera*

**economy** *n la economía f*

**Ecuadorian** *adj ecuatoriano -a*

**editor** *n el editor m, la editora f*

**educator** *n el educador m, la educadora f*

**eight** *n el ocho m*

**eighteen** *n el dieciocho m*

**eighth** *n el octavo m*

**eighty** *n el ochenta m*

**election** *n la elección f*

**electrical hookup** *n la conexión eléctrica f*

**elevator** *n el elevador m*

**eleven** *n el once m*

**e-mail** *n el e-mail m*

May I have your e-mail address? *¿Me puede dar su dirección de e-mail?*

e-mail message *mensaje de e-mail*

**e-mail, to send e-mail** *v enviar un e-mail* **p22**

**embarrassed** *adj avergonzado -a*

**embassy** n la embajada f

**emergency** n la emergencia f

**emergency brake** n el freno de emergencia m

**emergency exit** n la salida de emergencia f

**employee** n el empleado m, la empleada f

**employer** n el patrono m

**engine** n el motor m

**engineer** n el ingeniero m, la ingeniera f

**England** n Inglaterra

**English** n, adj el inglés m, la inglesa f

**Do you speak English?** ¿Habla inglés?

**enjoy, to enjoy** v disfrutar p22

**enter, to enter** v entrar p22

**Do not enter.** No entre.

**enthusiastic** adj entusiasmado -a

**entrance** n la entrada f

**envelope** n el sobre m

**environment** n el ambiente m

**escalator** n la escalera mecánica f

**espresso** n el café expreso m

**exchange rate** n la tasa de cambio f

**What is the exchange rate for US / Canadian dollars?** ¿Cuál es la tasa de cambio para los dólares americanos / canadienses?

**excuse (pardon)** v excusar, perdonar p22

**Excuse me.** Perdone.

**exhausted** adj exhausto -a

**exhibit** n la exhibición f

**exit** n la salida f

**not an exit** no es salida

**exit** v salir p23 (I leave salgo)

**expensive** adj caro -a

**explain** v explicar p22

**express** adj expreso -a ,

**express check-in** registro expreso

**extra (additional)** adj adicional

**extra-large** adj extra grande

**eye** n el ojo m

**eyebrow** n la ceja f

**eyeglasses** n los espejuelos m

**eyelash** n la pestaña f

**F**

**fabric** n la tela f

**face** n la cara f

**faint** v desmayar p22

**fall (season)** n el otoño m

**fall** v caer p23 (I fall caigo)

**family** n la familia f

**fan** n el abanico m

**far** lejos

**How far is it to _____?** ¿Cuán lejos es hasta _____?

**fare** n la tarifa f

**fast** adj rápido -a ,

**fat** adj gordo -a ,

**father** n el padre m

**faucet** n el grifo m

**fault** n la culpa f

**I'm at fault.** Es mi culpa.

It was his fault. *Fue su culpa.*

**fax** *n* el fax *m*

**February** *n* febrero

**fee** *n* el honorario *m*

**female** *adj* hembra

**fiancé(e)** *n* el prometido *m*, la prometida *f*

**fifteen** *adj* el quince *m*

**fifth** *adj* el quinto -a *m*

**fifty** *adj* el cincuenta *m*

**find** *v* encontrar, hallar **p22**

**fine (for traffic violation)** *n* la multa *f*

**fine** *bien*

I'm fine. *Estoy bien.*

**fire!** *n* el fuego *m*

**first** *adj* primero -a

**fishing pole** *n* la caña de pescar *f*

**fitness center** *n* el centro de gimnasia *m*

**fit (clothes)** *v* entallarse **p22, 35**

Does this look like it fits? *¿Esto parece que me entalla?*

**fitting room** *n* el probador *m*

**five** *adj* cinco

**flight** *n* el vuelo *m*

Where do domestic flights arrive / depart? *¿Adónde llegan / De dónde salen los vuelos domésticos?*

Where do international flights arrive / depart? *¿Adónde llegan / De dónde salen los vuelos internacionales?*

What time does this flight leave? *¿A qué hora sale este vuelo?*

**flight attendant** *asistente de vuelo*

**floor** *n* el piso *m*

ground floor *planta baja*

second floor *primer piso*

*\*Note that in Spanish, the second floor is called the first, the third is the second, etc.*

**flower** *n* la flor *f*

**flush (gambling)** *n* la escalera *f*

**flush, to flush** *v* bajar el inodoro **p22**

This toilet won't flush. *El inodoro no baja.*

**flute** *n* la flauta *f*

**food** *n* la comida *f*

**foot (body part, measurement)** *n* el pie *m*

**forehead** *n* la frente *f*

**formula** *n* la fórmula *f*

Do you sell infants' formula? *¿Venden fórmula para infantes?*

**forty** *adj* cuarenta

**forward** *adj* delante

**four** *adj* cuatro

**fourteen** *adj* catorce

**fourth** *adj* cuarto -a

one-fourth *un cuarto*

**fragile** *adj* frágil

**freckle** *n* la peca *f*

**French** *adj* francés

**fresh** *adj* fresco -a
**Friday** *n* el viernes *m*
**friend** *n* el amigo *m* la amiga *f*
**front** *adj* delantero
  **front desk** la recepción
  **front door** la puerta principal / puerta del frente
**fruit** *n* la fruta *f*
**fruit juice** *n* el jugo de fruta *m*
**full, to be full (after a meal)** *adj* lleno -a
**Full house!** *n* ¡Full house!
**fuse** *n* el fusible *m*

**G**

**gallon** *n* el galón *m*
**garlic** *n* el ajo *m*
**gas** *n* el combustible *m*, la gasolina *f*
  **gas gauge** indicador de combustible
  **out of gas** sin combustible
**gate (at airport)** *n* la puerta de salida *f*
**German** *adj* alemán, alemana
**gift** *n* el regalo *m*
**gin** *n* la ginebra *f*
**girl** *n* la chica *f*, la muchacha *f*
**girlfriend** *n* la novia *f*
**give, to give** *v* dar **p22** (I give doy)
**glass** *n* la copa *f*
  **Do you have it by the glass?** ¿Lo tienen por la copa?

  **I'd like a glass please.** *Quisiera una copa por favor.*
**glasses (eye)** *n* las gafas *f*
  **I need new glasses.** *Necesito gafas nuevas.*
**glove** *n* el guante *m*
**go, to go** *v* ir **p25**
**goal (sport)** *n* el gol *m*
**goalie** *n* el portero *m*
**gold** *adj* oro
**golf** *n* el golf *m*
**golf, to go golfing** *v* jugar golf **p35**
**good** *adj* bueno -a
**goodbye** *n* el adiós *m*
**grade (school)** *n* el grado *m*
**gram** *n* el gramo *m*
**grandfather** *n* el abuelo *m*
**grandmother** *n* la abuela *f*
**grandparent** *n* el abuelo *m*, la abuela *f*
**grape** *n* la uva *f*
**gray** *adj* gris
**great** *adj* grandioso -a
**Greek** *adj* griego -a
**Greek Orthodox** *adj* ortodoxo griego
**green** *adj* verde
**groceries** *n* los comestibles *m*
**group** *n* el grupo *m*
**grow, to grow (get larger)** *v* crecer **p23**
  **Where did you grow up?** *¿Dónde creciste?*

**guard** n el guardia m

  **security guard** guardia de seguridad

**Guatemalan** adj guatemalteco -a

**guest** n el invitado m, la invitada f

**guide (of tours)** n el / la guía m f

**guide (publication)** n la guía f

**guide, to guide** v guiar **p22**

**guided tour** n la excursión guiada f

**guitar** n la guitarra f

**gym** n el gimnasio m

**gynecologist** n el ginecólogo m

**H**

**hair** n el pelo m, el cabello m

**haircut** n el recorte de pelo m

  **I need a haircut.** Necesito un recorte de pelo.

  **How much is a haircut?** ¿Cuánto cuesta un recorte de pelo?

**hairdresser** n el peluquero m, la peluquera f

**hair dryer** n la secadora de pelo f

**half** n la mitad f

  **one-half** medio

**hallway** n el pasillo m

**hand** n la mano f

**handicapped-accessible** adj accesible para personas con impedimentos

**handle, to handle** v manejar **p22**

**handsome** adj guapo -a, bien parecido -a

**hangout (hot spot)** n el lugar de reunión m

**hang out (to relax)** v pasar el rato **p22**

**hang up (to end a phone call)** v colgar **p35** (like jugar)

**hanger** n la percha f

**happy** adj alegre

**hard** adj difícil (difficult), duro -a (firm)

**hat** n el sombrero m, el gorro m

**have** v tener **p29**

**hazel** adj color café

**headache** n el dolor de cabeza m

**headlight** n el foco delantero m

**headphones** n los audífonos m

**hear** v escuchar **p22**

**hearing-impaired** adj con impedimentos auditivos

**heart** n el corazón m

**heart attack** n el ataque cardiaco m, el ataque al corazón m

**hectare** n la hectárea f

**hello** n hola

**Help!** n ¡Ayuda!

**help, to help** v ayudar **p22**

**hen** n la gallina f

**her** adj de ella

**herb** n la hierba f

**here** n aquí

**high** adj alto -a

**highlights (hair)** n los destellos m

**highway** *n la autopista f*
**hike, to hike** *v excursionar* **p22**
**him** *pron él*
**Hindu** *adj hindú*
**hip-hop** *n hip-hop*
**his** *adj de él*
**historical** *adj histórico -a*
**history** *n la historia f*
**hobby** *n el pasatiempo m*
**hold, to hold** *v sujetar* **p22**
  **to hold hands** *sujetar las manos*
  **Would you hold this for me?** *¿Sujetas esto por mí?*
**hold, to hold (to pause)** *v esperar* **p22**
  **Hold on a minute!** *¡Espera un minuto!*
  **I'll hold.** *Espero.*
**hold, to hold (gambling)** *v quedar* **p22**
**holiday** *n el día de fiesta m*
**home** *n el hogar m, la residencia f*
**homemaker** *n la ama de casa f*
**Honduran** *adj hondureño -a*
**horn** *n la bocina f*
**horse** *n el caballo m*
**hostel** *n la hospedería f*
**hot** *adj caliente*
**hot chocolate** *n el chocolate caliente m*
**hotel** *n el hotel m*
  **Do you have a list of local hotels?** *¿Tiene una lista de hoteles locales?*

**hour** *n la hora f*
**hours (at museum)** *n el horario m*
**how** *adv cómo, cuánto (how much), cuántos (how many)*
**humid** *adj húmedo -a*
**hundred** *n cien m, cientos m*
**hurry** *v apresurar* **p22, 35**
  **I'm in a hurry.** *Tengo prisa.*
  **Hurry, please!** *¡Apresúrate por favor!*
**hurt, to hurt** *v herir* **p31** *(like querer)*
  **Ouch! That hurts!** *¡Ay! ¡Eso duele!*
**husband** *n el esposo m*

**I**
**I** *pron yo*
**ice** *n el hielo m*
**identification** *n la identificación f*
**inch** *n la pulgada f*
**indigestion** *n la indigestión f*
**inexpensive** *adj económico -a, barato -a*
**infant** *n el infante m*
  **Are infants allowed?** *¿Se permiten infantes?*
**information** *n la información f*
**information booth** *n el puesto de información m*
**injury** *n la lesión f*
**insect repellent** *n el repelente para insectos m*
**inside** *adentro*
**insult** *v insultar* **p22**

**insurance** n el seguro m
**intercourse (sexual)** n el coito m
**interest rate** n la tasa de interés f
**intermission** n el interludio m
**Internet** n el Internet m

> **High-speed Internet** Internet de alta velocidad
> **Do you have Internet access?** ¿Tienen acceso al Internet?
> **Where can I find an Internet café?** ¿Dónde puedo encontrar un ciber-café?

**interpreter** n el / la intérprete m f

> **I need an interpreter.** Necesito un intérprete.

**introduce, to introduce** v introducir p33 (like conocer)

> **I'd like to introduce you to ____.** Quisiera introducirle a ____.

**Ireland** n Irlanda
**Irish** adj irlandés, irlandesa
**is** v See be (to be). p27, 28
**Italian** adj italiano -a

**J**

**jacket** n la chaqueta f
**January** n enero
**Japanese** adj japonés / japonesa
**jazz** n el jazz m
**Jewish** adj judío -a

**jog, to run** v trotar p22
**juice** n el jugo m
**June** n junio
**July** n julio

**K**

**keep, to keep** v guardar p22
**kid** n el niño m

> **Are kids allowed?** ¿Se permiten niños?
> **Do you have kids' programs?** ¿Tienen programas para niños?
> **Do you have a kids' menu?** ¿Tienen un menú para niños?

**kilo** n el kilo m
**kilometer** n el kilómetro m
**kind** n el tipo m, la clase F (type)

> **What kind is it?** ¿Qué clase es?

**kiss** n el beso m
**kitchen** n la cocina f
**know, to know (something)** v saber p33
**know, to know (someone)** v conocer p33
**kosher** adj kósher

**L**

**lactose-intolerant** adj intolerante a la lactosa
**land, to land** v aterrizar p22
**landscape** n el paisaje m
**language** n el lenguaje m
**laptop** n la computadora portátil f

**large** *adj grande*

**last, to last** *v durar* p22

**last** *adv último -a*

**late** *adj tarde*

Please don't be late. *Por favor no estés tarde.*

**later** *adv luego, más tarde*

See you later. *Te veo luego.*

**laundry** *n la lavandería f*

**lavender** *adj lavanda*

**law** *n la ley f*

**lawyer** *n el abogado f*

**least** *n al menos f*

**least** *adj mínimo*

**leather** *n el cuero m*

**leave, to leave (depart)** *v salir* p23 (I leave *salgo*)

**left** *adj izquierdo -a*

on the left *a la izquierda*

**leg** *n la pierna f*

**lemonade** *n la limonada f*

**less** *adj menos*

**lesson** *n la lección f*

**license** *n la licencia f*

driver's license *licencia de conducir*

**life preserver** *n el salvavidas m*

**light** *n (lamp) la luz f*

**light (for cigarette)** *n la lumbre f*

May I offer you a light? *¿Puedo ofrecerle lumbre?*

**lighter (cigarette)** *n el encendedor m*

**like, desire** *v gustar* (to please) p34

I would like ____. *Me gustaría ____.*

**like, to like** *v gustar* (to please) p34

I like this place. *Me gusta este lugar.*

**limo** *n la limosina f*

**liquor** *n el licor m*

**liter** *n el litro m*

**little** *adj pequeño -a (size), poco -a (amount)*

**live, to live** *v vivir* p23

Where do you live? *¿Dónde vives?*

**living** *n la vida f*

What do you do for a living? *¿Qué haces para ganarte la vida?*

**local** *adj local*

**lock** *n el candado m*

**lock, to lock** *v cerrar con llave* p31 (like *comenzar*)

I can't lock the door. *No puedo cerrar la puerta con llave.*

I'm locked out. *Me quedé fuera sin llave.*

**locker** *n el casillero m*

storage locker *casillero de almacén*

locker room *vestuario*

**long** *adv mucho tiempo, bastante*

For how long? *¿Por cuánto tiempo?*

**long** *adj largo -a*

**look, to look** *v (to observe) mirar* p22

**I'm just looking.** *Sólo estoy mirando.*

**Look here!** *¡Mira aquí!*

look, to look *v* (to appear) *ver* **p23** (I see *veo*)

**How does this look?** *¿Cómo se ve esto?*

look for, to look for (to search) *v buscar* **p22**

**I'm looking for a porter.** *Estoy buscando un portero.*

loose *adj suelto -a*

lose, to lose *v perder* **p31** (like *querer*)

**I lost my passport.** *Perdí mi pasaporte.*

**I lost my wallet.** *Perdí mi cartera.*

**I'm lost.** *Estoy perdido -a.*

lost. See lose *perdido -a*

loud *adj ruidoso -a*

loudly *adv ruidosamente*

lounge *n el salón público m*

lounge, to lounge *v relajarse* **p22, 35**

love *n el amor m*

love, to love *v amar* **p22**

to love (family) *amar*

to love (a friend) *amar, querer*

to love (a lover) *amar*

to make love *hacer el amor*

low *adj bajo -a*

lunch *n el almuerzo m*

luggage *n el equipaje m*

**Where do I report lost luggage?** *¿Dónde reporto el equipaje perdido?*

**Where is the lost luggage claim?** *¿Dónde está el reclamo de equipaje?*

## M

machine *n la máquina f*

made of *adj hecho de*

magazine *n la revista f*

maid (hotel) *n la camarera f*

maiden *adj soltera*

**That's my maiden name.** *Ese es mi apellido de soltera.*

mail *n el correo m*

air mail *correo aéreo*

registered mail *correo certificado*

mail *v enviar* **p22**

make, to make *v hacer* **p30**

makeup *n el maquillaje m*

make up, to make up (apologize) *v hacer las paces* **p30**

make up, to make up (apply cosmetics) *v maquillar* **p22**

male *n el varón m*

male *adj masculino*

mall *n el centro comercial m*

man *n el hombre m*

manager *n el / la gerente m f*

manual (instruction booklet) *n el manual m*

many *adj muchos -as*

map *n el mapa m*

March (month) *n marzo*

market *n el mercado m*

flea market *mercado de pulgas / pulguero*

**open-air market** *mercado al aire libre*

**married** *adj casado -a*

**marry, to marry** *v casarse* **p22, 35**

**massage, to massage** *v dar masaje* **p22**

**match (sport)** *n el partido m*

**match** *n el fósforo m*

**book of matches** *libro de fósforos*

**match, to match** *v igualar, hacer juego* **p22, 30**

**Does this ___ match my outfit?** *¿Este ___ hace juego con mi vestido?*

**May (month)** *n mayo*

**may** *v aux poder* **p31**

**May I ___?** *¿Puedo?*

**maybe** *talvez*

**meal** *n la comida f*

**meat** *n la carne f*

**meatball** *n la albóndiga f*

**medication** *n la medicina f*

**medium (size)** *adj mediano -a*

**medium rare (meat)** *adj a medio cocer*

**medium well (meat)** *adj medio bien cocido*

**member** *n el miembro m*

**menu** *n el menú m*

**May I see a menu?** *¿Puedo ver un menú?*

**children's menu** *menú para niños*

**diabetic menu** *menú diabético*

**kosher menu** *menú kósher*

**metal detector** *n el detector de metales m*

**meter** *n el metro m*

**Mexican** *adj mexicano -a*

**middle** *adj de en medio*

**midnight** *n la medianoche f*

**mile** *n la milla f*

**military** *n el ejército m, la milicia f*

**milk** *n la leche f*

**milliliter** *n el mililitro m*

**millimeter** *n el milímetro m*

**minute** *n el minuto m*

**in a minute** *en un minuto*

**miss, to miss (a flight)** *v perder* **p31** (like *querer*)

**missing** *adj perdido -a, ausente*

**mistake** *n el error m*

**moderately priced** *adj de precio moderado*

**mole (facial feature)** *n el lunar m*

**Monday** *n el lunes m*

**money** *n el dinero m*

**money transfer** *transferencia de dinero*

**month** *n el mes m*

**morning** *n la mañana f*

**in the morning** *en la mañana*

**mosque** *n la mezquita f*

**mother** *n la madre f*

**mother, to mother** *v cuidar* **p22**

**motorcycle** *n la motocicleta f*

**mountain** *n* la montaña *f*
  **mountain climbing** escalado de montaña
**mouse** *n* el ratón *m*
**mouth** *n* la boca *f*
**move, to move** *v* mover **p23**
**movie** *n* la película *f*
**much** *n* mucho *m*, la gran cantidad *f*
**mug, to mug (someone)** *v* asaltar **p22**
  **mugged** *adj* asaltado -a
**museum** *n* el museo *m*
**music** *n* la música *f*
  **live music** música en vivo
**musician** *n* el músico *m*, la musica *f*
**muslim** *adj* musulmán
**mustache** *n* el bigote *m*
**mystery (novel)** *n* la novela de misterio *f*

**N**
**name** *n* el nombre *m*
  **My name is ___.** Me llamo ___.
  **What's your name?** ¿Cómo se llama? / ¿Cuál es su nombre?
**napkin** *n* la servilleta *f*
**narrow** *adj* angosto -a
**nationality** *n* la nacionalidad *f*
**nausea** *n* la náusea *f*
**near** *adj* cercano -a
**nearby** *adj* cercano -a
**neat (tidy)** *adj* limpio -a
**need, to need** *v* necesitar **p22**

**neighbor** *n* el vecino *m*, la vecina *f*
**nephew** *n* el sobrino *m*
**network** *n* la red *f*
**new** *adj* nuevo -a
**newspaper** *n* el periódico *m*
**newsstand** *n* el puesto de periódicos *m*
**New Zealand** *n* Nueva Zelanda
**New Zealander** *adj* neozelandés, neozelandesa
**next** *prep* próximo, al lado
  **next to** al lado de
  **the next station** la próxima estación
**Nicaraguan** *adj* nicaragüense, nicaragüeña
**nice** *adj* agradable
**niece** *n* la sobrina *f*
**night** *n* la noche *f*
  **at night** en la noche
  **per night** por noche
**nightclub** *n* el club nocturno *m*
**nine** *adj* nueve
**nineteen** *adj* diecinueve
**ninety** *adj* noventa
**ninth** *adj* noveno -a
**no** *adv* no
**noisy** *adj* ruidoso -a
**none** *n* el ninguno *m*
**nonsmoking** *adj* de no fumar
  **nonsmoking area** área de no fumar
  **nonsmoking room** habitación de no fumar
**noon** *n* el mediodía *m*

nose *n* la nariz *f*

novel *n* la novela *f*

November *n* noviembre

now *adv* ahora

number *n* el número *m*

> **Which room number?** *¿Cuál es el número de la habitación?*
>
> **May I have your phone number?** *¿Me puede dar su número de teléfono?*

nurse *n* la enfermera *f*

nurse *v* amamantar **p22**

> **Do you have a place where I can nurse?** *¿Tienen un lugar dónde pueda amamantar?*

nursery *n* la guardería infantil *f*

> **Do you have a nursery?** *¿Tienen una guardería infantil?*

nut *n* la nuez *f*

## O

o'clock *adv* en punto

> **two o'clock** *dos en punto*

October *n* octubre

offer, to offer *v* ofrecer **p33** (like conocer)

officer *n* el oficial *m*, la oficial *f*

oil *n* el aceite *m* ,

okay *adv* OK, de acuerdo

old *adj* viejo -a

olive *n* la aceituna *f*

one *adj* uno -a

one way (traffic sign) *adj* en una sola dirección

open (business) *adj* abierto -a

> **Are you open?** *¿Están abierto?*

opera *n* la ópera *f*

operator (phone) *n* el operador *m*, la operadora *f*

optometrist *n* el optómetra *m*, la optometra *f*

orange (color) *adj* naranjo -a

orange juice *n* el jugo de naranja *m*

order, to order (demand) *v* pedir **p32**

order, to order (request) *v* ordenar **p22**

organic *adj* orgánico -a

Ouch! *interj* ¡ay!

outside *n* afuera

overcooked *adj* sobrecocido -a

overheat, to overheat *v* sobrecalentarse **p31** (like comenzar), 35

> **The car overheated.** *El auto se sobrecalentó.*

overflowing *adv* desbordante

oxygen tank *n* el tanque de oxígeno *m*

## P

package *n* el paquete *m*

pacifier *n* el chupete *m*

page, to page (someone) *v* mandar a llamar **p22**

paint, to paint *v* pintar **p22**

painting *n* la pintura *f*

pale *adj* pálido -a

ENGLISH–SPANISH

**Panamanian** adj panameño -a

**paper** n el papel

**parade** n la parada f

**Paraguayan** adj paraguayo -a

**parent** n el padre m

**park** n el parque m

**park, to park** v estacionar p22

  **no parking** no estacione

  **parking fee** tarifa de estacionamiento

  **parking garage** estacionamiento

**partner** n el compañero m, la compañera f

**party** n el partido m

**party** n la fiesta f

  **political party** partido político

**pass, to pass** v pasar p22

  **I'll pass.** Yo paso.

**passenger** n el pasajero m, la pasajera f

**passport** n el pasaporte m

  **I've lost my passport.** Perdí mi pasaporte.

**pay, to pay** v pagar p22

**peanut** n el cacahuate m

**pedestrian** adj peatonal

**pediatrician** n el pediatra m, la pediatra f

  **Can you recommend a pediatrician?** ¿Puede recomendar un pediatra?

**permit** n el permiso m

  **Do we need a permit?** ¿Necesitamos un permiso?

**permit, to permit** v permitir p23

**Peruvian** adj peruano -a

**phone** n el teléfono m

  **May I have your phone number?** ¿Me puede dar su número de teléfono?

  **Where can I find a public phone?** ¿Dónde puedo encontrar un teléfono público?

  **phone operator** operadora

  **Do you sell prepaid phones?** ¿Venden teléfonos prepagados?

**phone** adj telefónico -a

  **Do you have a phone directory?** ¿Tiene un directorio telefónico?

**phone call** n la llamada telefónica f

  **I need to make a collect phone call.** Necesito hacer una llamada telefónica con cargos revertidos.

  **an international phone call** una llamada internacional

**photocopy, to photocopy** v fotocopiar p22

**piano** n el piano m

**pillow** n la almohada f

  **down pillow** almohada de plumas

**pink** adj rosado -a

**pint** n la pinta f

**pizza** n la pizza f

**place, to place** v colocar p22

**plastic** n el plástico m

**play** n la obra de teatro f

**play, to play (a game)** v jugar p35

**play, to play (an instrument)** v tocar **p22**

**playground** n el patio de recreo m

**Do you have a playground?** ¿Tienen un patio de recreo?

**please (polite entreaty)** adv por favor

**please, to be pleasing to** v agradar **p22**

**pleasure** n el placer m

**It's a pleasure.** Es un placer.

**plug** n el enchufe m

**plug, to plug** v enchufar **p22**

**point, to point** v señalar, apuntar **p22**

**Would you point me in the direction of____?** ¿Me pude señalar la dirección de____?

**police** n la policía f

**police station** n la estación de policías f

**pool** n la piscina f

**pool (the game)** n el billar m

**pop music** n la música pop f

**popular** adj popular

**port (beverage)** n el oporto m

**port (for ship)** n el puerto m

**porter** n el portero m, la portera f

**portion** n la porción f

**portrait** n el retrato m

**postcard** n la postal f

**post office** n el correo m

**Where is the post office?** ¿Dónde está el correo?

**poultry** n las aves de corral f pl

**pound** n la libra f

**prefer, to prefer** v preferir **p31** (like querer)

**pregnant** adj embarazada

**prepared** adj preparado -a

**prescription** n la receta f

**price** n el precio m

**print, to print** v imprimir **p23**

**problem** n el problema m

**process, to process** v procesar **p22**

**product** n el producto m

**professional** adj profesional

**program** n el programa m

**May I have a program?** ¿Me puede dar un programa?

**Protestant** n protestante m

**publisher** n el editor m

**Puerto Rican** adj puertorriqueño -a m / f

**pull, to pull** v halar **p22**

**pump** n la bomba f

**purple** adj morado -a

**purse** n la cartera f, el bolso m

**push, to push** v empujar **p22**

**put, to put** v poner **p23** (I put pongo)

## Q

**quarter** adj un cuarto

**one-quarter** un cuarto

**quiet** adj tranquilo -a

## R

**rabbit** n el conejo m

**radio** n el radio m

satellite radio *radio por satélite*

rain, to rain *v llover* **p31** (like *poder*)

**Is it supposed to rain?** *¿Se supone que llueva?*

rainy *adj lluvioso -a*

**It's rainy.** *Está lluvioso.*

ramp, wheelchair *n la rampa para sillas de ruedas f*

rare (meat) *adj crudo -a*

rate (for car rental, hotel) *n la tarifa f*

**What's the rate per day?** *¿Cuál es la tarifa por día?*

**What's the rate per week?** *¿Cuál es la tarifa por semana?*

rate plan (cell phone) *n el plan de tarifa m*

rather *adv preferiblemente*

read, to read *v leer* **p23**

really *adv verdaderamente*

receipt *n el recibo m*

receive, to receive *v recibir* **p23**

recommend, to recommend *v recomendar* **p31** (like *comenzar*)

red *adj rojo -a*

redhead *n el pelirrojo m, la pelirroja f*

reef *n el arrecife m*

refill (of beverage) *n el relleno m*

refill (of prescription) *n el reabastecimiento m*

reggae *adj reggae*

relative (family) *n el pariente m*

remove, to remove *v remover* **p31** (like *poder*)

rent, to rent *v alquilar* **p22**

**I'd like to rent a car.** *Quisiera alquilar un auto.*

repeat, to repeat *v repetir* **p32** (like *pedir*)

**Would you please repeat that?** *¿Puede repetir eso por favor?*

reservation *n la reservación m*

**I'd like to make a reservation for ___.** *Quisiera hacer una reservación para ___.*

restaurant *n el restaurante? m*

**Where can I find a good restaurant?** *¿Dónde puedo encontrar un buen restaurante.*

restroom *n el baño m*

**Do you have a public restroom?** *¿Tienen un baño público?*

return, to return (to a place) *v regresar* **p22**

return, to return (something to a store) *v devolver* (**p31**, like *poder*)

ride, to ride *v correr* **p23**

right *adj derecho -a*

**It is on the right.** *Está a mano derecha.*

**Turn right at the corner.** *Vira a la derecha en la esquina.*

rights *n pl los derechos m*

**civil rights** *derechos civiles*

**river** n el río m

**road** n la carretera f

**road closed sign** n el letrero de carretera cerrada m

**rob, to rob** v robar **p22**

I've been robbed. Me han robado.

**rock and roll** n rock and roll

**rock climbing** n la escalada de rocas f

**rocks (ice)** n las rocas f

I'd like it on the rocks. Lo quisiera en las rocas.

**romance (novel)** n la novela de romance f

**romantic** adj romántico -a

**room (hotel)** n la habitación f

room for one / two habitación para uno / dos

room service servicio de habitaciones

**rope** n la cuerda f

**rose** n la rosa f

**royal flush** n la escalera real f

**rum** n el ron m

**run, to run** v correr **p23**

**S**

**sad** adj triste

**safe (for storing valuables)** n la caja fuerte

Do the rooms have safes? ¿Las habitaciones tienen cajas fuertes?

**safe (secure)** adj seguro -a

Is this area safe? ¿Esta área es segura?

**sail** n la vela f

**sail, to sail** v zarpar **p22**

When do we sail? ¿Cuándo zarpamos?

**salad** n la ensalada f

**salesperson** n el vendedor m, la vendedora f

**salt** n la sal f

Is that low-salt? ¿Eso es bajo en sal?

**Salvadorian** adj salvadoreño -a

**satellite** n el satélite m

satellite radio radio satélite

satellite tracking rastreo por satélite

**Saturday** n el sábado m

**sauce** n la salsa f

**say, to say** v decir (**p32**, like pedir) (I say digo)

**scan, to scan** v (document) escanear **p22**

**schedule** n el itinerario m

**school** n la escuela f

**scooter** n la motoneta f

**score** n la puntuación f

**Scottish** adj escocés

**scratched** adj rayado -a

scratched surface superficie rayada

**scuba dive, to scuba dive** v bucear con tanques de oxígeno **p22**

**sculpture** n la escultura f

**seafood** n los mariscos m

**search** n la búsqueda f

hand search búsqueda a mano

**search, to search** *v buscar* **p22**

**seasick** *adj mareado -a*
  **I am seasick.** *Estoy mareado -a.*

**seasickness pill** *n la píldora para el mareo f*

**seat** *n el asiento m ,*
  **child seat** *asiento de niño*

**second** *adj segundo -a*

**security** *n la seguridad f*
  **security checkpoint** *punto de control de seguridad*
  **security guard** *guardia de seguridad*

**sedan** *n el sedán m*

**see, to see** *v ver* **p23 (I see** *veo*)
  **May I see it?** *¿Puedo verlo?*

**self-serve** *adj auto servicio*

**sell, to sell** *v vender* **p23**

**seltzer** *n el seltzer m*

**send, to send** *v enviar* **p22**

**separated (marital status)** *adj separado -a*

**September** *n el septiembre m*

**serve, to serve** *v servir* **p32 (like** *pedir*)

**service** *n el servicio m*
  **out of service** *fuera de servicio*

**services (religious)** *n el servicio m*

**service charge** *n el cargo por servicio m*

**seven** *adj siete*

**seventy** *adj setenta*

**seventeen** *adj diecisiete*

**seventh** *adj séptimo -a*

**sew, to sew** *v coser* **p23**

**sex (gender)** *n el sexo m*

**sex, to have (intercourse)** *v tener relaciones*

**shallow** *adj poco profundo -a*

**sheet (bed linen)** *n la sábana f*

**shellfish** *n el crustáceo m*

**ship** *n el barco m*

**ship, to ship** *v enviar* **p22**
  **How much to ship this to ____?** *¿Cuánto cuesta enviar esto ____?*

**shipwreck** *n el naufragio m*

**shirt** *n la camisa f*

**shoe** *n el zapato m*

**shop** *n la tienda f*

**shop** *v ir de compras* **p25**
  **I'm shopping for mens' clothes.** *Estoy comprando ropa de hombres.*
  **I'm shopping for womens' clothes.** *Estoy comprando ropa de mujer.*
  **I'm shopping for childrens' clothes.** *Estoy comprando ropa para niños.*

**short** *adj corto -a*

**shorts** *n los pantalones cortos m*

**shot (liquor)** *n el trago m*

**shout** *v gritar* **p22**

**show (performance)** *n el espectáculo m, la función f*
  **What time is the show?** *¿A qué hora es el espectáculo?*

show, to show v mostrar **p35**
(like *jugar*)

**Would you show me?**
*¿Puede mostrarme?*

shower n la ducha f

**Does it have a shower?**
*¿Tiene una ducha?*

shower, to shower v
ducharse **p22, 35**

shrimp n el camarón m

shuttle bus n el autobús de
transbordo m

sick adj enfermo -a

**I feel sick.** *Me siento
enfermo -a.*

side n el lado m

**on the side (e.g., salad
dressing)** *por el lado*

sidewalk n la acera f

sightseeing n el excursionismo m

sightseeing bus n el autobús
de excursión m

sign, to sign v firmar **p22**

**Where do I sign?** *¿Dónde
firmo?*

silk n la ceda f

silver adj plato -a

sing, to sing v cantar **p22**

single (unmarried) adj
soltero -a

**Are you single?** *¿Estás
soltero -a?*

single (one) adj sencillo -a,
individual

**single bed** *cama individual*

sink n el fregadero m

sister n la hermana f

sit, to sit v sentarse **p31, 35**
(like *comenzar*)

six adj seis

sixteen adj dieciséis

sixty adj sesenta

size (clothing, shoes) n la talla f

skin n la piel f

sleeping berth n el camarote
para dormir m

slow adj lento -a

slow, to slow v reducir la
velocidad **p33** (like *conocer*)

**Slow down!** *¡Reduzca la
velocidad!*

slow(ly) adv lentamente

**Speak more slowly.** *Hable
más lentamente.*

slum n el suburbio m

small adj pequeño -a

smell, to smell v oler **p31**
(like *poder*)

smoke, to smoke v fumar **p22**

smoking n el fumar m **p37**

**smoking area** *área de fumar*
**No Smoking** *No fumar*

snack n el bocadillo m

**Snake eyes!** n *¡Ojos de serpiente!, ¡Par de ases!*

snorkel n el tubo de res-
piración m

soap n el jabón m

sock n la media f

soda n la soda f, el refresco
m, la gaseosa f

**diet soda** *refresco de dieta*

soft adj suave

software n el software m

sold out adj vendido -a

**some** *adj* algún, alguno -a
**someone** *n* alguien
**something** *n* algo *m*
**son** *n* el hijo *m*
**song** *n* la canción *f*
**sorry** *adj* apenado -a
 I'm sorry. *Lo siento.*
**soup** *n* la sopa *f*
**spa** *n* el balneario *m*
**Spain** *n* España
**Spanish** *adj* español
**spare tire** *n* la llanta de
  respuesta *f*
**speak, to speak** *v* hablar **p22**
 Do you speak English?
 *¿Habla inglés?*
 Would you speak louder,
 please? *¿Podría hablar
 más alto, por favor?*
 Would you speak slower,
 please? *¿Podría hablar
 más lento, por favor?*
**special (featured meal)** *n* el
  especial *m*
**specify, to specify** *v* especificar **p22**
**speed limit** *n* el límite de
  velocidad *m*
 What's the speed limit? *¿Cuál
 es el límite de velocidad?*
**speedometer** *n* el velocímetro *m*
**spell, to spell** *v* deletrear **p22**
 How do you spell that?
 *¿Cómo se deletrea eso?*
**spice** *n* la especie *f*
**spill, to spill** *v* derramar **p22**
**split (gambling)** *n* la división *f*
**sports** *n* los deportes *m*

**spring (season)** *n* la primavera *f*
**stadium** *n* el estadio *m*
**staff (employees)** *n* el personal *m*
**stamp (postage)** *n* la
  estampilla *f*
**stair** *n* la escalera *f*
 Where are the stairs?
 *¿Dónde están las
 escaleras?*
 Are there many stairs?
 *¿Hay muchas escaleras?*
**stand, to stand** *v* pararse
  **p22, 35**
**start, to start (commence)** *v*
  comenzar **p31**
**start, to start (a car)** *v* encender **p31** (like *querer*)
**state** *n* el estado *m*
**station** *n* la estación *f*
 Where is the nearest_____?
 *¿Dónde está _____ más cer-
 cana?*
 gas station
 *la gasolinera*
 bus station
 *la estación de autobuses*
 subway station
 *la estación del metro*
 train station
 *la estación del tren*
**stay, to stay** *v* quedarse **p22, 35**
 We'll be staying for _____
 nights. *Me quedaré por
 _____ noches.*
**steakhouse** *n* el restaurante
  de parrilla *m*

**steal, to steal** v robar p22

**stolen** adj robado -a

**stop** n la parada f

> **Is this my stop?** ¿Ésta es mi parada?
>
> **I missed my stop.** Perdí mi parada.

**stop, to stop** v detener p29 (like tener)

> **Please stop.** Por favor deténgase.
>
> **STOP** (traffic sign) PARE
>
> **Stop, thief!** ¡Alto, ladrón!

**store** n la tienda f

**straight** adj recto -a, derecho -a, lacio -a (hair)

> **straight ahead** hacia delante
>
> **straight** (drink) sencillo
>
> **Go straight.** (giving directions) Siga derecho.

**straight** (gambling) n la escalera f

**street** n la calle f

> **across the street** al cruzar la calle
>
> **down the street** calle abajo
>
> **Which street?** ¿En cuál calle?
>
> **How many more streets?** ¿Cuántas calles más?

**stressed** adj estresado -a

**striped** adj a rayas

**stroller** n el cochecito para niños / bebés m

> **Do you rent baby strollers?** ¿Alquilan cochecitos para bebés?

**substitution** n la sustitución f

**suburb** n el barrio m

**subway** n el metro m

> **subway line** línea del metro
>
> **subway station** estación del metro
>
> **Which subway do I take for ___?** ¿Cuál metro tomo para ___?

**subtitle** n el subtítulo m

**suitcase** n la maleta f

**suite** n la suite f

**summer** n el verano m

**sun** n el sol m

**sunburn** n la quemadura de sol f

> **I have a bad sunburn.** Tengo una quemadura de sol mala.

**Sunday** n domingo m

**sunglasses** n las gafas de sol f

**sunny** adj soleado -a

> **It's sunny out.** Está soleado afuera.

**sunroof** n el techo corredizo m

**sunscreen** n el bloqueador de sol m

> **Do you have sunscreen SPF ___?** ¿Tienen bloqueador de sol SPF ___?

**supermarket** n el supermercado m

**surf** v surfear p22

**surfboard** n la tabla de surfear f

**suspiciously** adv sospechosamente

**swallow, to swallow** *v tragar* **p22**

**sweater** *n el suéter m*

**swim, to swim** *v nadar* **p22**

**Can one swim here?**
*¿Puedo nadar aquí?*

**swimsuit** *n el traje de baño m*

**swim trunks** *n el pantalón de traje de baño m*

**symphony** *n la sinfonía f*

**T**

**table** *n la mesa f*

**table for two** *mesa para dos*

**tailor** *n el sastre m*

**Can you recommend a good tailor?** *¿Puede recomendar un buen sastre?*

**take, to take** *v tomar, llevar* **p22**

**Take me to the station.** *Lléveme a la estación.*

**How much to take me to ____?** *¿Cuánto cuesta llevarme a ____?*

**takeout menu** *n el menú para llevar m*

**talk, to talk** *v hablar* **p22**

**tall** *adj alto -a*

**tanned** *adj bronceado -a*

**taste (flavor)** *n el sabor m*

**taste** *n (discernment) el gusto m*

**taste, to taste** *v probar* **p35** (like *jugar*)

**tax** *n el impuesto m*

**value-added tax (VAT)** *impuesto al valor agregado (IVA)*

**taxi** *n el taxi m*

**Taxi!** *¡Taxi!*

**Would you call me a taxi?** *¿Me puede llamar un taxi?*

**tea** *n el té m*

**team** *n el equipo m*

**Techno** *n el techno m*

**television** *n la televisión f*

**temple** *n el templo m*

**ten** *adj diez*

**tennis** *n el tenis m*

**tennis court** *cancha de tenis*

**tent** *n la tienda de campaña f*

**tenth** *adj décimo -a*

**terminal** *n (airport) el terminal m*

**Thank you.** *Gracias.*

**that (near)** *adj ese / eso / esa*

**that (far away)** *adj aquel / aquello / aquella*

**theater** *n el teatro m*

**them (m/f)** *ellos / ellas*

**there (demonstrative)** *adv ahí (nearby), allí (far)*

**Is / Are there ?** *¿Hay ?*

**over there** *allí*

**these** *adj éstos -as*

**thick** *adj grueso -a, espeso -a*

**thin** *adj delgado -a, flaco -a, fino -a*

**think** *v pensar* **p31** (like *comenzar*)

**third** *adj tercero -a*

**thirteen** *adj trece*

**thirty** *adj treinta*

**this** *adj este, esto, esta*

**those** *adj aquellos -as, esos -as*

**thousand** mil

**three** tres

**Thursday** n el jueves m

**ticket** n el boleto m

  **ticket counter** mostrador de venta de boletos

  **one-way ticket** boleto de ida

  **round-trip ticket** boleto de ida y vuelta

**tight** adj apretado -a

**time** n el tiempo m

  **Is it on time?** ¿Está a tiempo?

  **At what time?** ¿A qué hora?

  **What time is it?** ¿Qué hora es?

**timetable** n (train) el itinerario m

**tip (gratuity)** la propina f

**tire** n la llanta f

  **I have a flat tire.** Tengo una llanta vacía.

**tired** adj cansado -a

**today** n hoy

**toilet** n el inodoro m

  **The toilet is overflowing.** El inodoro se está desbordando.

  **The toilet is backed up.** El inodoro está tapado.

**toilet paper** n el papel higiénico m

  **You're out of toilet paper.** Se le acabó el papel higiénico.

**toiletries** n los artículos de tocador m

**toll** n el peaje m

**tomorrow** n mañana

**ton** n la tonelada f

**too (excessively)** adv demasiado -a

**too (also)** adv también

**tooth** n el diente m

  **I lost my tooth.** Perdí mi diente.

**toothache** n el dolor de dientes m

  **I have a toothache.** Tengo dolor de dientes.

**total** n el total m

  **What is the total?** ¿Cuál es el total?

**tour** n la excursión f

  **Are guided tours available?** ¿Hay excursiones guiadas disponibles?

  **Are audio tours available?** ¿Hay excursiones por audio disponibles?

**towel** n la toalla f

  **May we have more towels?** ¿Me puede dar más toallas?

**toy** n el juguete m

  **toy store** n la juguetería f

  **Do you have any toys for the children?** ¿Tiene juguetes para niños?

**traffic** n el tráfico m, el tránsito m

  **How's traffic?** ¿Cómo está el tráfico?

  **traffic rules** reglas de tránsito

**trail** n el sendero m
  **Are there trails?** ¿Hay senderos?

**train** n el tren m
  **express train** tren expreso
  **local train** tren local
  **Does the train go to \_\_\_?** ¿El tren va a \_\_\_\_\_?
  **May I have a train schedule?** ¿Me puede dar un itinerario de trenes?
  **Where is the train station?** ¿Dónde está la estación del tren?

**train, to train** v entrenar **p22**

**transfer, to transfer** v transferir **p31** (like querer)
  **I need to transfer funds.** Necesito transferir fondos.

**transmission** n la transmisión f
  **automatic transmission** transmisión automática
  **standard transmission** transmisión manual

**travel, to travel** v viajar **p22**

**travelers' check** n el cheque de viajero m
  **Do you cash travelers' checks?** ¿Ustedes cambian cheques de viajero?

**trim, to trim (hair)** v recortar **p22**

**trip** n el viaje m

**triple** adj triple

**trumpet** n la trompeta f

**trunk** n el baúl m **(luggage)** , el portaequipajes m **(in car)**

**try, to try (attempt)** v intentar **p22**, tratar **p22**

**try, to try on (clothing)** v medir **p32** (like pedir)

**try, to try (food)** v probar **p35** (like jugar)

**Tuesday** n el martes m

**turkey** n el pavo m

**turn, to turn** v virar, girar **p22**
  **to turn left / right** vire a la izquierda / derecha
  **to turn off / on** encender / apagar **p22**

**twelve** adj doce

**twenty** adj veinte

**twine** n la cuerda f

**two** adj dos

## U

**umbrella** n la sombrilla f

**uncle** n el tío m

**undercooked** adj crudo -a

**understand, to understand** v entender **p31** (like querer)
  **I don't understand.** No entiendo.
  **Do you understand?** ¿Entiende?

**underwear** n la ropa interior f

**university** n la universidad f

**up** adv arriba

**update, to update** v actualizar **p22**

**upgrade** n la mejora de categoría f

**upload, to upload** v cargar **p22**

**upscale** adj de más clase

**Uruguayan** adj uruguayo -a
**us** pron nosotros -as
**USB port** n el puerto USB m
**use, to use** v usar **p22**

**V**

**vacation** n la vacación m
  **on vacation** de vacaciones
  **to go on vacation** ir de vacaciones
**vacancy** n el vacante m
**van** n la furgoneta f, la van f
**VCR** n la videograbadora f
  **Do the rooms have VCRs?** ¿Las habitaciones tienen videograbadoras?
**vegetable** n el vegetal m
**vegetarian** n el vegetariano m, la vegetariana f
**vending machine** n la máquina de venta f
**Venezuelan** adj venezolano -a
**version** n la versión f
**very** muy
**video** n el video m
  **Where can I rent videos or DVDs?** ¿Dónde puedo alquilar videos o DVD?
**view** n la vista f
  **beach view** vista a la playa
  **city view** vista a la ciudad
**vineyard** n el viñedo m
**vinyl** n el vinilo m
**violin** n el violín m
**visa** n la visa f
  **Do I need a visa?** ¿Necesito una visa?

**vision** n la visión f
**visit, to visit** v visitar **p22**
**visually-impaired** adj con impedimentos visuales f
**vodka** n el vodka m
**voucher** n el vale m

**W**

**wait, to wait** v esperar **p22**
  **Please wait.** Por favor espere.
  **How long is the wait?** ¿Cuán larga es la espera?
**waiter** n el camarero f
**waiting area** n la área de espera f
**wake-up call** n la llamada de despertar f
**wallet** n la cartera f, la billetera f
  **I lost my wallet.** Perdí mi cartera.
  **Someone stole my wallet.** Alguien me robó mi billetera.
**walk, to walk** v caminar **p22**
**walker (ambulatory device)** n el andador m
**walkway** n la pasarela f
  **moving walkway** pasarela mecánica
**want, to want** v querer **p31**
**war** n la guerra f
**warm** adj caliente ,
**watch, to watch** v observar **p22**

**water** n el agua m
> **Is the water potable?** ¿El agua es potable?
> **Is there running water?** ¿Hay agua de llave?

**wave, to wave** v agitar las manos **p22**

**waxing** n la depilación con cera f

**weapon** n el arma m

**wear, to wear** v usar **p22**

**weather forecast** n el pronóstico del tiempo m

**Wednesday** n el miércoles m

**week** n la semana f,
> **this week** esta semana
> **last week** la semana pasada
> **next week** la próxima semana

**weigh** v pesar **p22**
> **I weigh ____.** Yo peso ____.
> **It weighs ____.** Pesa ____.

**weights** n las pesas f

**welcome** adv bienvenido
> **You're welcome.** Está bienvenido.

**well** adv bien
> **well done (meat)** bien cocido
> **well done (task)** bien hecho
> **I don't feel well.** No me siento bien.

**western** adj occidental, de vaqueros

**whale** n la ballena f

**what** adv qué
> **What sort of ____?** ¿Qué clase de ____?
> **What time is ____?** ¿A qué hora es ____?

**wheelchair** n la silla de ruedas f
> **wheelchair access** acceso para sillas de ruedas
> **wheelchair ramp** rampa para sillas de ruedas
> **power wheelchair** silla de ruedas eléctricas

**wheeled (luggage)** adj con ruedas

**when** adv cuándo

**where** adv dónde
> **Where is it?** ¿Dónde está?

**which** adv cuál
> **Which one?** ¿Cuál?

**white** adj blanco -a

**who** adv quién

**whose** adj de quién

**wide** adj ancho -a

**widow, widower** n la viuda f, el viudo m

**wife** n la esposa f

**wi-fi** n la red inalámbrica f

**window** n la ventana f, la ventanilla f,
> **drop-off window** ventanilla de entregas
> **pickup window** ventanilla de recogido

**windshield** n el parabrisas m

**windshield wiper** n el limpiaparabrisas m
**windy** adj ventoso -a
**wine** n el vino m
**winter** n el invierno m
**wiper** n el limpiaparabrisas m
**with** prep con
**withdraw** v retirar **p22**
**I need to withdraw money.**
Necesito retirar dinero.
**without** prep sin
**woman** n la mujer f
**work, to work** v trabajar,
funcionar **p22**
**This doesn't work.** Esto no
funciona.
**workout** n el ejercicio m
**worse** peor
**worst** lo peor
**write, to write** v escribir **p23**
**Would you write that down
for me?** ¿Podría escribir
eso para mí?
**writer** n el escritor m

**X**
**x-ray machine** n la máquina
de rayos X f

**Y**
**yellow** adj amarillo -a
**Yes.** adv Sí.
**yesterday** n ayer m
**the day before yesterday**
anteayer
**yield sign** n la señal de ceda
el paso f
**you** pron usted, tú, ustedes,
vosotros -as
**you (singular, informal)** tú
**you (singular, formal)** usted
**you (plural informal)**
vosotros -as **(rare)**
**you (plural formal)** ustedes
**your, yours** adj suyo -a, tuyo -a
**young** adj joven

**Z**
**zoo** n el zoológico m

**A**

abajo *down adv*

el abanico *m fan (hand-held) n*

la abeja *f bee n*

abierto -a *open (business) adj*

el / la abogado *m lawyer n*

la abolladura *f dent n*

abordar *to board v* **p22**

el abrigo *m coat n*

el abril *m April n*

la abuela *f grandmother n*

el abuelo *m grandfather n*

acampar *to camp v* **p22**

el accidente *m accident n*

el aceite *m oil n ,*

la aceituna *f olive n*

aceptar *to accept v* **p22**

Se aceptan tarjetas de crédito. *Credit cards accepted.*

la acera *f sidewalk n*

achicharrado -a *charred (meat) adj*

aclarar *to clear v* **p22**

el acné *m acne n*

actual *actual adj*

actualizar *to update v* **p22**

de acuerdo *Okay. adj adv*

el acumulador *m, la acumuladora f battery (for car) n*

adelante *forward adj*

el adelanto *m advance n*

adentro *inside adv*

el aderezo *m dressing (salad) n*

adicional *extra adj*

el adiós *m goodbye n*

la aduana *f customs n*

el aeropuerto *m airport n*

afroamericano -a *African American adj*

afro, africano *afro adj*

afuera *outside n*

¡Agarren al ladrón! *Stop, thief!*

la agencia *f agency n*

la agencia de alquiler de autos *f car rental agency*

la agencia de crédito *f credit bureau n*

el agnóstico *m,* la agnóstica *f agnostic n adj*

el agosto *m August n*

agotado -a *exhausted (person) adj, sold out (thing) adj*

agradable *nice adj*

agradar *to please v, to be pleasing to v* **p22**

el agua *m water n*

el agua caliente *hot water*

el agua frío *cold water*

el águila *m eagle n*

ahí *there (nearby) adv (demonstrative)*

ahora *now adv*

el aire acondicionado *m air conditioning n*

el ajo *m garlic n*

la albóndiga *f meatball n*

el alcohol *m alcohol n*

alegre *happy adj*

el alemán *m,* la alemana *f German n adj*

la alergia *f allergy n*

**alérgico -a** *allergic adj* ,
   **Soy alérgico / alérgica a ____.** *I'm allergic to ____.*
**algo** *m something n*
**el algodón** *m cotton n*
**alguien** *someone n*
**algún, alguno -a** *some adj*
**allá** *over there adv*
**allí** *there (far) adv (demonstrative)*
**la almohada** *f pillow n*
   **la almohada de plumas** *down pillow*
**el almuerzo** *m lunch n*
**alquilar** *to rent v*
**el alpinismo** *m mountain climbing n*
**alto -a** *high adj, tall adj*
   **alto** *high adj*
   **más alto** *higher*
   **lo más alto** *highest*
**la altitud** *f altitude n*
**el aluminio** *m aluminum n*
**amable** *kind (nice) n*
**la ama de casa** *f homemaker n*
**amamantar** *to breastfeed v* **p22**
**el amanecer** *m dawn n*
   **al amanecer** *at dawn*
**amar** *to love v* **p22**
**amarillo -a** *yellow adj*
**el ambiente** *m environment n*
**la ambulancia** *f ambulance n*
**americano -a** *American adj*
**el amigo** *m* / **la amiga** *f friend n*
**el amor** *m love n*
**ancho -a** *wide adj*

**el andador** *m walker (ambulatory device) n*
**el animal** *m animal n*
**ansioso -a** *anxious adj*
**el antibiótico** *m antibiotic n*
   **Necesito un antibiótico.** *I need an antibiotic.*
**los anticonceptivos** *m pl birth control n* ,
   **Estoy usando anticonceptivos.** *I'm on birth control.*
**anticonceptivo -a** *birth control adj*
   **Se me acabaron las pastillas anticonceptivas.** *I'm out of birth control pills.*
**el antihistamínico** *m antihistamine n*
**el año** *m year n*
   **¿Cuántos años tiene?** *What's your age?*
**apagar** *to turn off (lights) v* **p22**
**el apellido** *m last name*
   **Me quedé con mi apellido de soltera.** *I kept my maiden name.*
**apenado -a** *sorry adj*
   **Lo siento.** *I'm sorry.*
**apostar** *to bet v* **p35** *(like jugar)*
**apresurarse** *to hurry v* **p22, 35**
   **¡Apresúrate por favor!** *Hurry, please!*
**apretado -a** *tight adj*
**la apuesta** *f bet n*
   **Igualo tu apuesta.** *I'll see your bet.*

**apuntar** to point v **p22**

**aquel / aquello** that (far away) adj

**aquellos / aquellas** those adj pl

**aquí** here adv

**argentino -a** Argentinian adj

**el arma** m weapon n

**el arrecife** m reef n

**arriba** up adv

**el arte** m art n

la exhibición de arte exhibit of art

de arte art adj

el museo de arte art museum

el artesano m, la artesana f craftsperson / artisan n

**los artículos de tocador** m toiletries n

**el / la artista** m f artist n

**asaltar** to mug (assault) v **p22**

asaltado to get mugged

**asiático -a** Asian adj

**el asiento** m seat n

el asiento a nivel de orquesta orchestra seat

**la asistencia** f assistance n

la asistencia telefónica f directory assistance

**asistir** to attend v / to assist v **p23**

**el asma** f asthma n

Yo tengo asma. I have asthma.

**la aspirina** f aspirin n

**el asunto** m matter, affair

No te metas en mis asuntos. Mind your own business.

**el ataque cardiaco** m, **el ataque al corazón** m heart attack n

**ateo -a** atheist adj

**aterrizar** to land v **p22**

**el ático de lujo** m penthouse n

**los audífonos** m headphones n

**el audio** m audio n

**audio -a, auditivo -a** audio adj

**ausente** missing adj

**el Australia** m Australia n

**australiano -a** Australian adj

**el auto** m, **el automóvil** m, **el carro** m car n

la agencia de alquiler de autos car rental agency

**el autobús** m bus n

la parada de autobuses bus stop

el autobús de transbordo shuttle bus

el autobús de excursión sightseeing bus

**la autopista** f highway n

**de auto servicio** self-serve adj

**el avance** m advance n

**avergonzado -a** embarrassed adj

**las aves de corral** f pl poultry n

**¡Ay!** Ouch! interj

**ayer** m yesterday adv

**el día antes de ayer / anteayer** the day before yesterday adv

**la ayuda** f help n

**¡Ayuda!** Help! n

**ayudar** to help v p22

**azul** blue adj

## B

**el baile de salón** m ballroom dancing n

**bailar** to dance p22

**bajar el inodoro** to flush v p22

**bajo -a** low adj

**bajo** low adj

**más bajo** lower

**lo más bajo** lowest

**el balance** m balance (on bank account) n

**balancear** to balance v p22

**el balcón** m balcony n

**el balneario** m spa n

**bancario -a** bank adj

**la cuenta bancaria** bank account

**la tarjeta bancaria** bank card

**el banco** m bank n

**la banda** f band n

**la banda ancha** f broadband n

**bañarse** to bathe v p22, 35

**la bañera** f, **la tina de baño** f bathtub n

**el baño** m bathroom, restroom n, bath n

**¿Tienen un baño público?** Do you have a public restroom?

**el baño de caballeros** men's restroom

**el baño de damas** women's restroom

**barato** cheap adj

**barato** cheap

**más barato** cheaper

**lo más barato** cheapest

**el barbero** m barber n

**el barco** m boat n, ship n

**el barrio** m suburb n

**la batería** f battery (for car) n

**el baúl** m trunk (luggage) n

**el / la bebé** m f baby n

**de bebés, para bebés** for babies adj

**coches para bebés** baby strollers?

**comida para bebés** baby food

**beber** to drink v p23

**la bebida** f drink n

**la bebida complementaria** complimentary drink

**Quisiera una bebida.** I'd like a drink.

**bello -a** beautiful adj

**el beso** m kiss n

**bien** okay adv

**¿Está bien?** Are you okay?

**bien** well adv

**bien** fine adj

**Estoy bien.** I'm fine.

**bien parecido** m handsome adj

**bienvenido -a** welcome adj

**Está bienvenido.** You're welcome.

**bilingüe** *bilingual adj*

**el billar** *m pool (the game) n*

**el billete** *m bill (currency) n*

**la billetera** *f wallet n*

**biracial** *biracial adj*

**blanco -a** *white, off-white adj*

**el blanqueador** *m bleach n*

**el bloque** *m block n*

**el bloqueador de sol** *m sun-screen n*

**bloquear** *to block v p22*

**la blusa** *f blouse n*

**la boca** *f mouth n*

**el bocadillo** *m snack n*

**la bocina** *f horn n*

**la bola** *f ball (sport) n*

**la boleta de abordaje** *f boarding pass n*

**la boletería** *f box office n*

**el boleto** *m ticket n*

> **el mostrador de venta de boletos** *ticket counter*
> **el boleto de ida** *one-way ticket*
> **el boleto de ida y vuelta** *round-trip ticket*

**boliviano -a** *Bolivian adj*

**la bolsa** *f / **el bolso** m bag n*

**el bolso** *m purse n*

**la bomba** *f bomb n*

**la bomba** *f pump n*

**el borde de la acera** *m curb n*

**el bordo** *m board n*

> **a bordo** *on board*

**borroso -a** *blurry adj*

**la botella** *f bottle n*

**el braille americano** *m braille (American) n*

**el brandy** *m brandy n*

**el brazo** *m arm n*

**brillante** *bright adj*

**bronceado -a** *tanned adj*

**bronze (color de)** *bronze (color) adj*

**bucear** *to dive v p22*

**bucear con tanques de oxígeno** *to scuba dive v*

> **Buceo con tanques de oxígeno.** *I scuba dive.*

**bucear con tubo de respiración** *to snorkel v*

**el budista** *m,* **la budista** *f Buddhist n*

**bueno -a** *good adj*

> **buenos días** *good morning*
> **buenas noches** *good evening*
> **buenas noches** *good night*
> **buenas tardes** *good afternoon*

**el bufé** *m buffet n*

> **de tipo bufé** *buffet-style adj*

**el burro** *m donkey n*

**buscar** *to look for (to search) v p22*

**la búsqueda** *f search n*

> **búsqueda a mano** *hand search*

## C

**el caballo** *m horse n*

**el cabello** *m hair n*

**la cabra** f goat n
**el cacahuate** m peanut n
**el cachemir** m cashmere n
**caer** to fall v **p23** (I fall **caigo**)
**café (color de)** brown adj
**el café** m café n, coffee n
**el café helado** iced coffee
**el café expreso** m espresso n
**el cibercafé** Internet café
**la caja fuerte** safe (for storing valuables) n
**el cajero automático** m ATM n
**caliente** hot adj, warm adj
**el calipso** m calypso (music) n
**callado -a** quiet adj
**la calle** f street n
**calle abajo** down the street
**al cruzar la calle** across the street
**la cama** f bed n
**la camarera** f maid (hotel) n
**el camarero** m waiter n
**el camarón** m shrimp n
**el camarote** m berth n
**cambiar** to change (money) v / to change (clothes) v **p22**
**el cambio** m change (money) n
**el cambio de moneda** m currency exchange n ,
**la caminadora** f treadmill n
**caminar** to walk v **p22**
**la caminata** f walk n
**la camisa** f shirt n
**el campamento** m campsite n
**el campista** m camper n
**el campo para golpear pelotas** m driving range n

**Canadá** m Canada n
**canadiense** Canadian adj
**cancelar** to cancel v **p22**
**la cancha** f court (sport) n
**la canción** f song n
**el candado** m lock n
**cansado -a** tired adj
**cantar** to sing v **p22**
**la cantidad** f amount n
**la cantina** f bar n
**la cantina de piano** piano bar
**la cantina para solteros** singles bar
**la caña de pescar** f fishing pole n
**el cappuccino** m cappuccino n
**la cara** f face n
**cargar** to upload v **p22**
**el cargo de entrada** m cover charge (in bar) n
**el cargo por servicio** m service charge n
**la carie** f cavity (tooth cavity) n
**la carnada** f bait n
**la carne** f meat n
**caro -a** expensive adj
**la carretera** f road n
**el carro para dormir** m sleeping car n
**la cartera** f purse n, wallet n
**Perdí mi cartera.** I lost my wallet.
**Alguien me robó mi cartera.** Someone stole my wallet.
**casado -a** married adj
**casarse** to marry v **p22, 35**
**el casillero** m locker n

**casillero del gimnasio** *gym locker*

**casillero de almacén** *storage locker*

**el casino** *m casino n*

**el católico** *m*, **la católica** *f Catholic n adj*

**catorce** *fourteen n adj*

**el CD** *m*, **el disco compacto** *m CD n*

**el cebo** *m bait n*

**la ceda** *f silk n*

**la ceja** *f eyebrow n*

**celebrar** *to celebrate v* **p22**

**la cena** *f dinner n*

**el centímetro** *m centimeter n*

**el centro comercial** *m mall n*

**el centro de la ciudad** *m downtown n*

**el centro de gimnasia** *m fitness center n*

**cerca** *close, near adj*

**cerca** *close*

**más cerca** *closer*

**lo más cerca** *closest*

**cercano -a** *near, nearby adj*

**cercano** *near adj*

**más cercano** *nearer (comparative)*

**lo más cercano** *nearest (superlative)*

**el cerdo** *m pig n*

**cerrado -a** *closed adj*

**la cerradura** *f lock n*

**cerrar** *to close v* **p31** *(like comenzar)*

**cerrar con llave** *to lock v* **p31** *(like comenzar)*

**la cerveza** *f beer n*

**cerveza de barril** *beer on tap, draft beer*

**la chaqueta** *f jacket n*

**el cheque** *m check n*

**el cheque de viajero** *m travelers' check n*

**la chica** *f girl n*

**chino -a** *Chinese adj*

**el chocolate caliente** *m hot chocolate n*

**el chofer** *m driver n*

**el chupete** *m pacifier n*

**el cibercafé** *m cybercafé n*

**ciego -a** *blind adj*

**el cigarrillo** *m cigarette n*

**el paquete de cigarrillos** *pack of cigarettes*

**el cigarro** *m cigar n*

**cinco** *five n adj*

**el cincuenta** *m fifty n adj*

**el cine** *m*, **el cinema** *m cinema n*

**el cinturón** *m belt n*

**el cisne** *m swan n*

**la cita** *f appointment n*

**la ciudad** *f city n*

**el clarinete** *m clarinet n*

**claro -a** *clear adj*

**la clase** *f kind (type) n*

**¿Qué clase es?** *What kind is it?*

**la clase** *f class n*

**la clase de negocios** *business class*

**la clase económica** *economy class*

**la primera clase** *first class*

**clásico -a** *classical (music) adj*

**el club nocturno** *m nightclub n*

**la cobija** *f blanket n*

**cobrar** *to charge (money) v p22*

**cobre (color de)** *copper adj*

**a cobro revertido** *collect adj*

**el cochecito para niños / bebés** *m stroller n*

**la cocina** *f kitchen n*

**la cocina pequeña** *f kitchenette n*

**cocinar** *to cook v p22*

**el coito** *m intercourse (sexual) n*

**el colegio** *m college n, high school n*

**colérico -a, enojado -a** *angry adj*

**colgar** *hang up (to end a phone call) v p35* (like jugar)

**el coliseo** *m coliseum n*

**colocar** *to place v p22*

**colombiano -a** *Colombian adj*

**el color** *m color n*

**colorear** *to color v p22*

**el combustible** *m gas n*

**el indicador de combustible** *gas gauge*

**sin combustible** *out of gas*

**comenzar** *to begin v, to start (commence) v p31*

**comer** *to eat v p23*

**comer afuera** *to eat out*

**los comestibles** *m groceries n*

**la comida** *f food n*

**la comida** *f meal n*

**la comida diabética** *diabetic meal*

**la comida kósher** *kosher meal*

**la comida vegetariana** *vegetarian meal*

**cómo** *how adv*

**el compañero** *m*, **la compañera** *f partner n*

**compensar** *to make up (compensate) v p22*

**comportar** *to behave v p22*

**comprar** *to shop v p22*

**comprobar, verificar** *to check v p22*

**la computadora** *f computer n*

**la computadora portátil** *f laptop n*

**con** *with prep*

**el concierto** *m concert n*

**concurrido** *busy (restaurant) adj*

**la condición** *f condition n*

**en buena / mala condición** *in good / bad condition*

**el condón** *m condom n*

**¿Tienes un condón?** *Do you have a condom?*

**no sin un condón** *not without a condom*

**el conejo** *m rabbit n*

**la conexión eléctrica** *f electrical hookup n*

**la confirmación** f *confirmation* n

**confirmar** *to confirm* v **p22**

**confundido -a** *confused* adj

**la congestión** f *congestion (sinus)* n

**congestionado -a** *congested* adj

**la congestión de tránsito** f *congestion (traffic)* n

**conocer** *to know (someone)* v **p33**

**la consola de juegos** f *game console* n

**el contacto de emergencia** m *emergency contact* n

**la contestación** f *answer* n

Necesito una contestación. *I need an answer.*

**contestar** *to answer (phone call)* v, *to answer (respond to a question)* v **p22**

Contésteme por favor. *Answer me, please.*

**continuar** *to continue* v **p22**

**el contrabajo** m *bass (instrument)* n

**la contraseña** f *password* n

**el convertible** m *convertible* n

**el coñac** m *cognac* n

**la copa** f *glass (drinking)* n

¿Lo tienen por la copa? *Do you have it by the glass?*

Quisiera una copa por favor. *I'd like a glass please.*

**el corazón** m *heart* n

**la corona** f *crown (dental)* n

**la correa** f *belt* n

**la correa transportadora** *conveyor belt*

**correcto -a** *correct* adj

**corregir** *to correct* v **p23**

**el correo** m *mail* n / *post office* n

**el correo aéreo** *air mail*

**el correo certificado** *certified mail*

**el correo expreso** *express mail*

**el correo de primera clase** *first class mail*

**el correo certificado** *registered mail*

¿Dónde está el correo? *Where is the post office?*

**correr** *to ride* v / *to run* v **p23**

**la corrida de toros** f *bullfight* n

**la corriente** f *current (water)* n

**la cortadura** f *cut (wound)* n

**cortar** *to cut* v **p22**

**la corte** f *court (legal)* n

**la corte de tránsito** *traffic court*

**cortés** *courteous* adj

**corto -a** *short* adj

**coser** *to sew* v **p23**

**costarricense** *Costa Rican* n adj

**costar** *to cost* v **p35** (like *jugar*)

**cuánto** *how (much)* adv

¿Cuánto? *How much?*

¿Por cuánto tiempo? *For how long?*

**cuántos** *how (many)* adv

**country (la música)** f country-and-western adj

**crecer** to grow (get larger) v **p23**

¿Dónde creciste? Where did you grow up?

**la crema** f cream n

**cremoso -a** off-white adj

**crudo -a** rare (meat) adj, undercooked adj

**el crustáceo** m shellfish n

**a cuadros** checked (pattern) adj

**cuál** which adv

**cualquier -a** any adj

**cualquier cosa** anything n

**cuándo** when adv

**cuarenta** forty n adj

**cuarto** fourth n adj

un cuarto one quarter, one fourth

**el cuarto de cambio** m changing room n

**el cuarto de degustación** m tasting room n

**el cuarto de galón** m quart n

**cuatro** four n adj

**el cubismo** m Cubism n

**cuenta** f account n

**la cuerda** f rope n, twine n

**el cuero** m leather n

**cuidar** to mother v **p22**

**la culpa** f fault n

Es mi culpa. I'm at fault.
Fue su culpa. It was his fault.

**la cuna** f crib n

## D

**dañado -a** damaged adj

**dar** to give v **p25** (like ir)

**dar masaje** to massage v **p22**

**debajo** below adj

**décimo -a** tenth adj

**decir** to say v **p32** (like pedir) (I say digo)

**declarar** to declare v **p22**

**delantero -a** front adj

**deleitado -a** delighted adj

**deletrear** to spell v **p22**

¿Cómo se deletrea eso? How do you spell that?

**delgado -a** thin (slender) adj

**demasiado -a** too (excessively) adv

**la democracia** f democracy n

**la dentadura** f dentures, denture plate n

**el dentista** m dentist n

**la depilación con cera** f waxing n

**los deportes** m pl sports n

**derecho -a** right adj, straight adv

Está a mano derecha. It is on the right.
Vira a la derecha en la esquina. Turn right at the corner.
Siga derecho. Go straight. (giving directions)

**los derechos** m pl rights n pl

los derechos civiles civil rights

**derramar** to spill v **p22**

desacelerar *to slow* v **p22**

desaparecer *to disappear* v **p33** (like *conocer*)

el desayuno *m breakfast* n

la descarga *f download* n

descargar *to download* v **p22**

desconectar *to disconnect* v **p22**

el descuento *m discount* n

**el descuento de niños** *children's discount*

**el descuento de personas mayores de edad** *senior discount*

**el descuento de estudiantes** *student discount*

el desfile *m parade* n

desmayar *to faint* v **p22**

despedirse *to check out (of hotel)* v **p32, 35** (like *pedir*)

los destellos *m pl highlights (hair)* n

el destino *m destination* n

el detector de metales *m metal detector* n

detener *to stop* v **p29**

**Deténgase por favor.** *Please stop.*

detrás *behind* adj

devolver *to return (something)* v **p31** (like *poder*)

el día *m day* n

**el día antes de ayer / anteayer** *the day before yesterday*

**estos últimos días** *these last few days*

diabético -a *diabetic* adj

el día de fiesta *m holiday* n

la diarrea *f diarrhea* n

dibujar *m drawing (activity)* v **p22**

el dibujo *m drawing (work of art)* n

el diccionario *m dictionary* n

el diciembre *m December* n

diecinueve *nineteen* n adj

dieciocho *eighteen* n adj

dieciséis *sixteen* n adj

diecisiete *seventeen* n adj

el diente *m tooth* n

diez *ten* n adj

diferente *different (other)* adj

difícil *difficult* adj

el dinero *m money* n

**la transferencia de dinero** *money transfer*

la dirección *f direction*

**en una sola dirección** *one way (traffic sign)*

la dirección *f address* n

**¿Cuál es la dirección?** *What's the address?*

el disco *m disco* n

el diseñador *m*, la diseñadora *f designer* n

el disfraz *m costume* n

disfrutar *to enjoy* v **p22**

disponible *available* adj

la división *f split (gambling)* n

divorciado -a *divorced* adj

doble *double* adj

doce *twelve* n adj

la docena *f dozen* n

el doctor *m* / la doctora *f doctor* n ,

el dólar *m* dollar *n*

doler to hurt (to feel painful) *v*
p31 (like *poder*)

¡Ay! ¡Eso duele! Ouch! That
hurts!

el dolor de cabeza *m*
headache *n*

el dolor de dientes *m*
toothache *n*

Tengo dolor de dientes.
I have a toothache.

el domingo *m* Sunday *n*

dónde where *adv*

¿Dónde está? Where is it?

dondequiera, cualquier lugar
anywhere *adv*

dorado -a golden *adj*

dos two *n adj*

el drama *m* drama *n*

el drenaje *m* drain *n*

la ducha *f* shower *n*

ducharse to shower *v* p22, 35

durar to last *v* p22

duro hard (firm) *adj*

el DVD *m* DVD *n*

E

la economía *f* economy *n*

económico -a, barato -a inexpensive *adj*

ecuatoriano -a Ecuadorian
*adj*

la edad *f* age *n*

¿Qué edad tienes? What's
your age?

el editor *m*, la editora *f* editor, publisher *n*

el educador *m*, la educadora
*f* educator *n*

el efectivo *m* cash *n*

efectivo solamente cash
only

el ejercicio *m* workout *n*

el ejército *m* military *n*

él him *pron*

de él his *adj*

la elección *f* election *n*

el elefante *m* elephant *n*

el elevador *m* elevator *n*

ella *f* she *pron*

de ella hers *adj*

ellos / ellas them *pron pl*

el e-mail *m* e-mail *n*

¿Me puede dar su dirección
de e-mail? May I have your
e-mail address?

el mensaje de e-mail e-mail
message

la embajada *f* embassy *n*

embarazada pregnant *adj*

embarcar to ship *v* p22

la emergencia *f* emergency *n*

empacar to bag *v* p22

el empleado *m*, la empleada
*f* employee *n*

empujar to push *v* p22

encantado -a charmed *adj*

el encendedor *m* lighter (cigarette) *n*

encender to start (a car) *v*, to
turn on *v* p31 (like *querer*)

enchufar to plug *v* p22

el enchufe *m* plug *n*

**el enchufe adaptador** *m adapter plug n*

**encontrar** *to find v* **p35** (like *jugar*)

**el enero** *m January n*

**la enfermera** *f nurse n*

**enfermo -a** *sick adj*

**la ensalada** *f salad n*

**entallar** *to fit (clothes) v* **p22**

**entender** *to understand v* **p23**

**No entiendo.** *I don't understand.*

**¿Entiende?** *Do you understand?*

**la entrada** *f entrance n*

**entrar** *to enter v* **p22**

**No entre.** *Do not enter.*

**Prohibida la entrada.** *Entry forbidden.*

**entrenar** *to train v* **p22**

**entusiasmado -a** *enthusiastic adj*

**enviar** *to send v* **p22**

**enviar un e-mail** *to send e-mail v* **p22**

**el equipaje** *m baggage, luggage n*

**el equipaje perdido** *lost baggage*

**de equipaje** *baggage adj*

**reclamo de equipaje** *baggage claim*

**el equipo** *m team n / equipment n*

**el error** *m mistake n*

**la escalada** *f climbing n*

**la escalada de rocas** *rock climbing*

**para escalar** *climbing adj*

**el equipo para escalar** *climbing gear*

**escalar, subir** *to climb v* **p22, 23**

**escalar una montaña** *to climb a mountain*

**subir las escaleras** *to climb stairs*

**la escalera** *f stair n / flush, straight (gambling) n*

**la escalera real** *royal flush*

**la escalera mecánica** *f escalator n*

**escanear** *to scan (document) v* **p22**

**escocés** *Scottish adj*

**escribir** *to write v* **p23**

**¿Podría escribir eso para mí?** *Would you write that down for me?*

**el escritor** *m writer n*

**escuchar** *to listen v* **p22**

**la escuela** *f school n*

**la escuela intermedia** *junior high / middle school*

**la escuela de leyes** *law school*

**la escuela de medicina** *medical school*

**la escuela primaria** *primary school*

**la escuela superior / secundaria** *high school*

**la escultura** *f sculpture n*

**ese / eso / esa** *that (near) adj*

**esos / esas** *those (near) adj pl*

**la espalda** *f back n*

**español** *Spanish n adj*
**el especial** *m special (featured meal) n*
**la especie** *f spice n*
**especificar** *to specify v* **p22**
**el espectáculo** *m show (performance) n*
**los espejuelos** *m eyeglasses n*
**la espera** *f wait n*
**esperar** *to hold (to pause) v, to wait v* **p22**
**espeso -a** *thick adj*
**la esposa** *f wife n*
**el esposo** *m husband n*
**la esquina** *f corner n*
**en la esquina** *on the corner*
**la estación** *f station n*
**¿Dónde está la gasolinera más cercanía?** *Where is the nearest gas station?*
**la estación de policías** *f police station n*
**estacionamiento** *parking adj*
**estacionar** *to park v* **p22**
**no estacione** *no parking*
**el estadio** *m stadium n*
**el estado** *m state n*
**estadounidense** *American adj*
**la estampilla** *f stamp (postage) n*
**estar** *to be (temporary state, condition, mood) v* **p27**
**este / esta** *this adj*
**esto** *this n*
**éstos / éstas** *these n adj pl*

**estrecho -a** *narrow adj*
**estreñido -a** *constipated adj*
**estresado -a** *stressed adj*
**la excursión** *f tour n*
**excursionar** *to hike v* **p22**
**la excursión guiada** *f guided tour n*
**el excursionismo** *m sightseeing n*
**excusar, perdonar** *to excuse (pardon) v* **p22**
**Perdone.** *Excuse me.*
**exhausto -a** *exhausted adj*
**la exhibición** *f exhibit n*
**explicar** *to explain v* **p22**
**expreso** *express adj*
**el registro expreso** *express check-in*
**extra grande** *extra-large adj*

**F**
**facturar** *to bill v* **p22**
**la familia** *f family n*
**el fax** *m fax n*
**el febrero** *m February n*
**el festival** *m festival n*
**fino -a** *thin (fine) adj*
**firmar** *to sign v* **p22**
**Firme aquí.** *Sign here.*
**flaco -a** *thin (skinny) adj*
**la flauta** *f flute n*
**fletar** *to charter (transportation) v* **p22**
**fleteado** *charter adj*
**vuelo fleteado** *charter flight*
**la flor** *f flower n*

el foco delantero *m* headlight *n*

el formato *m* format *n*

la fórmula *f* formula *n*

el fósforo *m* match (fire) *n*

fotocopiar to photocopy *v* **p22**

frágil fragile *adj*

francés *m*, francesa *f* French *adj*

la frazada *f* blanket *n*

el fregadero *m* sink *n*

frenar to brake *v* **p22**

el freno *m* brake *n*

la frente *f* forehead *n*

del frente front *adj*

fresco fresh *adj*

frío -a cold *adj*

la fruta *f* fruit *n*

el fuego *m* fire *n*

las fuerzas armadas *f pl* armed forces *n pl*

¡Full house! Full house! *n*

fumar to smoke *v* **p22**

el fumar *m* smoking *n*

la área de fumar smoking area

no fumar no smoking

la función *f* show (performance) *n*

funcionar to work *v* **p22**

la furgoneta *f* van *n*

el fusible *m* fuse *n*

G

las gafas *f pl* glasses (spectacles) *n*

las gafas de sol *f pl* sunglasses *n*

la galleta *f* cookie *n*

el galón *m* gallon *n*

la ganga *f* deal (bargain) *n*

la gasolina *f* gas *n*

el gato *m*, la gata *f* cat *n*

el / la gerente *m f* manager *n*

el gimnasio *m* gym *n*

la ginebra *f* gin *n*

el / la ginecólogo -a gynecologist *n*

girar to turn *v* **p22**

el gol *m* goal (sport) *n*

el golf *m* golf *n*

el campo de golf golf course

gordo -a fat *adj* ,

el gorro *m* hat *n*

gotear to drip *v* **p22**

gracias thank you

el grado *m* grade (school) *n*

el gramo *m* gram *n*

la gran cantidad *f* a lot *n*

grande big *adj*, large *adj*

grande big, large ,
más grande bigger, larger ,
lo más grande biggest, largest

¡Grandioso! Great! *interj*

griego -a Greek *adj*

la grieta *f* crack (in glass object) *n*

el grifo *m* faucet *n*

gris gray *adj*

gritar to shout *v* **p22**

grueso -a thick *adj*

**el grupo** *m group n*
**el guante** *m glove n*
**guapo** *handsome adj*
**guardar** *to keep v* **p22**
**la guardería infantil** *f nursery n*
**el guardia** *m guard n*
**el guardia de seguridad** *security guard*
**guatemalteco -a** *Guatemalan adj*
**la guerra** *f war n*
**la guía** *f guide (publication) n*
**el / la guía** *m f guide (of tours) n*
**guiar** *to guide v* **p22**
**guiar, manejar** *to drive v* **p22**
**la guitarra** *f guitar n*
**gustar** *to please v* **p34**
**el gusto** *m taste (discernment) n*

**H**
**la habitación** *f room (hotel) n*
**hablar** *to speak v, to talk v* **p22**
**Se habla Inglés aquí.** *English spoken here.*
**hacer** *to do v, to make v* **p30**
**hacer efectivo** *to cash v* **p30**
**hacer efectivo** *to cash out (gambling)* **p30,**
**hacer juego** *to match v* **p30**
**hacer las paces** *to make up (apologize) v* **p30**
**hacia** *toward prep*
**halar** *to pull v* **p22**
**¿Hay ____?** *Is / Are there ____?*

**hecho de** *made of adj*
**la hectáre a** *f hectare n*
**la hermana** *f sister n*
**el hermano** *m brother n*
**el hielo** *m ice n*
**la máquina de hielo** *ice machine*
**la hierba** *f herb n*
**la hija** *f daughter n*
**el hijo** *m son n*
**el hindú** *m,* **la hindú** *f Hindu n*
**hip-hop** *hip-hop n*
**la historia** *f history n*
**histórico -a** *historical adj*
**el hogar** *m home n*
**la hoja del limpiaparabrisas** *f wiper blade n*
**hola** *hello n*
**el hombre** *m man n*
**hondureño -a** *Honduran adj*
**el honorario** *m fee n*
**la hora** *f hour n, time n*
**el horario** *m hours (at museum) n*
**la hospedería de cama y desayuno** *f bed-and-breakfast (B & B) n*
**la hospedería** *f hostel n*
**el hotel** *m hotel n*
**hoy** *today n*
**húmedo -a** *humid adj*

**I**
**la identificación** *f identification n*
**la iglesia** *f church n*

**igualar** *to match* v **p22**

**el impedimento** *m*, **la persona con impedimento** *f handicap* n

**con impedimentos auditivos** *hearing-impaired* adj

**el impresionismo** *m Impressionism* n

**imprimir** *to print* v **p23**

**el impuesto** *m tax* n

**impuesto al valor agregado (IVA)** *value-added tax (VAT)*

**la incapacidad** *f disability* n

**la indigestión** *f indigestion* n

**el infante** *m infant* n

**la información** *f information* n

**el ingeniero** *m*, **la ingeniera** *f engineer* n

**Inglaterra** *f England* n

**inglés, inglesa** *English* adj

**el inodoro** *m toilet* n

**el insecto** *m bug* n

**insultar** *to insult* v **p22**

**intentar** *to try (attempt)* v **p22**

**el interludio** *m intermission* n

**el Internet** *m Internet* n

**¿Dónde puedo encontrar un cibercafé?** *Where can I find an Internet café?*

**el / la intérprete** *m f interpreter* n

**intolerante a la lactosa** *lactose-intolerant* adj

**el invierno** *m winter* n

**el invitado** *m* / **la invitada** *f guest* n

**ir** *to go* v (See Future **p25**)

**ir a los clubes nocturnos** *to go clubbing* v (See Future **p25**)

**ir de compras** *to shop* v (See Future **p25**)

**Irlanda** *f Ireland* n

**irlandés, irlandesa** *Irish* adj

**italiano -a** *Italian* adj

**el itinerario** *m schedule* n, *timetable (train)* n

**izquierdo -a** *left* adj

## J

**el jabón** *m soap* n

**japonés, japonesa** *Japanese* adj

**el jazz** *m jazz* n

**el jefe** *m*, **la jefa** *f boss* n

**joven** *young* adj

**judío -a** *Jewish* adj

**el jueves** *m Thursday* n

**jugar golf** *to go golfing* v **p35**

**jugar** *to play (a game)* v **p22**

**el jugo** *m juice* n

**el jugo de fruta** *m fruit juice* n

**el jugo de naranja** *m orange juice* n

**el juguete** *m toy* n

**la juguetería** *f toy store* n

**el julio** *m July* n

**el junio** *m June* n

**K**

el kilo *m kilo n*

el kilómetro *m kilometer n*

kósher *kosher adj*

**L**

lacio -a *straight (hair) adj*

el lado *m side n*

> por el lado *on the side (e.g., salad dressing)*

al lado *next prep*

> del lado *next to*

largo *long adj*

> largo *long adj*
> más largo *longer*
> lo más largo *longest*

la lata *f can n*

el lavamanos *m sink n*

lavanda *lavender adj*

la lavandería *f laundry n*

la lección *f lesson n*

la leche *f milk n*

> el batido de leche *milk shake*

el lector de discos compactos *m CD player n*

leer *to read v* **p23**

lejos *far adj*

> más lejos *farther*
> lo más lejos *farthest*

el lenguaje *m language n*

lentamente *slowly adv*

el lente de contacto *m contact lens n*

lento -a *slow adj*

la lesión *f injury n*

el letrero de carretera cerrada *m road closed sign n*

la ley *f law n*

la libra *f pound n*

libre de impuestos *duty-free adj*

la librería *f bookstore n*

el libro *m book n*

la licencia *f license n*

> la licencia de conducir *driver's license*
> la placa de matrícula *automobile license plate*

el licor *m liqueur, liquor n*

el límite de velocidad *m speed limit n*

la limonada *f lemonade n*

la limosina *f limo n*

el limpiaparabrisas *m windshield wiper n*

limpiar *to clean v* **p22**

la limpieza en seco *f dry cleaning n*

limpio -a *clean neat (tidy) adj*

el litro *m liter n*

la llamada de despertar *f wake-up call n*

la llamada telefónica *f phone call n*

> la llamada con cargos revertidos *collect phone call*
> la llamada internacional *international phone call*
> la llamada de larga distancia *long-distance phone call*

**llamar** *to call (shout)* v **p22**

**llamar, telefonear** *to call (to phone)* v **p22**

**la llanta** f *tire* n

**la llanta de repuesta** *spare tire* n

**las llegadas** f pl *arrivals* n

**llegar** *to arrive* v **p22**

**lleno -a** *full* adj

**llevar** *to take* v **p22**

**llover** *to rain* v **p31** (like poder)

**lluvioso -a** *rainy* adj

**local** *local* adj

**la lona** f *canvas (fabric)* n

**luego, más tarde** *later* adv

**Hasta luego.** *See you later.*

**el lugar de reunión** m *hangout (hot spot)* n

**de lujo** *upscale* adj

**la lumbre** f *light (for cigarette)* n

**¿Puedo ofrecerle lumbre?** *May I offer you a light?*

**el lunar** m *mole (facial feature)* n

**el lunes** m *Monday* n

**la luz** f *light (lamp)* n

**la luz indicadora** *light (on car dashboard)*

**la luz del freno** *brake light*

**la luz de examinar el motor** *check engine light*

**el foco delantero** *headlight*

**la luz del aceite** *oil light*

## M

**la madre** f *mother* n

**¡Maldición!** *Damn!* expletive

**la maleta** f *suitcase* n

**el maletín** m *briefcase* n

**la mamá** f *mom* n, *mommy* n

**mandar a llamar** *to page (someone)* v **p22**

**manejar** *to handle* v **p22**

**Manejar con cuidado.** *Handle with care* .

**la mano** f *hand* n

**la mantequilla** f *butter* n

**el manual** m *manual (instruction booklet)* n

**la mañana** m *tomorrow* n adv

**la mañana** f *morning* n

**en la mañana** *in the morning*

**el mapa** m *map* n

**el mapa a bordo** *onboard map*

**el maquillaje** m *makeup* n

**maquillar** *to make up (apply cosmetics)* v **p22**

**la máquina** f *machine* n

**la máquina de rayos X** *x-ray machine*

**la máquina de venta** *vending machine*

**marcar** *to dial (a phone number)* v **p22**

**marcar directo** *to dial direct*

**mareado -a** *dizzy* adj / *seasick* adj ,

**el mareo de auto** m *carsickness* n

**los mariscos** *m seafood n*

**el martes** *m Tuesday n*

**el marzo** *m March (month) n*

**el masaje de espalda** *m back rub n*

**masculino** *male adj*

**el matador** *m bullfighter n*

**el mayo** *m May (month) n*

**la media** *f sock n*

**media libra** *half-pound*

**mediano -a** *medium adj (size)*

**la medianoche** *f midnight adv*

**la medicina** *f medicine n, medication n*

**medio -a** *half adj, one-half adj una*

**en medio** *middle adj*

**medio bien cocido** *medium well (meat) adj*

**a medio cocer** *medium rare (meat) adj*

**el mediodía** *noon n*

**medir** *to measure v / to try on (clothing) v* **p32** *(like pedir)*

**mejor** *best. See good*

**mejor** *better. See good*

**la mejora de categoría** *f upgrade n*

**la membresía** *f membership n*

**menos** *See poco*

**al menos** *f at least n*

**el menú** *m menu n*

**el menú para niños** *children's menu*

**el menú diabético** *diabetic menu*

**el menú de platos para llevar** *takeout menu*

**el mercado** *m market n*

**el mercado de pulgas / el pulguero** *flea market*

**el mercado al aire libre** *open-air market*

**el mes** *m month n*

**la mesa** *f table n*

**el metro** *m subway n / meter n*

**la línea del metro** *subway line*

**la estación del metro** *subway station*

**¿Cuál metro tomo para _____?** *Which subway do I take for _____?*

**mexicano -a** *Mexican adj*

**la mezquita** *f mosque n*

**el miembro** *m member n*

**el miércoles** *m Wednesday n*

**mil** *thousand n adj*

**el mililitro** *m milliliter n*

**el milímetro** *m millimeter n*

**la milla** *f mile n*

**el minibar** *m minibar n*

**el mínimo** *least. See little*

**el minuto** *m minute n*

**en un minuto** *in a minute*

**mirar** *to look (observe) v* **p22**

**¡Mira aquí!** *Look here!*

**la mitad** *f half n*

**la moneda** *f coin n*

la montaña *f mountain n*

**el escalado de montaña** *mountain climbing*

morado -a *purple adj*

el moreno *m,* la morena *f brunette n*

el mostrador *m counter (in bar) n*

mostrar *to show v* **p35** (like jugar)

**¿Puede mostrarme?** *Would you show me?*

la motocicleta *f motorcycle n*

la motoneta *f scooter n*

el motor *m engine n*

mover *to move v* **p31** (like poder)

la muchacha *f girl n*

mucho -a *much adj*

muchos -as *many adj*

la mujer *f woman n*

la multa *f fine (for traffic violation) n*

el museo *m museum n*

la música *f music n*

**la música pop** *pop music*

el musical *m musical (music genre) n*

músico -a *musical adj*

el músico *m musician n*

el musulmán *m,* la musulmana *f Muslim n adj*

muy *very*

# N

la nacionalidad *f nationality n*

nadar *to swim v* **p22**

**Nadar prohibido.** *Swimming prohibited.*

la naranja *orange n, orange (color) adj*

la nariz *f nose n*

el naufragio *m shipwreck n*

la náusea *f nausea n*

necesitar *to need v* **p22**

el negocio *m business n*

de negocios *business adj*

**el centro de negocios** *business center*

negro -a *black adj*

neozelandés, neozelandesa *New Zealander adj*

nicaragüense, nicaragüeña *Nicaraguan adj*

ninguno -a *none n*

la niña *f little girl n*

la niñera *f babysitter n*

el niño *m boy n, kid n*

los niños *m pl children n pl*

no *no adj adv*

la noche *f night n*

**a noche** *at night*

**en la noche** *at night*

**por noche** *per night*

de no fumar *nonsmoking adj*

**el área de no fumar** *nonsmoking area*

**el carro de no fumar** *nonsmoking car*

**la habitación de no fumar** *nonsmoking room*

el nombre *m name n*

**Me llamo ____. / Mi nombre es ____.** *My name is ____.*

¿Cómo se llama? / ¿Cuál es su nombre? *What's your name?*

el primer nombre *first name*

nosotros -as *we, us pron pl*

la novela *f novel n*

la novela de misterio *mystery novel*

la novela de romance *romance novel*

noveno -a *ninth n adj*

noventa *ninety n adj*

la novia *f girlfriend n*

el noviembre *m November n*

el novio *m boyfriend n*

nublado -a *cloudy adj*

Nueva Zelanda *f New Zealand n*

nueve *nine n adj*

nuevo -a *new adj*

la nuez *f nut n*

el número *m number n*

**O**

la obra de teatro *f play n*

observar *to watch v p22*

occidental *western adj*

ochenta *m eighty n adj*

ocho *m eight n adj*

octavo -a *eighth n adj*

tres octavos *three eighths*

el octubre *m October n*

ocupado -a *busy adj (phone line), occupied adj*

el oficial *m officer n*

la oficina del doctor *m doctor's office n*

ofrecer *to offer v p33 (like conocer)*

oír *to hear v*

el ojo *m eye n*

¡Ojos de serpiente! *Snake eyes! n*

oler *to smell v p23*

once *eleven n adj*

la onza *f ounce n*

la ópera *f opera n*

el operador *m,* la operadora *f operator (phone) n*

el oporto *m port (beverage) n*

el optómetra *m optometrist n*

ordenar *to order (request) v p22*

orgánico -a *organic adj*

el órgano *m organ n*

oro (color de) *gold (color) adj*

el oro *m gold n*

ortodoxo griego *Greek Orthodox adj*

la oscuridad *f darkness n*

oscuro -a *dark adj*

el otoño *m autumn (fall season) n*

otro -a *another adj ,*

**P**

el padre *m father, parent n*

pagar *to pay v p22*

el paisaje *m landscape (painting) n*

el pájaro *m bird n*

el pájaro carpintero *m woodpecker n*

el palco *m box (seat) n*

pálido -a *pale adj*

el pan *m* bread *n*

panameño -a *Panamanian adj*

el pantalón *m* pair of pants *n*

el pantalón de traje de baño *swim trunks n*

los pantalones cortos *shorts*

el pañal *m* diaper *n*

el pañal de paño *cloth diaper*

el pañal desechable *disposable diaper*

el papel *paper n*

el plato de papel *paper plate*

la servilleta de papel *paper napkin*

el papel higiénico *m* toilet paper *n*

el paquete *m* package *n*

el parabrisas *m* windshield *n*

la parada *f* stop *n*

la parada del autobús *bus stop*

paraguayo -a *Paraguayan adj*

pararse *to stand v* **p22, 35**

¡Par de ases! *Snake eyes! n*

PARE *STOP (traffic sign)*

el pariente *m*, la pariente *f* relative *n*

el parque *m* park *n*

el partido *m* match (sport) *n*

el partido político *m* political party *n*

el pasajero *m*, la pasajera *f* passenger *n*

el pasaporte *m* passport *n*

pasar *to pass (gambling) v* **p22**

la pasarela *f* walkway *n*

la pasarela mecánica *moving walkway*

pasar el rato *to hang out (relax) v* **p22**

el pasatiempo *m* hobby *n*

el pasillo *m* aisle (in store) *n* / hallway *n*

el patio de recreo *m* playground *n*

el pato *m* duck *n*

el patrono *m* employer *n*

el pavo *m* turkey *n*

el peaje *m* toll *n*

peatonal *pedestrian adj*

el distrito de compras peatonal *pedestrian shopping district*

la peca *f* freckle *n*

el / la pediatra *pediatrician n*

pedir *to order, request, demand v* **p32**

la pelea de gallos *f* cockfight *n*

la película *f* movie *n*

el peligro *m* danger *n*

el pelirrojo *m*, la pelirroja *f* redhead *n adj*

el pelo *m* hair *n*

el peluquero *m*, la peluquera *f* hairdresser *n*

el pensamiento *m* thought *n* / pansy *n*

pensar *to think v* **p31** (like conocer)

peor *worse. See bad*

lo peor *worst. See bad*

**pequeño -a** *small adj, short adj, little adj*

**pequeño** *small, little*
**más pequeño** *smaller, littler*
**lo mas pequeño** *smallest, littlest*

**la percha** *f hanger n*

**perder** *to lose v / to miss (a flight) v* **p31** *(like querer)*

**perdido -a** *missing adj, lost adj*

**el periódico** *m newspaper n*

**el permanente** *m permanent (hair) n*

**el permiso** *m permit n*

**permitir** *to permit v* **p23**

**el perro** *m dog n*

**el perro de servicio** *service dog*

**la persona** *f person n*

**la persona con impedimentos visuales** *visually-impaired person*

**el personal** *m staff (employees) n*

**el peruano** *m,* **la peruana** *f Peruvian n adj*

**pesar** *to weigh v* **p22**

**las pesas** *f pl weights n*

**la pestaña** *f eyelash n*

**el piano** *m piano n*

**el pie** *m foot (body part) n, foot (unit of measurement) n*

**la piel** *f skin n*

**la pierna** *f leg n*

**la pila** *f battery (for flashlight) n*

**la píldora** *f pill n*

**la píldora para el mareo** *f seasickness pill*

**la pinta** *f pint n*

**pintar** *to paint v* **p22**

**la pintura** *f painting n*

**la piscina** *f pool (swimming) n*

**el piso** *m floor n*

**el primer piso** *ground floor, first floor*

**la pizza** *f pizza n*

**el placer** *m pleasure n*

**Es un placer.** *It's a pleasure.*

**el plan de tarifa** *m rate plan (cell phone) n*

**¿Tiene un plan de tarifa?** *Do you have a rate plan?*

**el plástico** *m plastic n*

**plata** *silver (color) adj*

**la plata** *f silver n*

**plateado -a** *silver adj*

**el plato** *m dish n*

**la playa** *f beach n*

**poco -a** *little adj*

**un poco** *m bit (small amount) n*

**poco profundo -a** *shallow adj*

**poder** *to be able to (can) v, may v aux* **p31**

**¿Puedo ____?** *May I ____?*

**la policía** *f police n*

**el pollo** *m chicken n*

**poner** *to put (gambling) v* **p23** *(I put pongo)*

**¡Ponlo en rojo / negro!** *Put it on red / black!*

popular *popular* adj

por adelantado *in advance* adv

la porción *f portion (of food) n*

por favor *please (polite entreaty) adv*

el portaequipajes *m trunk (of car) n*

el portero *m,* la portera *f goalie n, porter n ,*

la postal *f postcard n*

el postre *m dessert n*

**el menú de postres** *dessert menu*

el precio *m price n*

**el precio de entrada** *admission fee n*

**de precio moderado** *moderately priced*

preferiblemente *preferably adj*

preferir *to prefer v* **p31** *(like querer)*

preguntar *to ask v* **p22**

preparado -a *prepared adj*

presentar *to introduce v* **p22**

**Quisiera presentarle a \_\_\_\_.** *I'd like to introduce you to \_\_\_\_.*

presupuestar *to budget v* **p22**

el presupuesto *m budget n*

la primavera *f spring (season) n*

primero -a *first adj*

el primo *m,* la prima *f cousin n*

el probador *m fitting room n*

probar *to taste v, to try (food) v* **p31** *(like jugar)*

el problema *m problem n*

procesar *to process (a transaction) v* **p22**

el producto *m product n*

profesional *professional adj*

profundo -a *deep adj*

el programa *m program n*

el prometido *m,* la prometida *f fiancé(e) n*

el pronóstico del tiempo *m weather forecast n*

la propina *f tip (gratuity)*

**propina incluida** *tip included*

protestante *Protestant n adj*

próximo -a *next prep*

**la próxima estación** *the next station*

el puente *m bridge (across a river) n / bridge (dental structure) n*

el puerco *m pig n*

la puerta *f door n*

**la puerta de salida** *gate (at airport)*

el puerto *port (for ship mooring) n*

el puerto USB *m USB port n*

puertorriqueño -a *Puerto Rican adj*

el puesto de información *m information booth n*

el puesto de periódicos *m newsstand n*

la pulgada *f inch n*

en punto *o'clock adv*

**dos en punto** *two o'clock*

la puntuación *f score n*

## Q

qué *what* adv

¿Qué hubo? *What's up?*

quedar *to hold (gambling)* v p22

quedarse *to stay* v p22, 35

la quemadura de sol *f* sunburn *n*

quemar *to burn* v p22

querer *to want* v p31

el queso *m cheese n*

quién *who* adv

¿De quién es ___? *Whose is ___?*

quince *m fifteen n adj*

el quinto *m fifth n adj*

el quiropráctico *m* chiropractor *n*

## R

la radio *m radio n*

la radio por satélite *satellite radio*

la rampa para sillas de ruedas *f wheelchair ramp n*

rápido -a *fast* adj ,

el rasguño *m scratch n*

el ratón *m mouse n*

rayado -a *scratched adj*

rayar *to scratch* v p22

a rayas *striped adj*

el rayazo *m scratch n*

el reabastecimiento *m* refill (of prescription) *n*

recargar *to charge (a battery)* v p22

la recepción *f front desk n*

la receta *f prescription n*

rechazado -a *declined adj*

Su tarjeta de crédito fue rechazada. *Your credit card was declined.*

recibir *to receive* v p23

el recibo *m receipt n*

el reclamo *m claim n*

recolectar *to collect* v p22

recomendar *to recommend* v p31 (like comenzar)

recortar *to trim (hair)* v p22

el recorte de pelo *m haircut n*

recto -a *straight adj*

la red *f network n*

la red inalámbrica *f wi-fi n*

reducir la velocidad *to slow* v p33 (like conocer)

¡Reduzca la velocidad! *Slow down!*

el refresco *m soda n*

el refresco de dieta *diet soda*

el regalo *m gift n*

el reggae *m reggae n*

el registro *check-in n*

el registro al borde de la acera *curbside check-in*

el registro electrónico *electronic check-in*

el registro expreso *express check-in*

regresar *to return (to a place)* v p22

relajarse *to lounge* v p22, 35

el reloj *m clock n, watch n*

el reloj despertador *alarm clock*

el **relleno** *refill (of beverage)* n

**remover** *to remove* v **p23, 31**
(like *poder*)

**repartir** *to deal (cards)* v **p23**

**Repárteme.** *Deal me in.*

el **repelente para insectos** m
*insect repellent* n

**repetir** *to repeat* v **p23, 32**
(like *pedir*)

**¿Puede repetir eso por favor?** *Would you please repeat that?*

la **reservación** m *reservation* n

el **resfriado** m *cold (illness)* n

**residencial** *home* adj

la **dirección residencial**
*home address*

el **número de teléfono residencial** *home telephone number*

el **restaurante** m *restaurant* n

el **restaurante de parrilla**
*steakhouse*

**retirar** *to withdraw* v **p22**

el **retiro** m *withdrawal* n

el **retraso** m *delay* n

el **retrato** m *portrait* n

la **revista** f *magazine* n

el **río** m *river* n

**rizado -a** *curly* adj

el **rizo** m *curl* n

**robado -a** *stolen* adj

**robar** *to rob* v, *to steal* v **p22**

la **roca** f *rock* n

**en las rocas** *on the rocks*

el **rock and roll** m *rock and roll* n

**rojo -a** *red* adj

**romántico -a** *romantic* adj

**romper** *to break* v **p23**

el **ron** m *rum* n

la **ropa interior** f *underwear* n

la **rosa** f *rose* n

**rosado -a** *pink* adj

el **rubio** m, la **rubia** f *blond(e)* n adj

**con ruedas** *wheeled (luggage)* adj

**ruidoso -a** *loud, noisy* adj 77

## S

el **sábado** m *Saturday* n

la **sábana** f *sheet (bed linen)* n

**saber** *to know (something)* v **p33**

el **sabor** m *taste, flavor* n

el **sabor a chocolate** *chocolate flavor*

la **sal** f *salt* n

**bajos en sal** *low-salt*

la **sala de espera** f *waiting area* n

la **salida** f *check-out* n / *departure* n / *exit* n

la **hora de salida** *check-out time*

**no es salida** *not an exit*

la **salida de emergencia**
*emergency exit*

**salir** *to leave (depart)* v **p23**
(*I leave* **salgo**)

el **salón público** m *lounge* n

la **salsa** f *sauce* n

**salvadoreño -a** *Salvadoran* adj

el **salvavidas** m *life preserver* n

**el sastre** *m tailor n*
**el satélite** *m satellite n*
  **la radio satélite** *satellite radio*
  **rastreo por satélite** *satellite tracking*
**secado -a** *dried adj*
**la secadora de pelo** *f hair dryer n*
**secar** *to dry v* **p22**
**seco -a** *dry adj*
**el sedán** *m sedan n*
**segundo -a** *second adj*
**la seguridad** *f security n*
  **el punto de control de seguridad** *security checkpoint*
  **la guardia de seguridad** *security guard*
**el seguro** *m insurance n*
  **el seguro para colisiones** *collision insurance*
  **el seguro de responsabilidad civil** *liability insurance*
**seguro -a** *safe (secure) adj*
**seis** *six n adj*
**el seltzer** *m seltzer n*
**la semana** *f week n ,*
  **esta semana** *this week*
  **la semana pasada** *last week*
  **la próxima semana** *next week*
  **una semana** *one week*
  **dentro de una semana** *a week from now*
**sencillo -a** *single n adj / simple adj*
  **sencillo** *straight up (drink)*

**el sendero** *m trail n*
**sentar** *to sit v* **p31** (like comenzar)
**señalar** *to point v* **p22**
**la señal de ceda el paso** *f yield sign n*
**separado -a** *separated (marital status) adj*
**el septiembre** *m September n*
**séptimo -a** *seventh n adj*
**ser** *to be (permanent quality) v* **p28**
**el servicio** *m service n*
  **fuera de servicio** *out of service*
**el servicio** *m service (religious) n*
**la servilleta** *f napkin n*
**servir** *to serve v* **p32** (like pedir)
**sesenta** *sixty n adj*
**setenta** *seventy n adj*
**el sexo** *m sex (gender) n*
**sí** *yes adv*
**siete** *seven n adj*
**la silla de ruedas** *f wheelchair n*
  **el acceso para sillas de ruedas** *wheelchair access*
  **rampa para sillas de ruedas** *wheelchair ramp*
  **la silla de ruedas eléctrica** *power wheelchair*
**sin** *without prep*
**la sinfonía** *f symphony n*
**sobre** *above adj*
**el sobre** *m envelope n*
**sobrecalentar** *to overheat v* **p31** (like comenzar)

**sobrecocido -a** *overcooked adj*

**la sobrina** *f niece n*

**el sobrino** *m nephew n*

**el socialismo** *m socialism n*

**la soda** *f soda n*

**el software** *m software n*

**el sol** *m sun n*

**soleado** *sunny adj*

**soltero -a** *single (unmarried) adj*

¿Estás soltero / soltera? *Are you single?*

**el sombrero** *m hat n*

**la sombrilla** *f umbrella n*

**la sopa** *f soup n*

**sordo -a** *deaf adj*

**sospechosamente** *suspiciously adv*

**suave** *soft adj*

**el subtítulo** *m subtitle n*

**el suburbio** *m slum n*

**suelto -a** *loose adj*

**el suéter** *m sweater n*

**la suite** *f suite n*

**sujetar** *to hold v p22*

sujetar las manos *to hold hands*

**el supermercado** *m supermarket n*

**surfear** *to surf v p22*

la tabla de surf *surfboard n*

**la sustitución** *f substitution n*

**suyo -a** *your, yours adj sing (formal)*

**T**

**la taberna** *f bar n*

**la talla** *f size (clothing, shoes) n*

**también** *too (also) adv*

**el tambor** *m drum n*

**el tanque de oxígeno** *m oxygen tank n*

**tarde** *late adj*

Por favor no llegues tarde. *Please don't be late.*

**la tarde** *f afternoon n*

en la tarde *in the afternoon*

**la tarifa** *f fare n / rate n*

**la tarjeta** *f card n*

la tarjeta de crédito *credit card*

¿Aceptan tarjetas de crédito? *Do you accept credit cards?*

la tarjeta de presentación *business card*

**la tasa de cambio** *f exchange rate n*

**la tasa de interés** *f interest rate n*

**el taxi** *m taxi n*

¡Taxi! *Taxi!*

la parada de los taxis *taxi stand*

**el té** *m tea n*

el té con leche y azúcar *tea with milk and sugar*

el té con limón *tea with lemon*

el té de hierbas *herbal tea*

**el teatro** *m theater n*

**el teatro de la ópera** *m opera house n*

**el techno** *m techno n (music)*

**el techo** *m roof n*

el techo corredizo *sunroof*

la tela *f* fabric *n*
telefónico *phone adj*
  el directorio telefónico *phone directory*
el teléfono *m* phone *n*
  el teléfono celular *cell phone*
  ¿Me puede dar su número de teléfono? *May I have your phone number?*
  el operador *m* / la operadora *f* de teléfono *phone operator*
  teléfonos prepagados *prepaid phones*
la televisión *f* television *n*
  la televisión por cable *cable television*
  la televisión por satélite *satellite television*
el templo *m* temple *n*
temprano *early adj*
tener *to have v* p29
  tener relaciones *to have sex (intercourse)*
el tenis *m* tennis *n*
tercero -a *third n adj*
el terminal *m* terminal (airport) *n*
la tía *f* aunt *n*
el tiempo *m* time *n*
la tienda *f* shop *n*, store *n*
  la tienda de campaña *f* tent *n*
la tintorería *f* dry cleaner *n*
el tío *m* uncle *n*
el tipo *m* kind (sort, type) *n*
la toalla *f* towel *n*

tocar *to touch v* / *to play (an instrument) v* p22
todo -a *all adj*
  todo el tiempo *all the time*
  Eso es todo. *That's all.*
tomar *to take v* p22
  ¿Cuánto tiempo tomará esto? *How long will this take?*
la tonelada *f* ton *n*
el torero *m* bullfighter *n*
el toro *m* bull *n*
la tos *f* cough *n*
toser *to cough v* p23
el total *m* total *n*
  ¿Cuál es el total? *What is the total?*
trabajar *to work v* p22
  Yo trabajo para _____. *I work for _____.*
el tráfico *m* traffic *n*
  ¿Cómo está el tráfico? *How's traffic?*
  El tráfico es terrible. *Traffic is terrible.*
tragar *to swallow v* p22
el trago *m* shot (liquor) *n*
el traje de baño *m* swimsuit *n*
la transacción *f* transaction *n*
la transferencia *f* transfer *n*
  la transferencia de dinero *money transfer, wire transfer*
transferir *to transfer v* p31 (like *querer*)
el tránsito *m* traffic *n*
  las reglas de tránsito *traffic rules*